EQUALITY & EXCELLENCE
in ANCIENT & MODERN
POLITICAL PHILOSOPHY

EQUALITY & EXCELLENCE
in ANCIENT & MODERN
POLITICAL PHILOSOPHY

Edited by

Steven Frankel & John Ray

SUNY PRESS

Published by State University of New York Press, Albany

© 2023 State University of New York

All rights reserved

Printed in the United States of America

No part of this book may be used or reproduced in any manner without written permission. No part of this book may be stored in a retrieval system or transmitted in any form or by any means including electronic, electrostatic, magnetic tape, mechanical, photocopying, recording, or otherwise without the prior permission in writing of the publisher.

For information, contact State University of New York Press, Albany, NY
www.sunypress.edu

Library of Congress Cataloging-in-Publication Data

Names: Frankel, Steven, 1968– editor. | Ray, John A., 1957– editor.
Title: Equality and excellence in ancient and modern political philosophy / edited by Steven Frankel and John Ray.
Description: Albany : State University of New York Press, [2023] | Includes bibliographical references and index.
Identifiers: LCCN 2022035443 | ISBN 9781438492780 (hardcover : alk paper) | ISBN 9781438492803 (ebook) | ISBN 9781438492797 (pbk. : alk paper)
Subjects: LCSH: Political science—Philosophy—History. | Equality—Political aspects. | Excellence.
Classification: LCC JA81 .E65 2023 | DDC 320.01—dc23/eng/20230106
LC record available at https://lccn.loc.gov/2022035443

10 9 8 7 6 5 4 3 2 1

*We dedicate this volume in gratitude
to the memory of Joseph Cropsey*

Contents

Acknowledgments ix

Introduction 1
    Steven Frankel and John Ray

1 Pursuing the Forms: Equality and Excellence
   in Plato's *Republic* and *Symposium* 9
    Stephanie A. Nelson

2 Equality and Excellence in the *Education of Cyrus* 33
    Nathan Tarcov

3 Splendid Equality in the *Nicomachean Ethics*: Munificence 53
    Ann Charney Colmo

4 How Excellence Bows to Equality in Aristotle's *Politics* 67
    Mary P. Nichols

5 First among Equals: Philosophers, Statesmen,
   and Citizens in Spinoza's Democracy 89
    Steven Frankel

6 Excellence and Equality in Fénelon's *Telemachus* 103
    Ryan Patrick Hanley

7 The Seductive Dangers of Equality and Excellence:
   The Moderating Wisdom of Montesquieu's Science of
   Ovidian Metamorphosis 121
    Frank J. Rohmer

8	Equality and Excellence in Rousseau's *Emile*, Book III *Pamela K. Jensen*	143
9	Hegel's Evaluation of Liberalism: Equality of Rights without Human Excellence *Andrea E. Ray*	159
10	Democracy, Nobility, and Freedom: The Political and Moral Aesthetics of Tocqueville *John C. Koritansky*	173
11	Does Kierkegaard Have a Concept of Excellence? *Christopher A. Colmo*	187
12	Nietzsche: The Indignity of Equality *Timothy Sean Quinn*	199
13	The Good and the Excellent: John Rawls's Egalitarian Liberalism *Michael Zuckert*	215
Bibliography		229
Contributors		241
Index		245

Acknowledgments

Ann Charney Colmo read every chapter as it was submitted and she communicated with each author about readability, grammar, and consistency. The quality of this volume would not be as high as it is without her gentle and thoughtful corrections. Thanks to her, we are all better writers. We also thank Nick Reynolds, an honors student at Xavier University, for preparing the bibliography. This work was made possible by a student research grant from the College of Arts and Sciences at Xavier University. We are grateful to the Hayek Fund for Scholars at the Institute for Humane Studies (IHS) for publication support.

A number of the contributors to this volume were either students or friends of Joseph Cropsey at the University of Chicago. We recall his gentle demeanor, graceful manners, and generous conversation. His magisterial lectures were infused with an urbane openness to ideas and enlivened by a quick dry wit. It is with deep gratitude that we dedicate this volume to his memory.

Introduction

STEVEN FRANKEL AND JOHN RAY

The idea for a volume of essays on "Equality and Excellence" arose out of a Tocqueville reading group at Xavier University that we held a number of years ago. Tocqueville saw that equality is the dominating passion of modern democracies. He thought that the Americans of his day had shown how equality could be combined with liberty to produce a stable democracy that would allow the talented to pursue their ambitions and perhaps even a version of aristocratic honor. He was not primarily interested in the Madisonian solution of institutional checks and balances in a diverse commercial republic but emphasized instead the doctrine of self-interest properly understood supported by religious beliefs, specifically those of Protestant Christianity. Yet as readers of the concluding chapters of volume two of *Democracy in America* know, Tocqueville was pessimistic that the excessive love of equality in democracies might ultimately be turned away from its tendency to undermine the liberty that excellence—whether as public or private virtue—needs to flourish. Equality would inevitably lead to a flattening and homogenization of democratic souls, typically obsessed with their own narrow interests. Individual men and women would be thwarted and overwhelmed by what Tocqueville called "soft despotism" to describe government as an irresistible parent guiding and limiting what can be done, said, and even thought. A dreary picture, to be sure, yet it is only one of many explorations on the tension between equality and excellence to emerge out of the history of political philosophy.

Analysis of the meaning and implications of equality has taken on renewed urgency in American life. Today, demands for racial justice and gender and sexual equality pervade our politics, threatening either to expose as fraudulent our national commitment to "equality under law," or to undermine that commitment by replacing individual rights with the group rights of identity politics. The times in which we live seem to call for sustained reflection on equality in the history of political philosophy. The chapters of this book capture the diversity of formulations of the tension between equality and excellence (and of the meaning of these terms) as well as of proposals to reconcile the two.

How, we wonder, in the long tradition of political philosophy has this age-old tension been understood? Is this tension a permanent reflection of human nature itself? Or, rather, is it simply a product of historical or other circumstances? Alternatively, what are the sources and types of human excellence? How critical is civic or personal virtue to a good society? And, of course, we must not shrink from asking, What is a good society? In addressing the tension between equality and excellence, we return, necessarily, to the question of justice.

Ancient Greek writers are critical of democracy from the point of view of nobility and wisdom, yet they do not simply dismiss the claims of equality. Readers of this volume will find in Plato, Aristotle, and Xenophon—the three writers we take to represent the best of ancient Greek political philosophy—both theoretical and practical grounds for respecting and promoting the claims of the many. Plato's *Symposium*, Aristotle's *Politics*, and Xenophon's *Education of Cyrus*, each in its own way, acknowledge human aspirations as universal.

Stephanie Nelson argues that while Plato's *Republic* promotes an ideal of Philosopher Rulers and has some exceedingly harsh things to say about democracy and equality, the dialogue that is in many ways its companion piece, the *Symposium*, grounds the philosophic pursuit of the Forms in a universal motivation. Even more paradoxically, although the *Republic* focuses on *aretē*, or excellence, it is, overall, much less interested in competition than the *Symposium*, the theoretical view of which is much more universal, but which is competitive throughout. Finally, the *Symposium*'s closing picture of Alcibiades, torn apart by competing views of the good, reflects the "almost-philosopher" of the *Republic*, setting up a dialogic relation between the *Republic*'s ideal city and the actuality of Athens. As such, the dialogues, taken together, force us to reconsider the relation between excellence and equality, not because democracy necessarily promotes philosophy, but because a doubtful system of values, such as that of a democracy, might finally be the more desirable option.

Nathan Tarcov observes that in his novel *The Education of Cyrus* Xenophon invents a quasi-Spartan ancient Persia formally devoted to freedom and equality, but where the well-off peers receive an education required for political office that the vast majority of hard-working commoners cannot afford. Cyrus's education is divided between his father's Persia, where he undergoes a warrior's austere and severe education in justice (as obedience to law), moderation, and military skills, and his grandfather's despotic and luxurious Media where justice means the ruler has everything. When Cyrus is appointed to command a Persian army, he works a moral, military, social, and political transformation of Persia that enables him to create and rule his quasi-universal empire. First, he transforms the moral outlook of the peers so as no longer to practice virtue for its own sake but to do so for rewards; second, he arms the commoners like the peers undermining the old hierarchy; third, he makes rewards proportionate to desert as judged by Cyrus himself. Thus he establishes a quasi-meritocracy where all have an equal opportunity under his despotic rule over an enormous multinational empire. Readers of *The Education of Cyrus* are left to wonder whether equality suits despotism as well as freedom.

We offer two views of Aristotle on the question of the relation between excellence and equality, one on the *Nicomachean Ethics* and one on the *Politics*. According to Ann Charney Colmo, munificence (*megaloprepeia*—splendid and fitting expenditure, especially for the city), although often overlooked in Aristotle's discussion of the moral virtues in the *Nicomachean Ethics*, discloses a surprising admixture of excellence and equality. The munificent outfits the city's triremes, with a view to the city's self-preservation—incidentally creating the need for the many to provide a strong navy. He gives the city opportunities to participate in the sacred things—for example, votive offerings—elevating all souls equally. He commissions beautiful art, monuments, buildings, bringing to all an education in the beautiful. As the discussion of the magnanimous is said to represent a "second" depiction—that of the philosopher (*Post. An.* 97b14–26)—so munificence reveals a "second" representation: that of the poet, who pleases and educates the many. Perhaps as important is that the poet needs the many—without an audience, his work would be futile. That need establishes a kind of mutual interchange between the poet and the many. Thus, munificence, one of the great virtues, provides on two levels the possibility of harmonizing the seemingly opposed qualities of equality and excellence.

Aristotle is famous for arguing that virtue is the end of political life, indeed, that "virtue must be a care for every city, or at least every one that is named so in truth." Yet as Mary P. Nichols shows in her chapter on the *Politics*, Aristotle gives a greater place to equality and freedom than is recognized. Nichols begins with his treatment of the family in Book 1 of the *Politics*. By attacking despotic rule of a husband over his wife, and of a father over his children, Aristotle prepares for his proposal of a form of rule that belongs to political life, a shared rule that he calls "political rule." Such rule is appropriate for human beings who are free and equal, in the sense that they are political by nature because they possess reason or speech. She then examines Aristotle's discussion of the claims to rule in Book 3, especially the claims of equality or free birth, wealth, and virtue. His famous sixfold classification of regimes gives the rule of the many in the common interest (polity) a central place, while he claims that the rule of "a king over everything," an individual of preeminent virtue, deprives the others in the community of the honors they deserve. Finally, Nichols shows how Aristotle's mixed regime of Book 4, including one based on a well-off middle class, and his regime in Book 7 that "we would pray for," mingle the principles of equality and excellence. Excellence or virtue must bow to equality, in reverence rather than submission, precisely because equality best allows excellence to flourish in the give and take of political life that requires citizens and statesmen to develop and exercise the virtues of moderation, justice, and prudence.

From the peaks of Greek antiquity, we turn first to representatives of classic modernity: Spinoza, Fénelon, and Montesquieu. In his chapter on Spinoza's *Theological-Political Treatise*, Steven Frankel begins by noting that Spinoza does little to conceal the distinction between the few and the many, along with his contempt for the latter. Nonetheless, he makes a strong case in favor of equality and democracy. According to Frankel, the key to understanding this apparent contradiction is Spinoza's doctrine of natural rights, which are rooted in our common striving for self-preservation in the state of nature. This striving or conatus has a political dimension in the sense that we interpret it in terms of freedom and choice. In addition, we privilege our individual perspective and do not recognize the wisdom of others. In this sense, nature does not privilege reason over passion. We are equal in the sense that we experience our conatus individually, according to our particular capacity and passions, and our evaluation of the good is particular to us as well. Natural right reflects the authority of our particular account of the good. In this practical sense, nature lends authority to the appearance of equality. Spinoza builds the case for democracy on this conviction even as he reminds philosophers of the superiority of reason.

We are delighted to include a chapter on Fénelon, a tremendously popular writer in the France of his day who deserves to be more widely read today. Ryan Patrick Hanley notes that Fénelon's chief contribution to political philosophy, his epic *Telemachus*, was written to instruct the heir of Louis XIV in the virtues of political rule. But the text also has another dimension. Conceived as a continuation of Homer's *Odyssey*, *Telemachus* also represents a Catholic archbishop's effort to provide an alternative to Homeric virtue. Hanley surveys Fénelon's novel synthesis of Christian conceptions of equality with ancient conceptions of political virtue in an effort to preserve greatness even within an ever more egalitarian world.

Frank Rohmer notes that though consistently cited as the most thorough proponent of the principle of separation of powers, Montesquieu was for more than two centuries an author more cited than carefully read. The seemingly disjointed character of his writings, involving multiple perspectives and lacking clear linear development, has understandably led those scholars who have seriously delved into the morass the author presents to varied and contradictory interpretations of his work. Intentionally perplexing, the desultory style of Montesquieu's three great works, *Persian Letters*, *Considerations on the Causes of the Greatness of the Romans and Their Decline*, and *The Spirit of the Laws*, reflects the complexity of a world of unfolding Ovidian Metamorphosis in which forms change into other forms as human nature is refracted by historical experience in which climate, geography, laws, and culture exert formative forces both physical and spiritual. Montesquieu's overriding purpose was to describe the motion of human things with a comprehensive science of politics, thereby deepening the appreciation of existing political orders, even if imperfect, to a decent and humane life and counseling moderation to those whose reformist impulses would impel them in the direction of perfectionist revolutionary zeal.

As the first great critic of early modernity, Rousseau is the turning point in the history of ideas. Pamela Jensen explores several aspects of the story of *Emile*, Rousseau's imaginary pupil, and "the magician-Socrates" and considers their implications for reconciling equality and excellence. She connects the issues of *amour-propre*, the need to promote a "constant curiosity" in *Emile*, and the introduction of the first book in Emile's education—the novel *Robinson Crusoe*. She suggests that in order to avoid a dangerous rivalry between the tutor or governor and Emile, Rousseau establishes a rivalry between Emile and Robinson Crusoe. Finally, she considers how

Rousseau the philosopher shields philosophy from attack and seeks to forge an alliance between philosophers and nonphilosophers; perhaps the best and for Rousseau the most important way to reconcile equality and excellence.

Andrea Ray observes that in *The Philosophy of Right*, Hegel describes liberal market-states as societies that both recognize individuals as equals insofar as they are all rights-bearers and deeply alienate those individuals from society by way of that recognition. Yet, unlike later theorists such as Marx, Hegel seeks to maintain much of the liberal state including property rights. Ray argues that Hegel instead approaches the problem of liberal alienation by examining how we are deficient under liberalism—how our self-actualization is hindered and how we fail to flourish as human beings within such a society. In doing so, Hegel suggests that the problem with liberalism is not so much that recognizing individuals as rights-bearers is wrong, as that such recognition is not enough. For a society to be conducive to human excellence, therefore, Hegel maintains that we must look beyond the form of life described by seventeenth-century liberalism to *Sittlichkeit*— an ethical order that permits a broader array of recognition by conceiving of the individual as deeply interwoven with the group without simply reducing the individual to a mere part of the group.

Our volume next turns to two additional thinkers of what we might call mature modernity, Tocqueville and Kierkegaard. Tocqueville distinguishes two forms of the love of equality, one "manly and legitimate," the other "debased." John Koritansky observes that Tocqueville's great work, *Democracy in America*, is intended to demonstrate the political and social structures whereby what we may call the nobler of these two forms can persist. Moreover, for Tocqueville, the sort of nobility that is potentially compatible with democracy is not merely a watered-down relic of aristocratic nobility but is rather a true reflection of human greatness.

Do all great thinkers have a concept of excellence? Christopher Colmo puts this question to Kierkegaard, and finds that his concept of excellence is embodied in men of excellence: Socrates, Shakespeare, or Mozart. But as these names make clear, excellence thus understood belongs to what Kierkegaard calls the aesthetic realm, the realm of more and less, where even excellence is finite. Excellence and mediocrity face a common despair in this finite realm where all is vanity. This despair fully embraced opens the way for all equally to imbue their individual talents with eternal validity as their task in life. Duty becomes a way to regain what despair took away.

We conclude the book with chapters on Nietzsche and Rawls, two contrary perspectives from postmodernity, the one despising equality for its betrayal of human greatness and the other insisting on equality as necessary to decent political life. As Timothy Sean Quinn shows, few thinkers have written so movingly about nobility, or with such undisguised hostility toward equality, as has Nietzsche. Quinn attempts to shape Nietzsche's concept of nobility in light of his rejection of liberalism by taking a synoptic look at writings across the entire ambit of his oeuvre, from the early essay "The Greek State" of 1871 to *Beyond Good and Evil*, which contains his most complete articulation of human nobility as it is manifest in the figure of the philosopher. Tracing Nietzsche's attack on equality on behalf of the dignity of philosophy in this fashion helps to clarify both the attractiveness of Nietzsche's views and their dangers.

John Rawls is universally recognized as a major theorist of egalitarian liberalism but less often noted is his concern with the conditions of excellence. Michael Zuckert traces the theme of excellence in Rawls's *A Theory of Justice*, and assesses its success as an effort to make room for excellence in a theory devoted primarily to equality. Although Rawls intends to reconcile equality and excellence, Zuckert finds that he has not done better than the liberal tradition in this elusive endeavor. Zuckert draws a conclusion fitting our book as a whole: it is "the tensions inherent in human nature and society that make anything but an imperfect and fraught reconciliation impossible."

The chapters of this book not only bear out Zuckert's conclusion, they also remind us that not every good principle can exist fully in a society at the same time. Excellence may need to give way to equality if there is to be justice; likewise, equality may need to moderate its demands if human excellence is to have the protective space it needs to flourish, to the benefit of all. If Tocqueville, our perceptive interpreter of American democracy, is correct, the danger to liberty in our time appears to come not from an excessive privileging of excellence—whether intellectual, moral, or civic—but from an unhealthy, because unreasoned, love of and demand for ever greater equality. However this may be, the chapters of this book will allow readers to gain a sweeping overview of the tension between equality and excellence as it has been articulated by political philosophers from Greek antiquity to modern times.

Chapter 1

Pursuing the Forms

Equality and Excellence in Plato's *Republic* and *Symposium*

STEPHANIE A. NELSON

Plato's *Republic* is notorious for its suggestion that *aretē* ("excellence" or "virtue") in its truest sense demands philosophy, and for the harsh things that Socrates has to say about democracy and its ideal of equality.[1] Some scholars, such as, most famously, Karl Popper in *The Open Society and Its Enemies*, have responded by attacking Plato as a totalitarian, while others have pointed out that for all his criticism of democracy, Socrates seems to have needed democratic Athens to practice his philosophic pursuits.[2] Another complication in Plato's view of the relation of excellence to equality, however, has gone largely unexplored. This is the view expressed in the dialogue that is in many ways the companion piece to the *Republic*, the *Symposium*, which describes a common, even universal, motivation behind the philosophic pursuit of Forms and which, apparently correspondingly, downplays the role of *aretē*. Here not only all humans, but even all living beings, are seen as driven by the same desire for immortality, a desire that moves some to the production of offspring, others to the production of political or artistic "children," and yet others toward the Forms. It seems that we all, according to our natures, seek the same good.[3] If so, true excellence, that is, a drive to eternal truths, may not be as opposed to equality as it had seemed.

There are other indications that equality and excellence may not be as opposed as they seem. While Plato discusses excellence in one dialogue and universality in the other, each shows signs of leading into the other. The *Republic* emphasizes hierarchy, and yet each level of the Divided Line, a line that could be either vertical or horizontal, seems to image the adjacent level, bringing out similarity as much as difference.[4] The hierarchy established also has some rather comic aspects, as with the notorious "nuptial number" (546a-d) or the elaborate calculation that the just live 729 times more pleasantly than the unjust (587b-e).[5] In contrast, the *Symposium*'s focus on universality leads to the ascent of the Ladder of Love and so to an apparent hierarchy. Moreover, after apparently having left considerations of *aretē* far behind, the Ladder of Love seems to return to it, concluding with the person who has seen beauty itself giving birth not merely to images of *aretē* but to true excellence (212a3-6). There seems to be a sort of equality, then, lurking behind the *Republic*'s focus on excellence, and a kind of excellence concealed within the universal drive of the *Symposium*.

And yet, before we congratulate ourselves on discovering that equality and excellence are perfectly compatible, we should wonder why Plato chose to stress excellence in contrast to equality in one dialogue, and equality in contrast to excellence in the other. Even if the qualities are related, it seems that the relation is fraught. In fact, and not surprisingly, it turns out that we cannot understand how excellence is related to equality until we know what excellence itself is, the question that also opens the *Republic*, at least in regard to justice (354b-c, 368e–369a). Socrates may believe that true excellence is wisdom but, as *Republic* Books 8 and 9 remind us, there are a number of challengers for the title. These challengers, I will argue, are also why, in the *Symposium*, Diotima's return to *aretē* leads into the sudden appearance of Alcibiades. The answer to our question concerning excellence and equality may be that there is no fixed answer, but rather a dynamic, ongoing, and even dialectical process in which ideas of equality and excellence establish themselves, are undermined, and reestablish themselves, each in relation to the other.[6]

The *Symposium* and *Republic* as Paired

As has often been observed, the *Republic* and *Symposium*, like a right and left hand, are both opposite and the same. The ways in which they are opposite may be most obvious. The *Republic* opens with Socrates "going down" from

Athens to the Piraeus (327a1), the *Symposium* with his devotee, Aristodemus, "going up" to town from Athens's older port, Phalerum (172a1).[7] The *Republic* opens with an injunction against speeches (344d, 348a, 350d-e) and its all-night conversation takes the place of dining (328a), while in the *Symposium* dining and drinking bracket an all-night series of speeches. The party crasher Alcibiades, arguably the main figure in the *Symposium* after Socrates, seems also to be the model for the "almost-philosopher" at the heart of the *Republic* (491a–495a)—the crucial figure who is not there.[8] The *Republic* critiques and banishes the playwrights; the *Symposium* includes and even celebrates them. The *Republic* essentially banishes *eros* from the city, while the *Symposium*, literally, is all about *Eros*. The Socrates of the *Republic* is, emphatically, his usual self (337a, 367d-e, 487e6, etc.), while the Socrates of the *Symposium* is very unusually self-sufficient, claims to have actual knowledge (177d), and is even wearing shoes (174a). One is immediate, opening with Socrates's "I went down yesterday to the Piraeus with Glaucon, the son of Ariston" (327a1), and the other begins with an elaborate set of distancing frames in which Glaucon (or a Glaucon) also plays a role (172c4).[9] And of course one is very, very long.

But while opposite, the two dialogues also reflect one another. As David Roochnik has beautifully shown, *eros,* in its absence, is as central to the *Republic* as it is to the *Symposium*.[10] Both dialogues are vitally about education, and, with the entry of Alcibiades in the *Symposium*, about the relation of education to the political. Both dialogues make a point of including women, the *Republic* in arguing that women are as capable as men of becoming Philosopher-Rulers, the *Symposium* showing us Diotima in essentially this role, guiding a rather hapless young Socrates. The *Republic* ends with a vision both comic and tragic: "pitiable to see and laughable and to be wondered at (θαυμασίαν)" (620a1); the *Symposium* centers around paired comic and tragic speeches and ends with Socrates forcing the tragic poet, Agathon, and the comic poet, Aristophanes, to agree that the same person can compose both comedy and tragedy (223d2–3). And perhaps most important, both center around the relation of "the good" to (as in Socrates's definition of justice) what is "one's own" (*Rep.* 441d-e, 462b-e, 465e–466c; *Symp.* 205d-e).[11]

A final, but also finally complicated similarity between the *Republic* and the *Symposium* lies in the relation of excellence to the Forms.[12] Without going into the question of whether Plato has any such thing as a "theory of the Forms," the Divided Line of *Republic* 6 and Diotima's Ladder of Love in the *Symposium* (*Rep.* 509d–511e; *Symp.* 210a–212b) are clearly parallel in positing the Forms as the ultimate objects of knowledge.[13] Moreover, just as the Ladder of Love culminates in the subject of *aretē* (212a3–6), the *Republic*'s argument that the City in Words models the soul of complete *aretē* implies that as the city requires a Philosopher-Ruler to be truly excellent, so also the soul must pursue the Forms in order to achieve true *aretē*.[14]

The complication arises from the fact that *aretē* in Greek has two rather different senses, and that both the *Republic* and the *Symposium* seem to choose the wrong one. At first glance it seems natural that the *Republic*, with its interest in hierarchy, focuses on excellence, while the *Symposium*, with its interest in the universal, does not. Equality and excellence, after all, are naturally opposed, as in Garrison Keeler's joke on Lake Wobegon, where all the children are above average. This is true, however, of only one sense of *aretē*, the competitive, Homeric sense in which *aretē* makes one *aristos*, the best, which is to say, better than others.[15] In the second sense, the sense that Socrates spells out early on in the *Republic* (335b-c, 352d–353e, and see 601d), the *aretē* of a thing is what enables it to do its essential work, so that the *aretē* of a knife is sharpness, the *aretē* of a racehorse is speed, etc. In this light the "excellence" of any given individual does not depend on superiority to others, and so is compatible with equality: not everyone can win at the Olympics, but it is perfectly possible for all the knives to be sharp.[16]

The *Republic*, hierarchy or no, is emphatically about *aretē* as what enables one to accomplish one's work. Plato reinforces this essentially noncompetitive sense of *aretē* in his emphasis on justice as doing one's own job (433d-e, 441d). He also underlines the move from justice to *aretē* more generally through some rather striking remarks, most amusingly Socrates's idea that if he identifies three of the four standard forms of excellence the fourth must be the one left over (428a).[17] And as *aretē* is essentially that which makes an x into a good x, it also makes sense that here Socrates's discussion of excellence leads to the Good (504d–509c). In contrast, in the *Symposium*, which has moved steadily away from a focus on *aretē*, Diotima's Ladder of Love closely parallels the Divided Line, but without the Good.[18]

This leads us to the other side of the complication. If the *Republic*, despite its focus on hierarchy, considers *aretē* in its noncompetitive form, the *Symposium*, despite its move toward the universal, is remarkably competitive. The *Republic* stresses the competition between Socrates and Thrasymachus in Book 1 (336b–338b, etc.) only to have it pointedly abate (450a-b, 498c, and see 500d–501e). In contrast, and despite the friendly celebration that is the dialogue's occasion, a sense of competition runs throughout the *Sympo-*

sium. As we will see, this culminates in the appearance of Alcibiades and so also, as I will argue, in a need to revaluate *aretē* and its relation to equality.

The *Republic*: Excellence without Equality

Despite these complications, the *Republic* and *Symposium* are deliberately cast as having opposite positions on the topics of excellence and equality. In the *Republic* Socrates requires a "longer road" (435d, 504b2) to lead to a Good even greater than "justice and the other things we went through" (Bk. 6 504d), a Good that is beyond even Being. In the *Symposium* the good appears in the much more general light of what anyone wants in order to be happy (204e–205a). As we will see below, the *Symposium* becomes ever more inclusive, and as it does so moves away from an initial focus on *aretē*. In contrast, the *Republic*, which is specifically a work about *aretē*, has little time for equality.[19] Long before we reach the critique of democracy, Socrates has gone out of his way to establish hierarchy as a basic principle of his City in Words.

The hierarchy of Socrates's ideal city appears even in its contrast to the society it grows out of. This, the "city of pigs" or the "city of utmost necessity," a society of those who "passing life in peace and with health, as is likely, and dying in old age, pass on such another life to their offspring" (372d2–5), is the most basic form of society according to Socrates, and probably the *Republic*'s most positive model of equality.[20] Socrates accordingly describes it as the true or healthy city, presumably because it is a city where vice has not yet entered in (372e7–8; 373d-e). In this light, however, it seems quite possible that it is also a society without virtue or excellence. Our search for *aretē* seems to necessitate leaving equality behind.

This does not mean, however, that all equality is eliminated. While Socrates is quite definite that we are born with unequal abilities, for example, his city is nonetheless, and necessarily, founded on what we would now term equality of opportunity. Far from being Popper's rigid caste system (45), Socrates goes out of his way not only to say, but also to reiterate, that children might well be born with abilities superior or inferior to those of their parents, and that the education given each child must suit his or her own particular abilities (415a-c, 423c-d). In this way, the class system represented by the metals of the Noble Lie is in fact a meritocracy. Plato is aware, as is anyone familiar with stock breeding (such as Glaucon, 459a), that traits are often, but not always, passed from parent to child.[21] As a result, the critical task of the City in Words is giving each child the education that suits his or her abilities—not the education that suits the abilities of his or her parents.

But while Socrates's City in Words is based on equality of opportunity, this does not make everyone equal. There remains a single objective standard of good that not everyone can attain. Moreover, the hierarchy of goods with which Glaucon initiated the conversation (357b-c) remains the salient issue. Just as Socrates's overall aim is to show that physical goods are not as valuable as goods of the soul, so also for the city. Both a soldier and a shoemaker may be good, for example, but a good soldier, it is implied, is better than a good shoemaker, as, even more critically, he (or she) is more important to society (421a, 434a-c). Hence also the culminating decision in Book 9 (580a–587e) ranks not only regimes, but also different ways of life, from best to worst.

Finally, the world of ideas, which the many are incapable of comprehending (493e–494a, and see 480a, 503b), is not only better and more important than the visible world, it, like its pleasures, is also more real (585b-d). Even further, it is more real because the visible world is merely derivative from it, as (in Socrates's notion, *Rep.* 596ec–598c) a picture is derivative from its model.[22] Hence, Socrates opens with and emphasizes the level of "images" as the essential way to understand the Divided Line (509d6–510a10) and then treats the visible world as itself an "image" to be employed in seeking the intelligible (510b–511b), making each level of the line essentially a reflection of the level above it.[23] Similarly, he describes the Philosopher-Ruler using the Forms as the model for the city he "sketches" (διαγράφω, ὑπογράφω, 500e–501c, and see 540a), itself one image out of the many that Socrates employs. Even in the Noble Lie, where there is an essential equality in all being born from the Earth (414c-e), Socrates seems to choose bronze and iron for the craftsmen, who work with the physical world (415a-c), at least partially because bronze seems a baser version of gold, and iron of silver.[24] In all these cases, as we saw above, this relation of substance and image brings out an underlying similarity, but it also makes us see that one is better than the other.

In this way, critics are perfectly right about Plato's nonegalitarian tendencies. If physical reality derives from a further, transcendent reality, that reality, which humans will never be equally able to appreciate, must be more important. Nor does it help that that ultimate truth seems rather unattainable.[25] It is true that Socrates's choice of the Sun as an image for the Good hardly suggests a steady gaze at the ultimate Forms.[26] Similarly, the progression up Diotima's ladder, taken over as it is by questions and indirect statements, "What then do we suppose it would be if it happened to someone . . . ?"; "Do you suppose . . . ?"; "Or do you not consider . . . ?" (211d8, 211e4, 212a1), is suddenly over just as we seem to be reaching the top. But while it might not be possible to stare steadily at the sun, one's eyes can be more or less adjusted to the light, as the allegory of the Cave reminds us. Similarly, while Diotima's ladder does not lead to a scenic observatory reserved for the elect, her focus on ascent (211b6, c2) still suggests a higher and a lower. Pure justice may be unachievable, but one act can still be more or less just than another. Even if we cannot attain absolute truth, one person may still get closer to it than another, and so, presumably, be closer to excellence.

Socrates and Democracy

The most important complication in the *Republic*'s opposition to equality, however, and one that resonates with the appearance of Alcibiades in the *Symposium*, is the argument that a Socrates could arise only in democracy. As Socrates points out (reinforced by the introduction of a new goddess to the city in the dialogue's first lines), a democracy's "supermarket of polities" (557d8) is the most appropriate place to look for a constitution "as we ourselves were doing just now" (557d5). In other words, democracy apparently provides the essential requirements for the *Republic*. Similarly, the Socrates of the *Apology* (37d-e) and *Crito* (53b-54a) is quite certain that no city except Athens could put up with him for even this long.[27] The intensely Athenian setting of Plato's dialogues makes Socrates and Athens seem as close a fit as Leopold Bloom and Dublin, and in the *Symposium*, at any rate, Socrates's persistence in Athens is implicitly contrasted with the departure of Agathon (172c) as well as of Pausanias and Alcibiades. It is of course true that the Athenian democracy put Socrates to death, but as Socrates himself pointed out, that may have been largely because the Thirty ran out of time (*Apology* 32e).

Here, however, there is an important qualification, to which we will return. If democracy is the only soil in which philosophy can grow, this is not because democracy promotes philosophy (which we may take, at least for now, as equivalent to excellence), but because it is the only polity that does not actively root it out.[28] In much the same way that relativism has to see even itself as relative, democracy promotes freedom and equality, and so allows for the free-thinking that enables philosophy to exist—just as it also allows for all the kinds of thinking that tend to the extermination of philosophy. The best we can say is that the *Republic* suggests that equality and excellence might coexist in a democracy for a while, until the great lazy horse, unperturbed by its inconsistency of principle, swats down the gadfly (*Apology* 30e).[29]

The *Symposium*: Equality without Excellence

In contrast to the *Republic*'s move from the equality of the City of Pigs to the hierarchical City in Words, the *Symposium* moves quite deliberately, if unobtrusively, from the elite to the universal, and in this sense from hierarchy to equality. That Phaedrus's first speech concerned the elite becomes clear when Pausanias opposes the "demotic" or "common" (πάνδημος) *eros* to the noble, "heavenly" (οὐράνιος) one described by Phaedrus (180c-d). Eryximachus then further expands the range, observing (in his own inimitably repetitious style) that *eros* "is not only in relation to the souls of humans in regard to the beautiful but also in regard to many other things and in other things, both the bodies of all living beings and in things that grow in earth and, so to speak, in everything that is" (186a4–7), while Aristophanes takes the unprecedented step of including even heterosexuals and women (though see 179b5 for a foreshadowing). As usual, the female, given an inch, takes a yard. Just as Eryximachus universalized Pausanias's two forms of *eros* (185e6–186b1), Diotima (though with a focus on the good rather than one's own, 204d-e, 205d-e, 212c) universalizes Aristophanes's connection of *eros* to our essential nature. She begins with what is "common to all human beings" (205a6) but soon moves to what is common to "mortal nature" (207d1) and "everything mortal" (208a7).

Just as the *Republic*'s focus on excellence leads the dialogue away from equality, the *Symposium*'s growing universality increasingly deemphasizes excellence. Phaedrus introduces the idea that Eros inspires the lover to great deeds deserving of honor (178d–179b, 180b5) and concludes that he is "the oldest of the gods and the most honored and powerful in regard to humans acquiring *aretē* and happiness both living and having ended life" (180b7–9). Pausanias then grabs the ball and runs with it, filling his speech with the idea of *aretē* (181e2, 184c2, c6, d1, e1; 185b1, b3, b5, c1). The emphasis, however, serves primarily as a contrast to what follows, since neither Eryximachus, nor Aristophanes, nor Diotima, until the very end of her speech, mentions *aretē*. After Pausanias uses the word eight times between 184c and 185c, the dialogue (with the exception below) goes eighteen pages (185c1–208d7) before it occurs again—and that mention is in a direct reference to Phaedrus's speech (208d7, 179b–180a).

The one speech that does not follow the pattern of increasing universality is Agathon's. Given Plato's care in setting up the speeches (for example, contriving Aristophanes's hiccups so that we notice the pairing of his comic speech with Agathon's tragic one), it is hard to see this as an oversight.[30] And in fact, Agathon's speech is unique in two ways: in resisting the move toward the universal, and in bringing back a focus on *aretē*.[31] Although Agathon uses the word only once (196b5), the heart of his speech, which demonstrates the justice, moderation, courage, and wisdom of Eros, is an elaborate joke on precisely the four standard forms of excellence discovered in the *Republic* (196b–197b). In other words, the *Symposium*'s focus on *aretē*, or excellence, returns precisely when the move toward the universal stops. Nor should we forget the name of the speaker, "Agathon," or the "Good," particularly notable to a man like Plato, whose father's name (*Republic* 327a1, 368a3 on his brothers) was "Ariston," or the "Best."

Plato also brings the idea of *aretē* back largely in order to undermine it. Agathon's defense of Eros's virtue is pointedly (and humorously) sophistic. The speech is the only one (before Diotima's closing words) to revive the idea of *aretē*, and also the only one to be directly refuted (201b-c). Similarly, while the occasion of the dialogue, Agathon's victory in the Lenaia of 416, should be a definitive demonstration of *aretē*, this comes into question when Agathon declares that the judgment of the wise outweighs that of the many. And not to end there, Socrates then undermines even this idea, which should be supremely Platonic, by pointing out that in this case the wise were among the many (194a-d). The rest of the refutation of Agathon, who with his lover, Pausanias, has been cited as an example of the all-male (193b), Socrates leaves to a woman.

Diotima's universalizing of *eros* is particularly striking following Agathon's speech and particularly marked as she opens by refuting the speech (201e–202e), apparently long before it was made. Her extension of *eros* from Aristophanes's basic principle of human nature (189d, 193b-d) to, essentially, a basic principle of nature altogether is underlined by other equalizing tendencies. *Eros* thus moves from being the beloved that Agathon portrayed to being the lover, and from having to wanting. Diotima also shifts the kind of wanting involved from wanting the beloved to any sort of wanting at all and, as an illustration, points out that all those who practice an expertise or *technē* are "makers" or "poets," although we single some out with the name (205b-d). It is a play on words, here from the particular to the universal, that Agathon (whose poetic skill has just been stressed (198b-c)) made the other way around—turning Eros, the "maker" of all things, into a poet of words in particular (196e–197a, and see 223d3).

As Diotima, in contrast to Agathon, universalizes, she also democratizes. While her Eros may be the child of both Resource ("Poros") and Poverty ("Penia") it is clearly Poverty (in implicit contrast to Agathon's feast) who has the more important role. As might be expected, given Socrates's appreciation for *aporia*, the only thing Poros does in Diotima's tale is to drunkenly pass out.[32] The agency is all Poverty's. Moreover, given Poverty's demonstrated ingenuity, it is not all that clear what Eros (who bears a distinct resemblance to our favorite, notoriously poor, philosopher, 203c-d) needed to inherit from his father. The further implications would be far clearer to Plato's audience than to us, since Athenians were not shy of recognizing that the people, or "demos," of "democracy" were primarily characterized by being poor (e.g., *Republic* 557a).

The *Symposium*'s sequence of speeches not only moves from an elite to a universal view, it also sets the stage for the arrival of Alcibiades through its arrangement into two groups.[33] The speeches of Aristophanes, Agathon, and Socrates/Diotima thus parallel those of Phaedrus, Pausanias, and Eryximachus. The lovers (of each other), Pausanias and Agathon, occupy the central place in each series and Eryximachus's final speech in the first series prepares the way for Diotima's, both in universalizing *eros* and in positing a harmony that will be disrupted by the next speaker. Eryximachus's universal harmony, moreover, is set in contrast to Heraclitus's "differing with itself it agrees with itself, as with the harmony of the bow and the lyre" (187a5–6)—a tension in unity that reappears in Aristophanes's round people. Similarly, the harmony that ends Diotima's account of the Ladder of Love is followed by Alcibiades, who disrupts all the systems of equality, excellence, the good, and one's own that have preceded him.

Alcibiades: The Aristocratic and the *Demos*

Alcibiades's disruption of the harmony suggested by Diotima appears most clearly in the way he reflects her return to the idea of *aretē*. Diotima reintroduces the idea first as an element in the ascent to true beauty (209a3, 209b8, 209e2), then at the end of the "lesser initiation" (210a1–3), and finally at the very conclusion of her speech, saying that one who sees beauty itself gives birth not to images (εἴδωλα) of *aretē* but rather, "laying hold of not an image but the truth," to true *aretē* (212a3–6).[34] An echo of the passage appears in Alcibiades's account of his attempted seduction of Socrates, when Socrates declares that Alcibiades must have seen an extraordinary beauty in him, and that, "If seeing this you are attempting to have something in common with me and exchange beauty for beauty, you intend to profit from me by not a little; you are attempting to acquire the truth of the beautiful in place of opinion and you mean in reality to change "'gold for bronze'" (218e4–19a2).

The contrast here between what is truly beautiful and what is beautiful only in opinion recalls Diotima's description of the ultimate desirability of the beautiful itself, as well as her contrast of images and true *aretē*. A more unsettling side of the comparison, however, emerges in Socrates's characterization of this as an exchange of gold for bronze, an idea that resonates not only with the *Republic*'s Noble Lie, but with another account as well, one that Socrates in the *Republic* says illustrates the "necessity of Diomedes" (493d5).[35]

The *Republic*'s "necessity of Diomedes" and the *Symposium*'s "bronze for gold" are connected by a passage in the *Iliad* where Glaucus exchanges his golden armor for Diomedes's bronze (6.224–36). They are also connected, however, by the context of the *Republic* reference, which describes the inevitability of yielding to the valuations of the many.[36] Moreover, the yielding that Socrates describes is the inevitable seduction of the "almost-philosopher" by the many and, as was suggested above, that "almost-philosopher" bears a striking resemblance to Alcibiades. In fact, as we will see, Alcibiades does seem to be torn between *aretē* as Socrates sees it and *aretē* as it is viewed by the many.[37] And while it may seem obvious, in all of these cases, that the "golden" option is the preferable one, there is a curious undertone. Of the trade made by Glaucus, Homer says that "there also Zeus, son of Cronus, took away Glaucus's wits, / who exchanged armor with Tydeus's son Diomedes, / gold for bronze, of a hundred oxen's worth for the worth of nine" (6.234–36). And yet, given that Diomedes is in the midst of his *aristeia* when he encounters Glaucus, an *aristeia* in which he will successfully attack even a god (5.336–465, 818–20), Zeus might not have taken all of Glaucus's wits when he made the trade. He may leave the battlefield with armor worth only nine oxen, but he also leaves with his life.[38]

Yet another difference between the *Symposium* and the *Republic* is that the *Republic*, in the person of its particular concern, justice (as 354b-c) centers on the question of what *aretē* actually is, while the *Symposium* never seems to even regard this as a question (in contrast see 194e–195a, 199c on Eros). Phaedrus introduces the idea of *aretē* and Pausanias runs with it, but for both *aretē* seems simply to distinguish the noble from the base—neither raises the question of what *aretē* actually consists in. The tendency is only underlined by Agathon's speech, which catalogues, very amusingly, the justice, moderation, courage, and wisdom of Eros, demonstrating only how completely the form of *logos* can be divorced from its content. The question of what *aretē* is has become only a plaything, as in the wonderful argument that Eros must be moderate, since it can master all [other] pleasures and desires (196c and see 201b10-c2). All of this changes, however, with the entrance of Alcibiades.

Entering, as he does, just after Diotima's contrast of true *aretē* to its images, Alcibiades makes us question what *aretē* actually is. For if Socrates appears in Aristodemus's and Alcibiades's accounts as like the whole and self-sufficient round person of Aristophanes's speech, Alcibiades is the round person whose halves are at war, and the war seems to be between two different views of *aretē*.[39]

In some ways, moreover, the conflict that appears in Alcibiades in regard to *aretē* is inherent to Athens itself, a system of radical equality built upon a Homeric ethos of excellence, captured even in the paradox of Aristodemus's name, the "best-common people."[40] The essence of the paradox appears in Alcibiades's (now the real Alcibiades) argument in Book 6 of Thucydides that he should lead the Sicilian Expedition (6.16). Far from concealing his attempt to outdo others, he boasts of his supremacy, and in the most aristocratic of ventures, the Olympic horse race, saying explicitly that one who has great thoughts may spurn equality ("nor is it unjust that one thinking greatly of himself should be not equal": οὐδέ γε ἄδικον ἐφ' ἑαυτῷ μέγα φρονοῦντα μὴ ἴσον εἶναι 6.16.4). And yet his ambition is to be supreme in a democracy. No one in Plato (one could really say, in fifth-century Athens) more completely embodies the ideals of *aretē* than Alcibiades, and yet what he aspires to is an excellence embedded in equality.

If the historical Alcibiades was divided by his need to pursue an aristocratic vision of *aretē* within a democracy, the Alcibiades of the *Symposium* is divided in an even more obvious way. He desires excellence, but both as the Athenians view it and as Socrates does, and, unfortunately for him, the two are diametrically opposed (216a-e).[41] Like Diotima, Alcibiades explicitly mentions *aretē* only at the end of his speech, when he points to the way in which Socrates, or here, his language, is also split, with a base and common exterior concealing elements that are most divine, and that contain the greatest images of *aretē* (θειοτάτους καὶ πλεῖστα ἀγάλματ' ἀρετῆς ἐν αὑτοῖς ἔχοντας 222a2–3).[42] The passage not only recalls Diotima's *eidola* of *aretē*, it also, essentially, reprises the topic Alcibiades opened with, his own sense of being torn between his desire to be honored by the many (216b4) and his desire to follow Socrates.

In short, what Alcibiades has introduced into the tension between equality and excellence is the extremely Socratic question of what excellence is (e.g., *Meno* 71b, 73c). Pursuit of the Forms, it seems, is no longer the only contestant. There have been indications of this possibility before. While Diotima seemed to reach true *aretē* at the top of her Ladder of Love (212a), the moment, as we saw, passed swiftly and in indirect questions. One of the things that young Socrates had to learn was that philosophers, lovers of wisdom, are therefore also those who are not wise (204a). It would be disingenuous to argue that Plato, and so Socrates, and so Diotima, do not feel that true excellence lies in wisdom, as the contest of *Republic* 9 seeks to demonstrate. Nonetheless, just as (I believe) it is necessary to take the dialogue form seriously, and not as sugar coating for an epistemological system, it is important to take seriously the reminder that Socrates's version of *aretē* is not the only one.

As the *Symposium* moved from Pausanias's focus on *aretē* to Diotima's account of an *eros* common to all life we might have expected the emergence as well of peace and harmony, perhaps, say, the harmony of Diotima's description of beauty itself: "being always itself in regard to itself, with itself, of one form" (211b2), or of the contemplative Socrates at the beginning of the dialogue. In fact what characterizes the dialogue, culminating in the war that is raging between Alcibiades's competing instincts, is competition. The humorous, or perhaps half-humorous, competition that runs throughout in regard to the speeches (177e, 186a, 189b-c, 194a, 198a-b, 212c-d) is introduced by Apollodorus's opening contentiousness (173c-d), Socrates's and Aristodemus's joking dispute over the relative goodness of Agamemnon and Menelaus, itself a contest with Homer (174b-c), by Socrates and Agathon's dispute on who has the greater wisdom (175d-e), Eryximachus's approach to drinking as a kind of contest (176c), and of course by the occasion of the feast, Agathon's victory in the dramatic competition.[43] Competition appears in the various speeches as well, in Pausanias's accounts of the contest between lover, beloved, and the law, in Aristophanes's round people challenging the gods, Agathon's correction of Phaedrus (195b-c), and in Diotima's account of how care for their offspring will lead the weakest beings to do battle with the strongest (207b). It continues in the contest between Socrates and Alcibiades over Agathon (213b-c, 223a) and has its coda in the philosopher's version of a dramatic competition when "Socrates forces [Aristophanes and Agathon] to agree" that the same man can write (or "make," ποιεῖν) both tragedy and comedy (223d2).[44] The great proponents of harmony, in contrast, are the comic Eryximachus (186d5–8, 187c-d), who leaves when things get too rowdy (223b), and Agathon (195c, 197c-e), who is immediately discredited.

A glance at the *Republic*'s "almost-philosopher" (*Republic* 490e ff.) also helps elucidate another competition, one not far under the surface of Alcibiades's speech in the *Symposium*. This is the competition between Athens and Socrates for Alcibiades, a competition that appears as well in the *Symposium*'s questioning whether Socrates is Alcibiades's lover or his beloved (213c-d, 214c-d, 218c-d, 222b-c, and see *Gorgias*, 481d-e, 519a-b, for a related use of Alcibiades). But while in the *Republic* what emerged most clearly was the unevenness of the odds, the *Symposium* focuses instead on the consequences for Alcibiades. They are not pretty. When set against Alcibiades's inner conflict, the self-contained, self-sufficient Socrates of the opening and of Alcibiades's speech (175a-b, 220c-d) comes to seem solipsistic. Even more so, the self-control (219d2–7, 220a-b, 221a-b) that resists Alcibiades can seem hubristic, and more like Aristophanes's round people than like the gods (190b-d, and see 175c8, 215b7).[45] And as the prologue reminded us of the date of the gathering, we know that the speeches of Thucydides's Book 6 are soon to occur, that Alcibiades, Eryximachus, and Pausanias will soon be involved in the scandal over the Eleusinian Mysteries, and that the disaster in Sicily is on the horizon.[46] The negative effects of Socrates's approach to *aretē*, it seems, will be felt by more than just Alcibiades.

Nor is the *Symposium* alone in reminding us that there is more than one view of *aretē*. The *Republic* takes a very roundabout way to establish what one feels should be its main point, that true *aretē* necessitates the rule of reason. Although Glaucon declares, before we are even halfway through the dialogue, that the conclusion to their quest is now obvious, Socrates insists on continuing (445a-e). Once the "digression" of Books 5–7 has established that only the philosopher can recognize the Forms that are the essence of reality (500b–501c, 518d-e, 540a), the superiority of the philosophic life seems only more evident. Socrates, however, still insists on describing all the possible regimes (543c–580a). This cements the victory of the City in Words, but it also reminds us of some very different view of what *aretē* consists in.

Republic Book 8, moreover, reminds us not only of the different views of *aretē*, but also of how intertwined these views are with what Aristotle calls our nature as a *politicon zōon* (*Politics* 1253a).[47] Different societies set different degrees of value on honor, pleasure, and freedom, and so suggest different kinds of human excellence to the individuals within them—and the individuals within them then shape the views held by their societies. Nor is it only the *polis* that forms our views of *aretē*; as Socrates's elaborate family histories demonstrate, we absorb a whole range of ideas about *aretē* from our earliest moments and in our most basic human associations, and these ideas are often in conflict. It might be that one form of human excellence is the best. *Republic* Book 8, however, makes it seem increasingly likely that human beings will continue to differ on the question.

What the *Republic*'s long pursuit of *aretē* has run up against is a necessity apparently left behind with the City of Pigs, the necessity of "some need they themselves [the citizens] have of one another" (372a1–2). And, as we recall, the fundamental characteristic of that city was equality. The same undertone sounds in Socrates's Noble Lie. Although it is, not surprisingly, Socrates's (and Hesiod's 468e8, 546e1) myth of the metals that tends to be remembered, the opening of the story is just as crucial, that we are all—equally—born from the earth, a motif that appears in tales of the Age of Cronos as well (*Laws* 4.713c–714a; *Statesman* 271a–274e). The idea would be familiar to everyone present, since Athens was notably invested in seeing its citizens as autochthonous, and in seeing autochthony as the basis of their equality (*Menexenus* 237b-c, 238a–239a). On the other hand, however, there is some ambivalence, since the Theban "sown men" (interestingly "spartoi") of the Phoenician story (414c) commenced to destroy one another (*Metamorphoses* 3.95–130).[48] Society, and the equality it demands, might be necessary, but it can also be dangerous. Or, in good dialectical fashion, we could say that society, and the equality it demands, might be dangerous, but it is also necessary.

As the opening of the Noble Lie implies, since we need society, we also need the basic level of equality that enables it to occur.[49] There is only so much hierarchy that we are willing to take. We appreciate Thrasymachus's scorn at the idea that rulers, like shepherds, govern for the sake of the sheep, even if he cannot logically defend it (343b–347a). Similarly, Socrates's insistence on describing the City in Words in terms generally used for the keeping of animals (451c-e, 459d–461c and see 375a–376b, etc.) has its desired effect: it is extremely off-putting. We may be willing to acknowledge that human beings are not altogether equal. We are not willing to acknowledge that they are as unequal as humans and beasts.

This same dialectic seems to occur between the *Symposium* and the *Republic*. As soon as we acknowledge something common to all, Plato pushes us to see where some must surpass others. As soon as we acknowledge that some must surpass others, Plato pushes us to see something common to all. Similarly, even as we seek to go farther, we cannot simply ignore the views of *aretē* that we grow up with, however mistaken they may be—as Socrates did not, finally, attempt to ignore them. The unusual Socrates of the *Symposium* may be as utterly self-absorbed, self-sufficient, and solipsistic at the opening of the dialogue as he was in Potidaea, but the more usual Socrates that we end with (223d8–11) passes his time, as he passed his very last moments, talking with others.

To return to the obvious, one cannot discover the relation of equality and excellence until one has asked what excellence is. As we have seen, the answer is more complicated than simply "philosophy." For example, the *Symposium*'s observation that the philosopher is a seeker after, and not a possessor of the virtue of wisdom seems to contradict the elaborate panoply of virtues given the philosophic soul at *Republic* 484a–87a. And even the panoply is not all that it seems. Socrates answers Adeimantus's initial misgiving by distinguishing who the real philosophers are (or would be), but this does not completely address the question. Finally, the philosopher's prime reason for not stealing or cheating seems to be that he (or she) doesn't value possessions, or even life, enough to make cheating or stealing worthwhile (485d–486b, 500b-c, and see *Apology* 40b-e). One does not need to be a Kantian to find this less than inspiring.

It is thus possible that excellence and equality are compatible in Plato exactly because he does not, generally speaking, think all that much of excellence, or at least of excellence as it is commonly viewed.[50] This might also explain the nonchalance with which Socrates acknowledges that the truly important study is one far beyond questions of excellence (*Republic* 504d). Moreover, a rather open view of the nature of *aretē*, along with an emphasis on equality, at least discourages the tendency of any given society to predetermine what excellence is, and, in this way, as with the necessity of *aporia*, might leave the path a little open for the possibility of seeking truth.

Unlike Tocqueville, Plato does not depict equality and freedom as being in tension with one another. Democracy, as Socrates portrays it in *Republic* 8, values the one precisely because it also values the other. Valuing freedom means that all pursuits must be seen as equally valid: none can be compelled, and none can be held as superior to another. Thus Socrates's democratic man, insisting always on his freedom, "having established all his pleasures on an equal footing," now drinks, now listens to the flute, now holds to strict diets and exercises, now practices philosophy, and now politics (561b3–4, 561c-d). It seems to be equality in this sense, the equality that refuses to make a decision, that is the best breeding ground for philosophy, just as it is for many varied forms of excellence.

However, what Tocqueville was to call "the tyranny of the majority" was no stranger, either to Plato or to Athens. Although Pericles praised Athens in exactly the terms of *Republic* 8, as leaving its citizens free to choose their own course (Thucydides 2.37), the *demos* was as capable of stamping out opinions that it disagreed with as the most strictly governed oligarchy, or the most puritanical New England village—as Socrates was to learn.[51] On the other hand, as Socrates also predicted (*Apology* 39c-d), there was always the chance that once the seed was set the plant could no longer be eradicated. By allowing any sort of *aretē* an opportunity to take root, democracy, in Plato's view, might be the best chance that true excellence has.

Plato's second letter describes his dialogues as coming not from himself, but from a Socrates made young and beautiful (314c). While some critics have excused, and others taken offence at, the depiction of democracy in *Republic* 8, it also seems possible that in it Plato has made democracy young and beautiful, promoting an ideal that Pericles also envisioned, but that Athens seldom lived up to. It is in a democracy such as this that equality can provide the environment in which excellence can truly be tested. The ideal city may be better suited to true excellence, but it remains an ideal.[52] Humans, who need to live together in some form of community, need to have some system of values, however provisional, and that system of values is bound to predispose us to a given view of excellence. In this light, while democracy, together with the equality it promotes, might be the *Republic*'s nearly worst form of government, in Churchill's phrase it may be the worst except for the other ones.

Notes

1. For convenience I use now fairly standard phrases such as the "City in Words," "Ladder of Love," "City of Pigs," or "Noble Lie," etc., while acknowledging some inaccuracy. "Logos" seldom means simply "word," for example; the "Ladder of Love" is actually more of a staircase; the "City of Pigs" is specified (for some

reason) as occupied by sows; and the *pseudos* of the "Noble Lie" could be merely "false" rather than a lie. For the last see, for example, Julia Annas, *An Introduction to Plato's Republic* (Oxford: Oxford University Press, 1981), 107–108; Malcolm Schofield, "The Noble Lie," in *The Cambridge Companion to Plato's Republic*, ed. G. R. F. Ferrari (Cambridge: Cambridge University Press, 2007), 138–39 and 149 on Hannah Arendt's view.

I would also like to take this occasion to express my enormous gratitude to Joe Cropsey for so much of inestimable value. I particularly recall his telling us that we could only get an A in his course on Hegel's *Philosophy of Right* if our paper was free of Hegel-speak. I still lament that there, as with so many of the challenges he set us, I was unable to rise to his level, but remain profoundly grateful for everything I learned from him and for the example he set us all.

2. Karl Popper, *The Open Society and Its Enemies: New One-Volume Edition* (Princeton: Princeton University Press, 2013) and see, in answer, Panos Eliopoulos, "The Political Dimension of Eros in Plato's Philosophy," in *The Poetry in Philosophy: Essays in Honor of Christos C. Evangeliou*, ed. Phillip Mitsis and Heather L. Reid (Sioux City, IA: Parnassos Press—Fonte Aretusa, 2021), 113–15; Lesley Brown, "How Totalitarian Is Plato's Republic?" in *Essays on Plato's Republic*, ed. E. N. Ostenfeld (Aarhus: Aarhus University Press, 1998), 13–27.

For Plato's pro-democratic side see David Roochnik, *Beautiful City: The Dialectical Character of Plato's Republic* (Ithaca: Cornell University Press, 2008), 78–92; Gregg Recco, *Athens Victorious: Democracy in Plato's Republic* (Lanham, MD: Lexington Books, 2007); Samantha Deane, "The Education of Tyrants: Democratic Education in the *Republic*," in *Philosopher Kings and Tragic Heroes: Essays on Images and Ideas from Western Greece*, ed. Heather L. Reid and Davide Tanasi (Sioux City, IA: Parnassos Press—Fonte Aretusa, 2016), 159–70; and for a counterargument, Donald Morrison, "The Utopian Character of Plato's Ideal City," in Ferrari, *Companion*, 241–44.

Others who have discussed Plato's involvement with Athenian politics include Arlene W. Saxonhouse, *Athenian Democracy: Modern Mythmakers and Ancient Theorists* (Notre Dame: University of Notre Dame Press, 1996); Josiah Ober, *Political Dissent in Democratic Athens: Intellectual Critics of Popular Rule* (Princeton: Princeton University Press, 2001) and *Mass and Elite in Democratic Athens: Rhetoric, Ideology, and the Power of the People* (Princeton: Princeton University Press, 1989); Danielle Allen, *Why Plato Wrote* (West Sussex: Blackwell, 2010); Sara Monoson, *Plato's Democratic Entanglements: Athenian Politics and the Practice of Philosophy* (Princeton: Princeton University Press, 2000).

3. An idea, incidentally, not unlike *Phaedrus* 246e–247e. The *Phaedrus*, which has a good claim to be considered a companion dialogue to the *Symposium* and *Republic* (notice that Phaedrus is the "father of the *logos*" at *Symposium* 177d5) also has each soul follow in the train of its own god (248a), following the *Republic*'s idea of "each to his own" but with greater equality.

4. Interestingly, Socrates also does not specify whether the intelligible or the visible sections of the line are larger. The element of ascent, of course, will enter into the *Republic* with the Image of the Cave.

5. See Roochnik, *Beautiful City*, 61–69 for the deliberate absurdity of the "marriage number."

6. Roochnik, *Beautiful City*, overall makes a compelling argument that the *Republic* itself follows a similar dialectical trajectory.

7. See Eva Brann, *The Music of the Republic: Essays on Socrates' Conversations and Plato's Writings* (Philadelphia: Paul Dry Books, 2004), 241.

8. For Alcibiades as the almost-philosopher and for further references see Mark Ralkowski, "A Contest Between Two Lives: Plato's Existential Drama," in *Athletics, Gymnastics, and Agon in Plato*, ed. Heather Reid, Mark Ralkowski, and Coleen Zoller (Sioux City, IA: Parnassos Press—Fonte Aretusa, 2020), 102–103. For a structural similarity between the *Symposium* and the *Republic* and for Alcibiades's appearance see Louis Ruprecht Jr., *Symposia: Plato, The Erotic and Moral Value* (Albany: State University of New York Press, 1999), 33–36.

9. See Stanley Rosen, *Plato's Symposium* (New Haven: Yale University Press, 1968), 12–14. Translations are my own.

10. Roochnik, *Beautiful City*, esp. 3–7, 51–77; Paul Ludwig, "Eros in the Republic," in Ferrari, *Companion*, 202–203.

11. Ludwig in Ferrari, *Companion*, overall.

12. See Ludwig in Ferrari, *Companion*, 217–22 for a miniature Ladder of Love in the *Republic*.

13. For various views on whether Plato has a "theory of Forms" see Terence Irwin, *Plato's Ethics* (New York: Oxford University Press, 1995), 148–69; Annas, *Introduction*, 217–18, 232–41; Brann, *Music*, 320–22; Stephanie Nelson, "Between Being and Becoming: Comedy, Tragedy, and the *Symposium*," in *Thinking the Greeks: A Volume in Honor of James M. Redfield*, ed. Lillian Doherty and Bruce King (London and New York: Routledge, 2018), 112; Charles Griswold, "Plato's Metaphilosophy: Why Plato Wrote Dialogues," in *Platonic Writings; Platonic Readings*, ed. Charles Griswold (University Park: Pennsylvania State University Press, 1988), 147–49; Drew Hyland, *Finitude and Transcendence in the Platonic Dialogues* (Albany: State University of New York Press, 1995), 165–97.

14. For various views of the Socratic idea that knowledge is virtue see Diskin Clay, *Platonic Questions: Dialogues with the Silent Philosopher* (University Park: Pennsylvania State University Press, 2000), 191–200; F. C. C. Sheffield, *Plato's Symposium: The Ethics of Desire* (Oxford: Oxford University Press, 2006), 134; Lloyd Gerson, "A Platonic Reading of Plato's *Symposium*" in *Plato's Symposium: Issues in Interpretation and Reception*, ed. James Lesher, Debra Nails, and Frisbee Sheffield (Washington, DC: Center for Hellenic Studies, 2006), 65–66 and Lloyd Gerson, "Plato's Rational Souls," *The Review of Metaphysics* 68 (2014): 37–59. See also Alexander Nehemas, *Virtues of Authenticity: Essays on Plato and Socrates* (Princeton: Princeton University

Press, 1999), 27–58; Irwin, *Ethics*, 203–22; and Christopher Rowe, "The Place of the *Republic* in Plato's Political Thought," in Ferrari, *Companion*, 47–49.

15. On the essentially competitive nature of Greek society see Jure Zovko, "Agōn as Constituent of the Socratic Elenchos," 173–84 and Lee Coulson, "The Agōnes of Platonic Philosophy: Seeking Victory Without Triumph," 211–22, both in Reid et al., *Athletics* and both citing Jacob Burckhardt, *The Greeks and Greek Civilization*, ed. Oswyn Murray, trans. Sheila Stern (New York: St. Martin's Press, 1998), 71, 162. For Homer see *Iliad* 6.208, 11.784 on the proper goal as "always to be best and be eminent over others"; A. W. H. Adkins, *Merit and Responsibility: A Study in Greek Values* (Oxford: Oxford University Press, 1960), 30–85 and for a critique of Adkins, Margalit Finkelberg, "Timē and Aretē in Homer," *The Classical Quarterly* 48 (1998): 14–28.

16. See Aryeh Kosman, "Justice and Virtue: The *Republic*'s Inquiry into Proper Difference" in Ferrari, *Companion*, 116–37; Nehemas, *Authenticity*, xxxi–ii, 318–20.

17. See Annas, *Introduction*, 110–12 for problems with the argument.

18. Although the discussion does begin with the good in the more basic sense of 204e–206a. While Beauty and the Good are not identical (see *Symposium* 201b10-c2) they seem to have corresponding roles, as C. H. Kahn, "Plato's Theory of Desire," *Review of Metaphysics* 41 (1987): 77–103, at 91, 101; Plato, *The Symposium*, trans. R. E. Allen (New Haven: Yale University Press, 1991), 21: "the account of Beauty itself at 210a–212a anticipates the account of the Good in Republic VI, 506b–509b."

19. Annas, *Introduction*, 176–78 and see Richard Kraut, 52: "One of Plato's great contributions to political philosophy lies precisely here, in his recognition of the importance of this unequal relationships among human beings" ("Ordinary Virtue from the *Phaedo* to the *Laws*," in *Plato's Laws: A Critical Guide*, ed. Christopher Bobonich (Cambridge: Cambridge University Press, 2010); Coleen Zoller, "Plato's Rejection of the Logic of Domination" in Reid et al., *Athletics*, 223–38.

20. See Rowe in Ferrari, *Companion*, 44, for a comparison of the City of Pigs to the Age of Cronus (*Laws* 4.713c–14a, *Statesman* 271a–74e), traditionally a time of equality. Note also that, as in the Noble Lie, these humans are born from the earth, further discussed below. Morrison in Ferrari, *Companion*, 252, sees the City of Pigs as the true city where each does his job.

21. On the Noble Lie and the difficulty of breeding true see Brann, *Music*, 125–28.

22. See Nehemas, *Authenticity*, xxxii–xxxiv, 138–58; Annas, *Introduction*, 181 on few being able to comprehend the Forms.

23. See Brann, *Music*, 100–101, 151–94 and 264–65, 357 for the level of visible things and the leval of mathematical objects as necessarily equal. For the same relation on the Ladder of Love see R. Patterson, "The Ascent in Plato's *Symposium*," *Proceedings of the Boston Area Colloquium in Ancient Philosophy* 7 (1991): 193–214.

24. Bronze and iron, of course, also reflect the Bronze Age of the Heroes and the current, degenerate Iron Age, an order somewhat altered by Hesiod as well (*Works and Days* 143–79 and see 468e8, 546e1).

25. See F. C. White, "Virtue in Plato's *Symposium*," *Classical Quarterly* 54 (2004): 366–78 for the pursuit itself as the aim; Harry Neumann, "Diotima's Concept of Love," *American Journal of Philology* 86 (1965): 37–38.

26. Dante's eagle (*Paradiso* 1.47–48, 20.31–37), who is able to stare at the Sun, reflects a Christian take on this idea.

27. Brann, *Music*, 90–92, 144, 145–46; Roochnik, *Beautiful City*, 2, 80–82.

28. For democracy as essentially formless, see Arlene Saxonhouse, "Democracy, Equality, and Eide: A Radical View from Book 8 of Plato's *Republic*," *American Political Science Review* 92 (1998): 273, and for the freedom of democracy being primarily from tyranny, Paul Woodruff, *First Democracy: The Challenge of An Ancient Ideal* (New York: Oxford University Press, 2005), 67.

29. See Joseph Cropsey in regard to the *Apology*: "Athens is not simply 'the city,' it is a democracy." *Plato's World: Man's Place in the Cosmos* (Chicago: University of Chicago Press, 1995), 145.

30. Or, as Joyceans inevitably quote at these moments (and, incidentally, in a context that casts Plato and Aristotle as the artist's Scylla and Charybdis): "A man of genius makes no mistakes. His errors are volitional and are the portals of discovery" (James Joyce, *Ulysses* 9.228–29).

31. For Agathon's focus on *aretē* see Gerald Mara, *Socrates' Discursive Democracy: Logos and Ergon in Platonic Political Philosophy* (Albany: State University of New York Press, 1997), 197.

32. For *aporia* see, for example, *Meno* 80a-b and as exhibited here in Socrates' mini-dialogue with Agathon, introduced by the mention at 198b2; Plato, *The Symposium*, ed. and trans. C. J. Rowe (Oxford: Aris and Phillips, 1998), 168, 177.

33. For the two groups of speeches see Nehemas, *Authenticity*, 306.

34. See also *Republic* 586a; Plato, *The Symposium*, ed. Kenneth Dover (Cambridge: Cambridge University Press, 1980), 159 for the *eidola* of pleasure. Anthony Hooper. "The Memory of Virtue: Achieving Immortality in Plato's *Symposium*," *The Classical Quarterly* 63 (2013): 543–57 comments on the oddness of the account here and on the relation to Alcibiades.

35. In contrast see *The Republic of Plato*, trans. with notes by Allan Bloom (New York: Basic Books, 1968), 462–63.

36. The similarity of Glaucus's name to Glaucon's (*Symposium* 172c4, as well as the *Republic*) is also striking, and see also the Glaucus of *Republic* Bk. 10, 611d.

37. Ralkowski in Reid et al., *Athletics*, 87–106.

38. See Homer, *The Iliad*, ed. G. S. Kirk, vol. II: Books 5–8 (Cambridge: Cambridge University Press, 1995), 189–91 for comments on this passage.

39. See Ruprecht, *Symposia*, 72, on Aristophanes and Alcibiades as reflecting a motif of "two becomes one"; Nelson in Doherty and King, *Thinking*, 113, 120–21.

40. See Stephanie Nelson, *Aristophanes' Tragic Muse: Tragedy, Comedy, and the Polis in Classical Athens* (Leiden: Brill, 2016), 233–34.

41. Eliopoulos in Mitsis and Reid, *Poetry*, 112; Gregory Vlastos, *Socrates: Ironist and Moral Philosopher* (Ithaca: Cornell University Press, 1991), 33–42.

42. See C. D. C. Reeve in Lesher et al., *Issues*, 124–46 on the *agalmata* as a clue to where Alcibiades went wrong.

43. For Plato making the Lenaia competition, where Agathon's victory occurred, seem like the more important City Dionysia see D. Sider, "Plato's *Symposium* as Dionysian Festival," *Quaderni Urbinati di Cultura Classica* 33 (1980): 41–56; Plato, *Symposium*, trans. Rowe, 129. For other accounts of competition in the dialogue see Marie-Élise Zovko in Reid et al., *Athletics*, 143; and Steven Robinson, "The Contest of Wisdom between Socrates and Agathon in Plato's *Symposium*," *Ancient Philosophy* 24 (2004): 81–100.

44. See Jure Zovko and Coulson, both in Reid et al., *Athletics*, on the relation of *elenchos* and competition.

45. For the contention that Socrates has harmed Alcibiades see Michael Gagarin, "Socrates' *Hubris* and Alcibiades' Failure," *Phoenix* 31 (1997): 22–37; Martha Nussbaum, *The Fragility of Goodness: Luck and Ethics in Greek Tragedy and Philosophy* (Cambridge: Cambridge University Press, 1986), 165–99, and 183 for Socrates's "psychological distance" and for an answer, Ruprecht, *Symposia*, 57–69. Elsewhere see Rosen, *Symposium*, xxxv, 21–23, 37–38; R. Duncan, "Plato's *Symposium*: The Cloven Eros," *Southern Journal of Philosophy* 15 (1977): 277–90. For pro-Socrates views see C. D. C. Reeve, "A Study in Violets," 124–46 in Lesher et al., *Interpretation*; A. W. Nightingale, *Genres in Dialogue: Plato and the Construct of Philosophy* (Cambridge: Cambridge University Press, 1995), 115–19; J. Jirsa, "Alcibiades' Speech in the *Symposium* and its Origins," 280–92 in *Plato's Symposium, Proceedings of the Fifth Symposium Platonicum Pragense*, ed. A. Havlíček and M. Cajthaml (Prague: Oikoumene, 2007) and more generally J. J. Cleary, "Erotic Paideia in Plato's *Symposium*," 125–46 in the same volume.

46. Rosen, *Symposium*, 7–8; Debra Nails, "Tragedy Off-Stage," 179–207 in Lesher et al., *Interpretation*; Nussbaum, *Fragility*, 168–71 dates to 404 and the return of Alcibiades. The apparent reference to Sparta's division of Mantinea in 385 (193a2) could also refer (significantly) to Alcibiades's defeat at Mantinea in 418, Xenophon, *Hellenica* 5.2.5–7; Plato, *Symposium*, ed. Dover, 119; Plato, *Symposium*, trans. Rowe, 159.

47. See Hyland, *Finitude*, 35–57, esp. 40–42 for a comparison to Marx's view of humans as "species-being" and a contrasting atomistic view in tension with this in the *Republic*.

48. On the Athenians as autochthonous see Casey Stegman, "Remembering Atlantis: Plato's "Timaeus-Critias," the Ancestral Constitution, and the Democracy

of the Gods," *Political Theory* 45 (2017): 240–60; Brann, *Music*, 125–28. See Schofield in Ferrari, *Companion*, 160–61 and 154 for Cadmus and the dragon teeth, and for further references. For the relationship between autochthony and Athenian politics see Christopher Pelling, "Bringing Autochthony Up-to-Date: Herodotus and Thucydides," *Classical World* 102 (2009): 471–83; Carol Dougherty, "Democratic Contradictions and the Synoptic Illusion of Euripides' *Ion*" in *Dēmokratia: A Conversation on Democracies, Ancient and Modern*, ed. Josiah Ober and Charles Hedrick (Princeton: Princeton University Press, 1996), 249–70.

49. See Cropsey, *World*, 165: "All things in the world being as they have been described, the natural human suspicion of human superiority gives rise to the urgent need for a presence and judgment above suspicion."

50. See Thucydides 7.86.5 on Nicias as one who more than any other Greek of Thucydides's time practiced *aretē* as it was commonly held (ἀρετὴν νενομισμένην).

51. Popper, *Open Society*, 177, calls *Republic* 8 a "caricature" of the Funeral Oration's tolerance, citing Plato's *Menexenus* as another parody of the oration. See also Annas, *Introduction*, 299–301 and 230: "Plato presents democracy as defined by a tolerant pluralism, but Athens was a populist democracy, with a clearly defined way of life separating those with power from those without, and about as tolerant of openly expressed nonconformity as McCarthyite America." In contrast, see Rowe in Ferrari, *Companion*, 28–39 for similar criticism of the current political climate in the *Gorgias*, *Euthdemus*, etc.

52. See Morrison in Ferrari, *Companion*, for the City in Words as not an impossible ideal but a paradigm and for further references.

Chapter 2

Equality and Excellence in the *Education of Cyrus*

NATHAN TARCOV

Purpose and Genre of the Book

Some general remarks about Xenophon's *Education of Cyrus* are in order before focusing on our theme of equality and education in that work. Xenophon begins with some reflections about how difficult it is to rule human beings. Democracies, monarchies, oligarchies, and tyrannies have been overthrown; even the masters of households cannot keep their servants obedient, whether few or many.[1] Herds of cattle and horses obey their keepers more willingly than human beings obey their rulers, allow their keepers to use the profits as they wish, and never unite against them, unlike human beings who unite most against whomever they perceive to be attempting to rule them. Xenophon reports that he almost concluded it is easier for a human being by his nature to rule all other animals than to rule human beings. Yet Cyrus with "a little army of Persians" acquired many human beings, very many cities, very many nations with different languages, all obeying him, even those who never saw him, some willingly, others conquered, in all of whom Cyrus implanted both fear of himself and desire to gratify him so they were governed by his judgment. This achievement led Xenophon no longer to think ruling human beings is impossible or even difficult if one does it knowledgeably. In fact, the historical Cyrus created the greatest empire up to that time, conquering the whole of what we now call the

Middle East, which the Greeks called "Asia," and becoming in Cyrus's own words "king of the world."[2] Xenophon therefore examined Cyrus's birth, nature, and education that enabled him to excel at ruling human beings: in effect, an inquiry into the possibility of ruling human beings, especially a multinational empire acquired and ruled by one man. With an eye on our theme, we can already say that Xenophon is concerned both with an ordinary kind of inequality, between rulers and ruled, and with an extraordinary kind, between Cyrus and practically all other rulers or would-be rulers, and with excellence at acquiring and exercising rule.

After the announced purpose of the work, we should next consider its genre or literary character. Machiavelli in chapter XIV of his *Prince* names it (the only book he names as offering a model for princes) as one of the "histories" a prince should read to consider the actions of excellent men. He refers to it as "the life of Cyrus written by Xenophon,"[3] so if we follow Machiavelli, we might call it a history or a life or biography, though its stated purpose should qualify it also as a work of political science or political philosophy.

Machiavelli in his *Discourses on Livy*, however, writes that Xenophon "*makes* Cyrus seize Armenia through deception" and "*makes* him deceive his maternal uncle Cyaxares, king of the Medes."[4] Cicero in the first letter to his younger brother Quintus says the book was "written by Xenophon not faithfully to history but as a model of just rule."[5] Similarly, Hume in his essay "Of the Balance of Power" writes of Xenophon's book, "that elegant composition should be supposed altogether a romance."[6] In other words, in important respects Xenophon's book is a novel, perhaps the first novel, a work of fiction albeit historical fiction.[7] As such, it sticks to the basic historical facts—the prince of this little country conquered and ruled a vast empire—but Xenophon freely invents episodes, including some of the most striking and memorable ones. He not only invents speeches by his characters like other ancient historians, but invents characters (as Thucydides may do with Diodotus), including some of the most interesting ones in the book. Xenophon engaged in what writers and readers now call "world building," inventing societies and relations among them.

Persia

Xenophon's invented pre-Cyrus Persia is an austere quasi-Spartan constitutional monarchy where the king obeys the law.[8] The society is divided between a few thousand families of rich peers (*homotimoi*, those of equal honor) and more than a hundred thousand families of poor commoners (*dēmotoi*) working as farmers and craftsmen.[9] By law every family can send their sons to be educated in the agora to become able to fight as hoplites at close quarters, hold office, and after twenty-five years of such military service, become elders (*geraiteroi*), members of a senate that judges all matters and elects officials. In practice, however, the commoners cannot afford to spare their sons from work to send them to school, so they serve only as light infantry fighting at a distance (I 2.15, 5.5, II 1.9–11) and have no share in political power. The regime thus is a de jure democracy that offers formally equal access to education and political rights, but is a de facto gerontocratic timocracy, oligarchy, or aristocracy.

The boys (*paides*) from families who can afford it are educated together in one quarter of the agora among the government buildings, ruled and taught by twelve elders—one for each tribe. There they train with bow and spear and learn justice (as obedience to rules prohibiting theft, robbery, deceit, insult, and ingratitude) by accusing each other of such injustices, defending themselves at trial, and sometimes serving as judges, which also accustoms them to give an account (*logos*) and take others' accounts (1.2.6–8, 1.4.3). Those judged guilty or who make false accusations or who judge contrary to law are beaten by their elders. Since their rulers spend most of the day judging cases (1.2.6), the boys must be constantly committing such crimes or accusing each other of doing so. The boys also learn moderation (*sophrosunēn*), which seems to mean obeying their rulers, distinguished from the continence (*enkrateian*) in food and drink they are taught by eating only bread and greens, drinking only water, and seeing older boys and youths doing the same.

Starting at sixteen or seventeen they spend ten years as youths or cadets (*ephēboi*) ruled by twelve mature men, sleep and train in another quarter of the agora, join the king on hunts, compete in contests, and serve as police and guards for the city (1.2.9–12).[10] Sleeping in the agora among the government buildings is not only for the sake of guarding the city but also for moderation, "for this age seems especially in need of care."[11] Spending the night sleeping in public among the other cadets presumably limits their sexual activities—even married cadets are expected not to be absent often. Their severe education in justice, moderation, and continence is achieved through punishment, habituating deprivation, competition, and example rather than through exhortation. There is no education in wisdom as such.

After ten years as cadets, the graduates are recognized as mature men able to fight abroad in close combat as hoplites and hold office. They can sleep at home but must still turn up in the agora at dawn and be available for campaigns for twenty-five more years, after which they serve as elders.

This education cultivates a certain kind of excellence. Both the elders appointed to rule the boys and the mature men appointed to rule the youths are those thought able to make them "best" (*beltistous*) (1.2.5). "Best" might mean as good as they can be made (under the circumstances?), or better than the commoners who cannot afford to attend school, or best simply. The competitions and contests with prizes for the winners indicate the youths themselves share the concern for being best. Excellence in this sense of superiority is as such at odds with equality as equal achievement and honor for it. Cyrus himself is eager to be and be considered the best in everything among his age group and by hard work succeeds in being so (1.3.15, 1.4.4–5, 1.5.1). The meaning of the excellence this education aims at is clarified by the parallel statement about the rulers of the mature men: they are those who seem able to make them especially able to carry out the orders and commands of the greatest office.[12] This entails obedience, fighting skills, and the endurance of heat, cold, hunger, thirst, and lack of sleep. That all this is preparation for war is most manifest in Xenophon's explanation that the cadets' hunting is "the truest of the exercises that pertain to war. For it habituates them to rise at dawn and to endure cold and heat, it exercises them in marches and running" and to shoot with the bow and throw the spear (1.2.10). In short, these Persians are educated in the excellence of warriors. If such excellence requires full-time education and practice, it cannot be provided to everyone, but depends on a fundamental inequality between those who can afford to devote themselves to it and those who provide the necessities of life for all, in the case of Persia the peers and the commoners.

Media

Xenophon's Persia contrasts sharply with his Media, ruled despotically by its king, lording it over a luxurious hedonistic court.[13] The Medes at court wear makeup and wigs, purple robes, and jewelry, eat sumptuous meals with many dishes and sauces, and drink wine to intoxication, unlike the unadorned Persians with their simple garments and diet (1.3.2–11). In Media there is no public education as in Persia.

The contrast between these two societies is especially crucial to *The Education of Cyrus* since Cyrus himself was half-Mede and half-Persian, the son both of Cambyses, the constitutional king of Persia, and of Mandane, daughter of Astyages, the despotic king of Media. Cyrus was divided between the kingdoms not only by birth but by his education divided between these two societies, exemplifying two different kinds of equality: equality under the law and equality under a despot. Around age twelve his austere and severe education among the boys in Persia was interrupted when he spent three or four years in Media at the court of Astyages (1.3–4), initially accompanying his mother on a presumably brief visit, but remaining at his grandfather's invitation over his mother's objections. As a good Persian boy, young Cyrus was disgusted by the lavish feasting and excessive drinking at the Median court, continued to eat and drink in the measured Persian mode, and accepted the plethora of meats his grandfather offered him only to distribute it among the servants who had helped him or his mother. But as a boy who loved beauty and honor (*philokalos kai philotimos*), he welcomed the fancy clothes and jewelry his grandfather gave him, though he gave them away to the boys with whom he had played and competed when he left to return to Persia. There they would be out of place and likely the subject of mockery. He even gave the splendid Median robe he was wearing to Araspas, the boy to whom he was especially attached (1.4.26, 5.1.2). He kept the horses (1.4.25) and, I assume, the custom-made armor (1.3.14, 1.4.18).

Xenophon does not fully articulate young Cyrus's attitude toward the ultimate form of inequality he encounters in Media, that between a despot and his subjects. Young Cyrus, however, seems to have enjoyed benefiting from his grandfather's ability to provide him with whatever he wanted, whether horses, armor, animals to hunt, or boys his age to play with (1.3.14).

The most explicit political contrast between Persia and Media is provided by Cyrus's mother, Mandane, when trying to dissuade Cyrus, still around twelve years old, from staying longer at her father's court (1.3.15–18). She first asked him how he would learn justice far from his teachers in Persia. He claimed he already knew it for the teacher appointed him as judge as knowing justice precisely. He was beaten, however, for judging it better to let a big boy keep the big tunic he had taken from a small boy and leave his little tunic to the small boy. He was appointed to judge according to the law, not according to what is better (*beltion*) or fitting (*harmottontos*), since the lawful (*to nomimon*) is just (*dikaion*), the violent (*biaion*) unjust. Would giving each what is fitting be true equality and justice? If young Cyrus thought the teacher's appointing him judge would show his mother he already knew justice, the rest of the story showed the teacher was disappointed. Perhaps he hoped she would think the beating taught him Persian justice. Or would the teacher's resort to force call into question his distinction between violence and law? Might Cyrus therefore be tempted to take things by force and again give each what is fitting rather than follow the law? In any case, he adds that if he needs any more instruction, his grandfather will teach him.

Cyrus's response leads Mandane to explain to him that the same things are not agreed to be just in Media and in Persia, for his grandfather is the master (*despotēs*) of everything in Media, but in Persia to have equality (*to ison*) is held or enacted (*nomizetai*) to be just (*dikaion*). His father, she says, is the first to do what is ordered by the city, and the law, not his own soul, is his measure. She drastically warns Cyrus that he'll be whipped to death if he returns home having learned from his grandfather not the kingly (*basilikou*) but the tyrannical (*tyrannikon*) way, in which one person is supposed to have more (*pleion echein,* to get the advantage, the root of *pleonexia,* greediness for more than one has, more than one's fair share, more than others) than everyone. Her warning is not entirely off the mark: when Cyrus returns to Persia a few years later, the other boys mock him as having learned to live for pleasure till he proves them wrong by eating and drinking as simply as they, sharing his portions at feasts, and showing his endurance, respect for his elders, and obedience to rulers (1.5.1).

Thus, only when faced with the danger that Cyrus might jeopardize his status in Persia or even his life by learning justice in Media does his mother enlighten him as to the despotic or tyrannical character of his grandfather's rule. She thereby also makes explicit what we have already inferred, that justice is understood in Persia as the lawful, not necessarily as producing the better or more fitting outcome. Most important for our theme, she adds that in Persia to have equality is held to be just. This equality is first of all equality under the law, which everyone from king to commoner must obey. There obviously is, however, inequality of wealth, as the peers, presumably living off the income from their estates where commoners do the work, can afford to send their sons to the school, whereas the commoners have to put their sons to work to make ends meet. Yet there is a fundamental sort of equality in that everyone has something of his own, whereas no Mede has anything the king cannot claim as his. And despite the inequality of wealth in Persia, there is an equality of mode of living as the peers eat and dress no more luxuriously than the commoners.[14]

Cyrus attempts to reassure his mother by arguing that since her father is very clever at teaching others to have less rather than more, having taught all the Medes to have less than him, she should be confident that Cyrus won't learn from him to have more (*pleonektein,* to be greedy). Cyrus's response assumes the subjects of a tyrant learn to accept his tyranny rather than wish to be tyrants themselves and that he will learn to imitate his grandfather's subjects rather than his grandfather himself. His subsequent career challenges that assumption. Xenophon's immediately following sentence is that Cyrus kept prattling many such things, but at last his mother left though Cyrus stayed and was brought up there (1.4.1).[15] Xenophon tempts readers to dismiss Cyrus's arguments as childish prattle, but we may regret that he does not report Cyrus's many other such arguments.

In the following three or four years of his self-directed education in Media, Cyrus continues his pursuit of a sort of excellence. He told his mother that while he was the best with bow and spear at home, in Media he was inferior in riding to those his age, which vexed him exceedingly, so he wished to stay and become the best rider (1.3.15). He cannot stand being inferior in anything, certainly not in anything pertaining to warfare, but has to excel and become the best. He succeeds quickly in becoming first the equal of the boys his age in horsemanship and then their superior. He also acquires a sort of leadership among the boys owing to his charm, his modestly carried superiority in their contests, and his influence with his doting grandfather. He even wins over their fathers by visiting them and showing his attachment to their sons, so if they need something from the king, they tell their sons to ask Cyrus to get it for them, which Cyrus does owing to his kindness (*philanthrōpian*) and love of honor (*philotimian*) (1.4.1). Cyrus's pursuit of a warrior's excellence in Media culminates in a hunt in which he kills a deer and a boar (1.4.5–15), and a cavalry battle in which he demonstrates tactical intelligence, leads a charge, and slays Assyrian invaders (1.4.16–24). In both he displays reckless daring and delight in bloodshed.

Erotic Interlude

Before we leave behind Cyrus's education in Media, we should note his encounter with another sort of unequal relationship. Xenophon somewhat apologetically concludes his account of Cyrus's time in Media with a *paidikou logou,* which we may translate as a story pertaining to a beloved boy, in this case Cyrus (now fifteen or sixteen, almost an ephebe, no longer a boy). It is common in Greek writings about love such as Plato's or Xenophon's *Symposia* to distinguish between lover (*erastēs*) and beloved (*eromenos* or *paidika*) especially if the lover is a young or adult man and the beloved a boy or youth, as if love were commonly (though not necessarily always) one-sided and unrequited. Artabazus, a character invented by Xenophon, introduced here a Mede who was a very noble and good man (*andra mala kalon k'agathon*) or gentleman, who had for some time been struck by Cyrus's beauty (*kallei*), managed to steal two or three kisses from Cyrus as he was about to depart from Media by pretending to be his relative, taking advantage of the Persian custom to kiss relatives on the mouth when separating or reuniting (1.4.27–28).[16] Cyrus gave Artabazus the kisses he desired, but there was no sign Cyrus returned his enduring love at this point or later, so the story fits the one-sidedness usually attributed to pederastic relations. The difference of age entails one sort of inequality (reversed by Cyrus's status as prince and later as general), but the one-sidedness entails a different sort of inequality, with the lover at the mercy of the beloved, compelled to please him to receive any favors. One-sided love is found not only in pederastic love: Xenophon later tells the dramatic story of the unrequited love of Araspas for Panthea, the captive queen of Susa, said to be the most beautiful woman in Asia, two characters probably invented by Xenophon (6.1.31–33).[17] Love can, however, be equal or mutual, as in the conjugal cases Xenophon presents of the love between the Armenian prince Tigranes and his wife and between Panthea and Abradatas, the king of Susa.

The relations between equal and mutual or unequal and unrequited eros and excellence or virtue are ambiguous. Artabazus's unrequited love for Cyrus drives him to a great deed to please Cyrus, ably persuading most of the Median army to abandon their king, Cyaxares, and follow Cyrus, whereas Araspas's unrequited love for Panthea drives him to threaten to take her by force if she will not have intercourse with him voluntarily. The mutual conjugal loves of Tigranes and his wife and of Panthea and Abradatas inspire them to noble lives and deeds on behalf of Cyrus (3.1.41–43, 7.1.21, 8.4.1, 8.4.24, 6.1.45–51, 6.4.2–11, 7.3.2–16).

Cyrus is by nature an affectionate (*philostorgos*) boy who quickly becomes familiar (*oikeios*) with and attached (*ēspazeto*) to other boys his age, especially to Araspas (1.3.2, 1.4.1, 1.4.26), and delights in doing them favors, and later as general he enjoys dining with his men while mixing serious and amusing conversation (2.2–3.1, 8.4), but he is never said to love anyone in the erotic sense. His marriage to Cyaxares's daughter secures for him the throne of Media, and though she is said to have been very beautiful and always wanted to marry Cyrus, there is no mention of love or affection on his part (8.5.17–20, 28). The only time I recall when he is said to love (*eran*), the object of his love is horsemanship (1.4.5). We should not conclude that he is simply unerotic and incapable of love: he declines Araspas's suggestion that he go see Panthea, fearing (one of the few times he admits to fearing anything; 6.1.13, 8.7.7) that he would keep visiting her and gazing at her and would neglect what he had to do (6.1.7–8, 6.1.16). He is afraid of falling in love and avoids temptation. What he achieves as general, conqueror, and ruler is not for the sake of pleasing any beloved.

Cyrus's Revolution

Xenophon presents Persia as a loyal ally of Media (rather than a resentful, conquered, subject people as in Herodotus), so when Media is threatened by an imminent invasion by what Xenophon calls Assyria, which historians now call the neo-Babylonian empire, Cyrus's uncle Cyaxares, having succeeded Astyages as Median king, asks Persia to send troops with Cyrus as commander. The Persian authorities send Cyrus as commander of a force of a thousand hoplite peers and thirty thousand light infantry commoners (1.5.4–5). Cyrus immediately sets out to work a moral, military, social, and political transformation of Persia that enables him to create and rule his quasi-universal empire.[18]

The first step Xenophon has Cyrus take is to transform the moral outlook of the peers. He assembles and addresses his thousand peers before they set out (1.5.6–14). He first compliments them for doing since childhood what the city holds noble and abstaining from what it holds base, but then he denigrates the moral outlook they inherited, admitted that he cannot see what good their ancestors acquired for Persia or for themselves by devoting their lives to practicing the deeds of virtue. He declares that he does not think human beings practice any virtue for the good ones to have no more than the bad, but rather they abstain from present pleasures not to abstain forever but to have much more future enjoyment they practice military training not to fight forever but to gain much wealth, much happiness, and great honors for themselves and the city. Finally, he praises them as lovers (*erastas*) of praise. To put it bluntly, he urges them to reject the ancestral practice of virtue for its own sake and use virtue merely as a means to acquire pleasures, rewards, and praise. He does not point out to them that if they do so they can no longer claim to be the moral superiors of the commoners.

Xenophon has Cyrus take the second step immediately upon his arrival in Media when he persuades Cyaxares to make breastplates, shields, and swords like those of the peers for the commoners he has brought, to transform them from light infantry to hoplites so they can fight the enemy hand-to-hand (2.1.9–10). Cyrus first announces this change to the peers (2.1.11) as meant to allay any fear they might have at being outnumbered by the enemy hand-to-hand. He says it belongs to them to sharpen the commoners' souls, "for it belongs to the ruler not only to make himself good, but he must also take care that the ruled will be as good as possible [*beltistoi*]." We recall that this was the task of the elders who ruled and taught the boys and of the mature men who ruled or commanded the cadets. Does this mean the commoners now get a version of the education the peers got to make them as good as the peers? One of the peers suggests that Cyrus rather than the peers should announce their elevation to the commoners (2.1.12–13) so they will esteem being placed in the ranks of the peers more highly and hold it more securely as conferred by the king's son and their general. This would be likely to transfer the commoners' loyalty to Cyrus rather than to the peers or council of elders especially the farther from home they campaigned and the longer they served under Cyrus.[19] We should note that Cyrus urged Cyaxares not to be discouraged by the small number of peers he brought since though few the peers easily rule the other Persians who are many (2.1.3). This implied they should be a match for many Assyrians, as if their rule at home over the many commoners depended on their military superiority. Could they still rule at home once the commoners achieved military equality?

Nothing openly said during the introduction of the arming of the commoners to fight among the peers expressed concern that the peers might resent or even fear this change. Later at a dinner with his officers and their guests, when Cyrus asks whether the newly armed commoners seem inferior owing to not having been educated like the peers, some of the officers provoke much laughter by telling stories making fun of them. Cyrus, however, praises them as easily pleased and obedient, saying he does not know what sort of soldiers one should pray for more than ones like them (2.2.1–10).

Cyrus next addresses the commoners (2.1.14–19). He admits they do not share equally in the fatherland, excluded not by the peers but by the necessity to provide sustenance, even though they were born and raised in the same land, their bodies are not inferior, and their souls should not be inferior. But now, he announces, they will have the same weapons, take the same risks, have the same desire for victory, and deserve the same share of the fruits of victory as the peers. Justified as an emergency measure of military necessity,[20] Cyrus's arming the commoners like the peers and promising them an equal share in the fatherland and an equal opportunity to achieve and show their excellence effectuated an egalitarian social and political revolution. He himself worked to make all the men better through his own example, exercises, tactical lessons, and contests with prizes for the victors, opportunities for promotion, hunts, and games (2.1.20–29).

Cyrus even extends a sort of equality to the camp servants whom his uncle provided, who presumably are not Persians, making sure they have an equal share of the provisions and are honored so they will be trustworthy, knowledgeable in military things, intelligent, eager, quick, and steady (2.1.31).

The third step in Cyrus's revolution adds an element of merit-based inequality to the military equality bestowed on the commoners. At the dinner mentioned above, Chrysantas, one of Xenophon's invented characters (whom Cyrus later seats in the place of honor at dinners because he performs not only what Cyrus has ordered but what he knows would be better for Cyrus and advises Cyrus on what to say, so that Cyrus judges him better for Cyrus than Cyrus is himself, 8.4.10–11), says some of the commoners are better and some are worth less, but all would consider themselves to deserve an equal share (*isomoirein*) of anything good. Yet he holds nothing is more unequal (*anisōteron*) for human beings than for the bad and the good to merit equal shares (2.2.17–18). This conclusion echoes Cyrus's first speech to the peers back in Persia ("I think no virtue is practiced by human beings so that those who become good have no more than the bad" [1.5.9]), but puts both the claim of the less deserving and his own opposed judgment in terms of equality, equality as getting an equal share as opposed to equality as all getting what they deserve. The justice of the latter may depend on everyone's having an equal opportunity to do well and deserve greater honors and rewards, which has been achieved by arming the commoners to fight alongside the peers.

Xenophon makes Cyrus respond to Chrysantas by asking whether it would be best to hold a council of the army to decide whether all should share equally in anything good they get or to give honors according to their deeds (2.2.18). Chrysantas asks why Cyrus should hold a discussion instead of announcing what he would do, as he did with the contests (2.2.19). Cyrus explains that the soldiers consider command of the army fairly (*isōs*)[21] his, so he can justly set contests, but they consider what they acquire campaigning to be theirs in common, so they all should decide on how to divide it. Chrysantas asks whether Cyrus supposed the multitude would vote not for equal shares but for the superior to have more (*pleonektein*) honors and gifts (2.2.20). Cyrus answers he supposed so since "we" advocate it, to deny that who toils and benefits the community most deserves the most would be shameful, and it would appear even to "the worst" to be expedient (*sumpheron*) for the good to have more (*pleonektein*).

Xenophon does not make Cyrus explain how it would be expedient, perhaps because it should be obvious even to the least deserving that giving greater rewards and honors to the soldiers contributing most to the community would motivate them to do so, thereby benefiting all, even those who contribute and receive least.

Cyrus's answers or questions in response to Chrysantas thus amount to a nearly proto-Rawlsian justification of inequality: giving more to those whose deeds contribute more to the community is just so long as (1) even those who contribute and receive least are benefited and recognize it is expedient, and (2) it is agreed to at a meeting of all.

Xenophon then reveals another motive for unequal distribution that Cyrus did not publicly announce (2.2.21). This policy was for the sake of the peers: they would be better if they knew they would be judged by their deeds and obtain what they deserved, and this seemed to him the right time to hold the vote *when the peers hesitated over the crowd sharing equally* (*isomoirian*). Presumably the peers, owing to their belief in their superiority, would be reassured that they would benefit disproportionately from distribution of honors and rewards based on each individual's deeds.

Cyrus then urges that those soldiers who want less of a share of labor but more of a share of everything good should be purged from the army. Otherwise, they might easily corrupt others, since wickedness is more attractive than virtue, by appealing to present pleasures (1.2.23–25). The fundamental obstacle to the widespread attainment of excellence or virtue is that it is hard, whereas its opposite is easy, the premise for Cyrus's insistence on rewarding or honoring virtue and punishing or shaming vice. Cyrus adds portentously that the replacements of the purged need not be confined to fellow Persians but could be recruited from any human beings who might contribute most. This foreshadows his putting together and ruling a huge army, including not only Persians but Medes, Armenians, Chaldeans, Hyrcanians, and even Assyrians, and the vast multinational empire that army acquired and maintained.

Cyrus assembles all the soldiers the day after the dinner discussion. He announces to them that the enemy is approaching and the victors will possess the goods of the vanquished, so each man will have to fight zealously. He poses the loaded question whether virtue would be practiced more if those who labor and risk more get more honor or if they know being bad makes no difference and all get equal shares (2.3.1–4).

Chrysantas, introduced by Xenophon as a man neither tall nor strong looking but excelling in prudence, is the first to respond (2.3.5–6). He suggests that Cyrus proposed the discussion to test whether anyone would show himself as thinking he should share equally in what others gain by virtue even if he does nothing noble and good. Chrysantas thereby helps Cyrus shame into silence anyone who would argue for equal shares. He proceeds bravely and cleverly to risk incurring contempt by playing the part of one of Cyrus's "worst" men who recognize it would be in their interest for the good men to have more. He admits that he is neither swift nor strong and by what he would do with his body would not be the best or second or thousandth or perhaps even ten thousandth, yet he knows that if the stronger act vigorously and they are victorious, he will share in something good as much as would be just, but if the bad do nothing and the good are dispirited and they are defeated, he will get more than he wished of something far from good. He speaks only of his bodily weakness, saying nothing of his mind or soul, even though here and elsewhere he displays his superior courage and intelligence.

Pheraulas

The next to speak is Pheraulas, another character invented by Xenophon, introduced here as a Persian commoner "somehow [*pōs*] even from childhood[22] well acquainted[23] with and pleasing to Cyrus, in body and soul not like an ignoble man" (2.3.7–15).[24] He stresses the equality of their situation: all equally starting in a contest of virtue, training their bodies the same way, all required to obey their commanders and honored by Cyrus for doing so, preparing to fight the enemy in a mode all human beings understand by nature. He says the commoners might compete with the peers, judged by Cyrus, who loves (*philein*) those he sees to be good no less than himself. He argues that though the peers are proud to have been educated to endure hunger, thirst, and cold, the commoners learned to do so from necessity. He concludes that he is willing to enter the contest and be honored by

Cyrus as he deserves and advises the commoners to enter this battle against the educated.

Pheraulas makes clear that Cyrus would be the judge of their deserts and rewards, which was not stated in the question Cyrus posed to the soldiers. Much as receiving their new arms from Cyrus would attach the commoners to him, so his being the judge of deserts and rewards would make all those desirous of honor and reward eager to please him, and all those honored and rewarded grateful to him. A system of merited rewards and honors in an army of more than thirty thousand men (that would later grow to around two hundred thousand) might seem to require an omniscient judge, but Cyrus has established a hierarchy of officers, commanders of units of five, ten, fifty, a hundred, a thousand, and ten thousand, that can closely observe the men and officers under them and forward recommendations for honors and rewards and promotions up the chain of command to Cyrus (2.1.22–24, 4.1.1–2).

The revolutionary character of Cyrus's policy is underlined by Pheraulas's presentation of the commoners' contest as being against the peers more than against the enemy. If the commoners fight as well as the peers against the enemy, they will defeat the peers by disproving their claim to superiority. His argument calls into question the necessity of the education to which Xenophon devoted the second chapter of the work. Although the peers lead and set an example for the others in Xenophon's account of Cyrus's first victorious battle (3.3.59, 70), there is no indication that the commoners fall short, and no distinction is made between them and the peers in later battles. No mention is made of Pheraulas himself in the accounts of the battles, and what role he might have played in them is left to our imagination.

The next mention of Pheraulas does not occur till the last book, where he appears as one of the most important and wealthiest men in Cyrus's empire. Only here do we learn more of his backstory. When Pheraulas spoke in favor of unequal rewards for merit, all we learned was that he was a Persian commoner "somehow even from childhood well acquainted with and pleasing to Cyrus, in body and soul not like an ignoble man." Pheraulas befriends a young man from Sakia and invites him to dinner (8.3.25–32–50). The Sakian, impressed by Pheraulas's furniture and furnishings and many servants, asks if he was so rich at home. Pheraulas answers that back home he lived by the work of his hands on a small farm, but his father managed to have him educated with the young sons of the peers till he became a youth and had to work on the farm to support his father.

Pheraulas explains that everything the Sakian sees was given to him by Cyrus. We can infer that it was during his years at school that he became "well acquainted with and pleasing to Cyrus." Already as a boy Cyrus was able to see past the Persian social hierarchy and recognize superior qualities in a commoner.

One of Pheraulas's duties at this later stage is to organize Cyrus's processions from his palace to the sanctuaries where he sacrifices to the gods (8.3.1–20). Xenophon explains that these were one of the arts Cyrus contrived to make his rule respected. He deliberates with Pheraulas as to how to arrange the processions to seem most beautiful to those of good will and most frightening to those of ill will. The procession begins with bulls and horses for the sacrifices, then Cyrus himself in a chariot, clad in a purple and white tunic, red pants, and a purple robe, made to look taller, four thousand spearmen, his bodyguard of three hundred, and tens of thousands of his cavalry. Troops with whips keep the crowds in order. Pheraulas orders the leaders in advance where to march and what to wear as if he were greater than they, provoking envy among them. Xenophon says Cyrus chose Pheraulas for this because he believed him to be intelligent, a lover of beauty (*philokalon*, the term Xenophon applied to young Cyrus at 1.3.3), and orderly. Pheraulas is the arch-example of the opportunity offered by Cyrus's transformation of Persia that rewards ability and loyalty to Cyrus with wealth, power, and honor.

Cyrus the Great King

After the armies of the Assyrians and their allies are defeated, first Sardis and then Babylon captured, and the Assyrian king killed, Cyrus orders the Babylonians to give up their arms, distributes their land and houses to his Persians and allies according to their deserts, and makes the Babylonians work their land and serve them as their masters (7.5.33–36). He justifies this radical inequality by the "eternal law" that the bodies of those in a captured city and their possessions belong to the conquerors and by the claim that their conquest was only against aggressors. He insists further that the ruling class has to deserve to rule by continuing to practice virtue and being better than the ruled, superior in moderation, continence, and the science of war (7.5.72–79). Apparently yielding to his friends' entreaties, Cyrus moves into the palace of the king and chooses eunuchs as his bodyguards and servants and ten thousand Persian spearmen to guard the palace in this huge hostile city and accompany him when he goes out (7.5.37–70). Thus, he replaces the Assyrian as the Great King of Asia.

The leading Persians and allies are expected to report every day to the gates of the palace mounted and armed and offer themselves to Cyrus to be used as he wishes. Those who do not report "voluntarily" find their possessions confiscated by Cyrus's friends (8.1.6, 1.16–20). He prefers ruling as "a seeing law" who puts human beings in order, sees who is out of order, and punishes them to ruling by written laws (8.1.22). Thus, he rules with absolute power like his Median grandfather rather than his Persian father, who ruled subject to the laws and the council. But like a good Persian, he himself sets an example of moderation, continence, piety, justice toward friends and allies, and exercise of the military arts, and rewards those who follow his example (8.1.12, 1.23–39). He and his associates in the Median manner make themselves look more beautiful and taller than they are by nature, wearing beautiful robes, elevator shoes, jewelry, and makeup (VIII 1.40–41, 2.8). He gives so much gold to his friends, though he knows they would return it if needed, that they prefer him to each other, even to their brothers, fathers, and children (8.1.48, 8.2.7–9, 8.2.15–18, 8.2.28). He employs many so-called Eyes and Ears of the King to report what would benefit him. Since no one knows who the Eyes and Ears are and the king listens to everyone who has heard or seen something important,[25] people have to be on their guard with everyone and never say anything unfavorable to Cyrus (8.2.10–11). He holds contests with prizes, arousing rivalry and strife among the best, and among the losers in disputed contests envy toward the winners and hatred toward the judges. Those who wish to be first in his friendship envy each other and wish each other out of the way rather than cooperate to do something good. In these ways he contrives for those who are superior to love (*philein*) him more than each other (8.2.26–28). Many of these devices are characteristic of tyranny.[26]

When Cyrus returns to Persia after settling affairs in Babylon, his father King Cambyses addresses him before the Persian elders and officials and warns him not to try to "rule Persians as you do others for your advantage [*epi pleonexia*]" (8.5.24; Cyrus seems to have obeyed this compact, visiting Persia only every few years to make customary sacrifices even after succeeding his father as its king). I have to regard this as the authoritative characterization within the book of Cyrus's rule of his empire. If Cyrus's rule of his empire was despotic and in many ways tyrannical, however benevolent to the few friends who elevated and honored him (8.2.1–13), we need to consider its relation to the excellence he promoted and the equality he granted.

Autocracy, Empire, Equality, and Excellence

The excellence or virtue that Cyrus himself possessed was, as the opening of the book declared, that of acquiring and maintaining a great multinational empire. He encountered and expressed some admiration for other ways of life with the virtues they entailed, most notably those of lovers in the cases of Tigranes and his wife and of Panthea and Abradatas, and of something like philosophy (3.1.14, 3.1.38–39, 6.1.41–43), but he did not devote himself to them. The excellence or virtue in others that Cyrus modeled, rewarded, and enforced is essentially related to the despotic character of his rule, though its emphasis on moderation, continence, piety, and military exercise overlapped with the virtues of pre-Cyrus Persia. The excellence Cyrus most highly honored and rewarded, however, was supreme loyalty and service to him, the excellence demanded by despots. From the beginning, he taught that virtue was to be pursued not for its own sake but for rewards (1.5.8–10). Rewards for such virtue seem to require an omniscient and omnipotent authority, human or divine, to bestow them.

Such virtue ultimately proves unsustainable. The controversial final chapter of the book (8.8) details the moral, political, and military decline of Persia after Cyrus's death.[27] Despite his deathbed injunctions to his two sons urging unity and fraternity, civil war between them ensued and cities and nations revolted. The conduct of his sons may be understood as evidence either of Cyrus's failure as an educator[28] or of his exceptional, irreplaceable ability to rule extolled in the opening pages of the book. If the latter, his establishment of a form of government that could work well only under someone like him was a disastrous mistake.[29] Xenophon reports that by his time Persians were marked by impiety, untrustworthiness, injustice, drunkenness, laziness, and inattention to military exercise, the opposites of the virtues honored both by Cyrus and by pre-Cyrus Persia. We may ask how Cyrus could be responsible for Persia's degeneration since he left Persia to rule itself in its old way while he ruled the rest of his empire autocratically. We may imagine that young men eager for wealth and honor growing up in Persia heard tales from older relatives serving in the empire and went to serve Cyrus and help rule the empire, where their children in turn were educated (7.5.86), infecting Persia with the mores of its empire.

The relation of Cyrus's autocratic imperial rule to the equality he instituted remains to be considered. Both replacing the fake equality of oligarchic Persia with real equality of opportunity by arming the commoners equally with the peers and granting an equal role in his empire to Medes, Hyrcanians, Armenians, and even some Assyrians enabled Cyrus to build the tremendous army that acquired and maintained his empire. The loyalty of the heavily armed commoners and men of the favored nations (along with Cyrus's network of spies and informers) might have deterred any attempts at a coup by discontented peers. Although there have been other autocrats who have sided with the common people rather than the elite, it would be a mistake to conclude that such equality necessarily eventuates in despotism. Machiavelli recommends in *The Prince* that princes side with the people against the *grandi* and arm at least some of them, but he also stresses the importance of arming the people for republics and devoted much of his career in government to forming a popular militia.[30] He holds up Cyrus as one of the most excellent of those who became princes by their own virtue, as a model of liberality with what was not his, deception, chastity, humanity, and affability, but curiously, given his own stress on arming the people in *The Prince* and the *Discourses*, Machiavelli does not mention in either book that Cyrus armed the commoners, though he does so in a letter.[31]

Notes

1. I generally follow the translation of Wayne Ambler, Xenophon, *The Education of Cyrus* (Ithaca: Cornell University Press, 2001), occasionally translating myself from Xenophon, *Cyropaedia*, ed. Walter Miller, 2 vols. (Cambridge: Harvard University Press, 1914, 1968). Parenthetical references to it are by book, chapter, and subsection, e.g., 1.1.1.

2. *The Cylinder of Cyrus* in Miller, Appendix 2, 2: 459.

3. Niccolo Machiavelli, *The Prince,* trans. Harvey C. Mansfield, 2nd ed. (Chicago: University of Chicago Press), 60 (ch. 14).

4. Nicolo Machiavelli, *Discourses on Livy,* trans., Harvey C. Mansfield and Nathan Tarcov (Chicago: University of Chicago Press, 1996), 155 (2.13.1), emphases added. Cf. Leo Strauss, *Thoughts on Machiavelli* (Chicago: University of Chicago Press, 1958), 139, 161.

5. Cicero, *Letters to Quintus and Brutus, Letter Fragments, Letter to Octavian, Invectives, and Handbook of Electioneering,* ed. D. R. Shackleton Bailey (Cambridge: Harvard University Press, 2002), 24 (1.1.23); my translation.

6. David Hume, "Of the Balance of Power," in *Essays Moral Political and Literary,* ed. Eugene F. Miller, rev. ed. (Indianapolis: Liberty *Classics,*1985), 332.

7. Cf. James Tatum, *Xenophon's Imperial Fiction: On the Education of Cyrus* (Princeton: Princeton University Press, 1989); Philip Stadter, "Fictional Narrative in the *Cyropaideia,*" in *Xenophon*, ed. Vivienne J. Gray (Oxford: Oxford University Press, 2010), 367–400; and Michael Reichel, "Xenophon's *Cyropaedia* and the Hellenistic Novel," in *Xenophon,* ed. Gray, 418–38.

8. On Xenophon's Persia, see Christopher Nadon, *Xenophon's Prince: Republic and Empire in the Cyropaedia* (Berkeley: University of California Press, 2001), 29–42. On its relation to Xenophon's portrayal of Sparta, see Christopher Tuplin, "Xenophon, Sparta and the *Cyropaedia*," in *The Shadow of Sparta*, ed. Anton Powell and Stephen Hodkinson (London: Routledge, 1994), 134–64.

9. Xenophon writes that "it is said the Persians are about a hundred twenty thousand" (1.2.15). Miller's note to this sentence claims "the number is meant to include the nobility only, the so called 'peers' (*homotimoi*) and not the total population of Persia." This is extremely improbable given that only one thousand peers accompany Cyrus's army (1.2.5) and none seem present in the second army (5.5.3), and it is difficult to imagine that number exercising at once in the agora. I assume it includes both peers and commoners, though probably only the adult males.

10. Xenophon refers to pre-Cyrus Persia as a polis or city.

11. Cf. "Regime of the Lacedaemonians," 3, trans. Catherine S. Kuiper and Susan D. Collins, in Xenophon, *The Shorter Writings*, ed. Gregory A. McBrayer (Ithaca: Cornell University Press, 2018): "a great spiritedness is naturally implanted in those of such an age, hubris is especially uppermost, and the strongest desires for pleasures take hold of them."

12. Walter Miller's note plausibly suggests this refers to "a Council of Elders, under the presidency of the king." *Cyropaedia*, 13n1.

13. See Nadon, *Xenophon's Prince*, 42–54.

14. Cf. Thucydides's contrast between Athenians and Spartans in this respect at 1.6.

15. The verb *lalein* can mean either childishly prattle or speak in general. The sentence is customarily separated from Cyrus's argument as the start of a new chapter and despite its *men de* construction translated as two sentences, obscuring the relation between Cyrus's arguments and his mother's leaving.

16. On homosexual love in Xenophon see Clifford Hindley, "Xenophon on Male Love," in *Xenophon*, ed. Gray, 72–110.

17. This story was dramatized by Tristan L'Hermite in his play *Panthée* of 1637, in *le theatre complet de tristan l'hermite*, ed. Claude K. Abraham, Jérôme W. Scheitzer, and Jacqueline Van Baelen (Tuscaloosa: University of Alabama Press, 1975), 125–216, and by Thomas Maurice in his play *Panthea, or The Captive Bride: A Tragedy: Founded on a Story in Xenophon* of 1789 (Ecco Print Editions).

18. On Cyrus's transformation of Persia see Nadon, *Xenophon's Prince*, 55–76.

19. Cf. Machiavelli on this phenomenon in Rome, *Discourses on Livy* 3.24.

20. Like Lincoln's Emancipation Proclamation.

21. The adverb *isos* means "fairly" as well as "equally"; the adjective means both fair and equal.

22. The word *oikothen* can mean "from home," "from childhood," or "from the beginning."

23. The word *sunēthēs* can mean "well acquainted" or "intimate."

24. On Pheraulas's speech see Nadon, *Xenophon's Prince*, 71–76.

25. Xenophon puts this in the present tense as true of Persia in his time.

26. Cf. Aristotle, *Politics* 5.11 1313b6–17, 1314a16–18.

27. For the controversy over the significance and authenticity of this chapter see, e.g., Tatum, *Xenophon's Imperial Fiction*, 217–25; Bodil Due, *The Cyropaedia* (Aarhus: Aarhus University Press, 1989), 16–22; Nadon, *Xenophon's Prince*, 139–46; and Vivienne J. Gray, *Xenophon's Mirror of Princes* (Oxford: Oxford University Press, 2011), 246–63.

28. Plato's *Laws* 694a–695e.

29. Cf. Machiavelli, *Discourses on Livy*, 1.9.2 and 1.11.4.

30. Machiavelli, *The Prince*, chs. 9, 20; *Discourses on Livy*, 1.6.3, 1.30.2, 1.43; Christopher Lynch, *Machiavelli on War*, forthcoming, ch. 1.

31. Machiavelli to Vettori, 26 August 1513, *Machiavelli and His Friends: Their Personal Correspondence,* trans. and ed. James B. Atkinson and David Sices (DeKalb: Northern Illinois Press, 1996), 259.

Chapter 3

Splendid Equality in the *Nicomachean Ethics*
Munificence

Ann Charney Colmo

Is it possible to reconcile excellence and equality? Aristotle says lack of excellence (*aretē*—often translated as "virtue") is due to lack of education (*NE* 1104b11–13). This statement helps us understand that a resolution of the opposition between excellence and equality through education exists in the *Nicomachean Ethics*[1]—in a place where excellence reaches its highest point: that of the great virtues.

In the *Nicomachean Ethics* there are two virtues that are designated "great" (*megalo-*). Each virtue focuses on greatness in the person who possesses it, greatness in the objective with which it is concerned, and greatness in the manner and nobility with which that person carries out the objective. These are the only two moral virtues that cannot be attained by all human beings—not even by all the virtuous. These great virtues would seem to show excellence farthest removed from equality. The better known virtue is *megalopsychia*, literally greatness of soul, often translated as "magnanimity" (*NE* 1123a35–1125a35). This greatness of soul, magnanimity, consists in justly estimating oneself as worthy of great honors or deeds, justly because one is worthy of them in truth.[2]

But the less well-known great virtue is where the conjunction of excellence and equality is achieved. This second great virtue is munificence (*megaloprepeia NE* 1122a18–1122a34), literally great fittingness, or conspicuously splendid spending.³ The one who possesses this virtue is able to expend large sums of money on projects that are fitting (-*prepeia*) and noble or beautiful. The expenditures of the munificent on great projects are undertaken with great pleasure; he must spend lavishly, without exacting calculation of the outlay. Yet the end product is *prepeia*—exactly fitting the occasion, just right, and clearly seen to be so.

Munificence is "a fitting expenditure on a great thing, such as constructing a trireme, or sponsoring a sacred embassy" (*NE* 1122a23–25), paying for a play's costumes or scenery, or providing funds for a statue to adorn the city. Expenditures must be great and must fit the purpose of the expenditure. They must be made for the sake of the noble (*tou kalou: NE* 1122b7); Aristotle adds that nobility is common to all the virtues. What is not common to all the virtues, however, is that the work (*poiesis*) that is *achieved* must be noble, which in this instance carries another connotation of the Greek word *to kalon*: beautiful (*NE* 1122b16).⁴ By requiring that the work of the munificent be fitting, Aristotle makes it clear that a great public work that was not beautiful would lose its fitting character. Even the trireme is decorated in a beautiful manner (Thucydides, *The Peloponnesian War* 6.31).

We are rather surprised to learn that this ability is a virtue. After all, it involves the accomplishment of a work completely external to the doer: it involves the kind of action that Aristotle in Book I of the *Nicomachean Ethics* says is apart from the activity itself, whereas virtue is an activity (*NE* 1094a4–5). In producing his work, the munificent is only indirectly involved in the execution of it. He is literally what we today call a "producer," not the sculptor, not the playwright, nor the director. The finished work is as dependent on the artist or artisan as on the one who furnishes the money—perhaps more so—though the choice of artist is the task of the munificent. While the virtue of liberality or generosity (*eleutheria*), the small-scale version of munificence, concerns *giving* to *others*—the recipient must be deserving—munificence is concerned with *spending* on *things* (*NE* 1122a20). In addition, munificence requires that the doer have accumulated or inherited a great deal of wealth. But wealth, even when justly gained (certainly a requirement for munificence), doesn't seem to depend on one's decency or good nature, but—especially, but not only, when inherited—rather on qualities that are accidental to moral virtue. In fact, munificence seems to require, or even be, some kind of art (*technē*), "bringing something [external] into existence which may either exist or not" (*NE* 1140a12–13).

The ability of the artist is not necessarily connected with any moral virtue whatsoever (*NE* 1140a17–20).

Given all this, why is *wealthy* expenditure a virtue, especially a great virtue, for Aristotle? A preliminary answer: munificence is a special type of spending—public spending, splendid, and in great amounts, for the common good—and it is an opportunity for the wealthy to perform noble actions that can be used or appreciated by all the citizens. In order to be munificent, in other words, a person must have great wealth, but that person must also act in a splendid way to benefit the city, that is to say, all the people in common equally.[5] Private expenditures of wealth are in harmony with munificence, but munificence pure and simple must involve splendid *public* benefactions. By the very activity of their virtue, the munificent can serve to educate and to raise the city up and beautify the city. In this way, the munificent may reconcile excellence and equality.

The examples that Aristotle gives of munificence make clear what we have stated, that the canvas on which the munificent person works is the public realm. At least, great expenditures are esteemed when they are for the common association, and when they involve objects for which it is fitting to wish to be publicly honored. His great and noble expenditures arouse wonder or admiration (*thaumastos*) in the spectator (*theōria NE* 1122b15–22).

When a munificent action is to outfit a trireme or to underwrite the production of a play, we see that the munificent participates in the country's most basic aims: life or security (*sōtēria*) and living well. As Aristotle says in the *Politics* (1252b28–30), the city comes into being for life, but its end is living well.[6] The munificent, then, is a necessary part of the city's self-preservation and of the city's good life.

But the munificent also provides the means for the city to care for its gods, publicly and fittingly. Thus, he commissions public sacrifices and sacred embassies. His is a virtue that is a necessity to the city in the highest degree, and in the highest things. Bringing beautiful sacred things to the public also furnishes the city with an education that is open to all, both because it aims at the beautiful and because it is free—"liberal" in both senses of the word. An education about beauty in the context of the gods enhances both in the mind of the citizen. Here again, the munificent's actions or works make excellence and equality compatible.

"The munificent," Aristotle says, "resembles a knower (*epistēmoni*), since he is able to contemplate what is fitting and to spend great amounts in a suitable way" (*NE* 1122a35–36). The munificent person must know a number of other things, particularly politics and economics, such as, for example, that his wealth depends on the stability of the regime and relative harmony among the citizens. The munificent person must know the laws that provide for and guard inheritance, and, more important, be aware that the value of his money is a function of the city's continued repayment of its debts (*Politics* 1276a8–14), and of the full faith and credit of its currency (*NE* 1133a28–32). The laws may also shape the munificent:

Legally required participation in religious festivities that include competitive artistic displays can foster habits of mutual friendliness and fraternity between families, while cultivating appreciation for thought-provoking works of art and graceful wit; by compelling the wealthier to patronize these public events, the law can stimulate in the rich, and in the rest, through their example, not only generosity but also tasteful magnificence [munificence].[7]

A historical fact about munificent expenditures, implied in the quote above, is that these expenditures were *expected* of wealthy citizens in the *polis* (Bartlett and Collins, 72n10)—by law or by convention. Interestingly, they were called *leitourgiai*—liturgies. But the *fact* of this historical fact is that during the times of spirited democracy in Athens these liturgies were *extorted* from the wealthy: do something for us with your money, or lose it. A litany of liturgies, the wealthy person's account of the public benefactions he had made to the city, was often used as a defense against envy in demotic lawsuits.[8] You will not find this mentioned by Aristotle (except indirectly, in the *Politics* 1309a13–21). Why not? Because the liturgy of munificence is not performed to deter envy: it is not a virtue unless it is done for the sake of the noble, with pleasure and without stinting (*NE* 1122b6).

The objects of the munificent person's public benefactions also underline the fact that the interest of the regime is the same as that of the munificent. For example, the rise of the Athenian navy gave even more importance to the contributions of the wealthy. At the same time, in a compelling way, the Athenian navy made the wealthy more dependent on the *dēmos,* the majority of the citizens. Thus, in his military expenditures, the munificent also benefits the entire city, not only the many, but also the military elements of the city and the rulers who must protect the city.[9] Aristotle's discussion of munificence in the *Nicomachean Ethics* downplays the continual strife in Athens between the wealthy and the *demos*—which reached a peak when the Athenian navy flourished—and its triremes, though funded and commanded by the wealthy,[10] achieved their successes through the *dēmos* (and *metics* and slaves) who powered them. This necessity led to the predominance of democracy and equality in the Athenian *polis,* despite its occasional turn to oligarchy.[11]

The reciprocal relation between the city and the munificent reminds us of Aristotle's discussion of reciprocity and justice in Book V of the *Nicomachean Ethics* (see especially 1132b32–1133a5). Aristotle in fact implicates the munificent in reciprocity.

> [T]he city stays together by means of proportional reciprocity. . . . If people do not [seek to do good to others in return for their good deeds], there is no mutual exchange (*metadosis*) that comes about—and people stay together through mutual exchange. Hence too people place a Shrine to the Graces along the roadway, to foster reciprocal giving, for this belongs to gratitude: one ought to serve in return someone who has been gracious, and ought oneself, the next time, to take the lead in being gracious. (*NE* 1132b34–1133a5)

The Shrine to the Graces might be the very type of sacred monument for which the city needs the expenditure of the munificent. The Shrine calls to mind civic reciprocity.[12] The munificent by funding such monuments would also be recognizing the city's role in his being in a position to be munificent. He himself needs the people to be conscious of his benefactions to them, in order that they feel gratitude to him. Finally, the example of this Shrine points to the importance of the munificent regarding the gods, or the divine protection of Providence needed by the city.

While the virtue of munificence benefits the city, however, it also makes the munificent in his virtuous actions *dependent on* the city to the highest degree. The munificent must know what is fitting to his particular city, whether it concern the city's basic needs or the city's gods. He must enlist the help of others—priests, poets, or pilots—to produce his splendid works. Since the practice of his virtue results in an external, splendid work, there must be spectators to admire his works and to honor them. He needs the city itself and its harbors as a locus for the fulfillment of his ambition.

The munificent is not only connected to and dependent on the regime as a whole, but also to the most important parts of the regime. In Book VII of the *Politics*, Aristotle lists the parts of the city that necessarily belong to it, "whatsoever it is without which the city would not be" (*Pol* 1328b2–24). These parts are the farmers, the artisans ("for living needs instruments"), the military, the wealthy (for its own needs and for the requirements of war), priests ("fifth and primary"), and judges ("of advantage and justice among the citizens," "sixth and most necessary of all"). Thus, there are six parts necessary to the very existence of the city. Of these six, the activity of the munificent touches on five, through common meals, spectacles and plays, the triremes, his own wealth, and the sacred rituals which he funds.[13] The interdependence of the city and the munificent inheres in his virtue.

The munificent is, as we have seen, uniquely in a position to unite the various elements of the city, especially those who contribute excellence and those whose participation in the city bring with it claims for equality. These may, of course, have opposing views of the best for the city. All parts of the city—including the decent and the many—are capable of being the cause of faction or stasis,[14] especially regarding the most important questions of a regime: how property should be distributed, and who should share in rule. The distribution of property, whatever the means of distribution chosen by the regime, if it is not executed with care, will result in envy and anger. Yet in his instructive debate between the many poor and the few wealthy in Book III of the *Politics* (1281a15–29), Aristotle indicates that neither the rich nor the poor can distribute the property or wealth of the other without injustice. One might expect that the decision about the distribution of property could be left safely with the decent (*epieikeis*). This, however, would require that the decent rule—the distribution of property is subsumed under the other tendentious question, that of rule. But Aristotle discounts the claim of the decent to rule on the grounds that it excludes the many from office. The many have several just reasons for their claim to rule. The city, to live well, must be self-sufficient. This is not possible without the many, and without the work of the many, dedicated to supplying the requisites for living. Aristotle indicates a way in which the many (or a particular multitude) might claim superiority over the few or the one best: the collective judgment of the many may include expertise in many aspects of a work—each one of the many knowledgeable about one of its parts (*Pol* 1281b1–23). Aristotle exemplifies the collective superiority of the many by the contributions they may make to enhance a public meal. It is not an accident that a public meal is one of the things that Aristotle lists among the contributions of the munificent. The interests, and even sometimes the type of contributions, of the excellent and the equal coincide.

The decent complain that the base should not govern about more important matters than do they themselves. Yet enmity in the city is at its most threatening when the many, being many, are excluded.[15] Aristotle expresses the dilemma in this way: "It is not safe for them to participate in the highest offices (for injustice and imprudence would necessarily cause them to act unjustly in some things and to err in others) but yet not to admit them and for them not to participate is fearful, for when there are a number of persons disenfranchised (*atimoi*) and in poverty, the city then is necessarily full of enemies" (*Pol* 1281b26–31). The city cannot continue to exist when a majority of its people do not wish it to.[16] The city must recognize the claims of the many, therefore, or live with powerful enemies within—and not just outside—its borders.

The possibility of enmity between the different parts of the city—those who claim the force of virtue, military strength, wealth, or freedom—creates a need for the great virtue of munificence. If anything could, the expenditures of the munificent could siphon off the envy and distrust that exist between the rich and the poor. The existence of a number of beautiful public works may make the many feel less poor—and confident in their collective judgment of them. Moreover, the works of the munificent, whether public or private, involve the many in the doings of the "worthies" (*axiōmati*)— even in ancient Athens, a splendid wedding might attract the interest of all the city (*NE* 1123a23)—bringing a sense of connection among the citizens.

The munificent, by working on a grand, public scale also serves as an example to the well-off of generosity, the kind of material giving that is possible equally on a small and a large scale, equally in the private and the public sphere. The emphasis in our time on service and philanthropy— though it might not be possible today to sponsor an aircraft carrier—and its recognition by political leaders indicates that munificence as well as generosity have a place—perhaps especially—in a liberal society. Turning the well-off toward the virtue of generosity would build another bridge between them and the multitude. Public spectacles bring the city together quite literally. The munificent person thus turns the most potentially inimical political divisions into an occasion for *philia*, a necessity for a true community of citizens.[17]

When Aristotle discusses the fitting expenditure of the munificent, he also talks about those who aim for what is fitting, but miss the mark (*NE* 1123a20–34). The person who fails to bring about the fitting because of excess is the vulgar (*banausos*), who believes that the quantity of the outlay of funds is the key to munificence. His desire, however, rather than to achieve the beautiful, is to cause the admiration that the munificent arouses—though he is more likely to create derision, as will the parsimonious, who "laments each great expenditure, and tries to spend the least amount possible, destroying the beautiful for some trifle." Aristotle also ridicules the poor who would try to emulate the munificent, spending beyond their means. A poor person who tries to be munificent is foolish (*ēlithios*).

"But these vices do not bring reproach," Aristotle says, "because they are neither harmful to a neighbor nor extremely unseemly." They do, however, create a comic effect, and bring laughter, rather than admiration.

Munificence is a moral virtue that brings in several intellectual virtues besides prudence, which operates in all the moral virtues. In addition to art (*technê*), we have seen that another of the intellectual virtues is brought in: *epistēmē*. "The munificent resembles a knower (*epistēmoni*)" (*NE* 1122a35).[18] This knowledge is concerned with eternal things, which exist of necessity and which cannot vary (*NE* 1139b23–25). This is indeed a strange thing to say about the munificent, who concerns himself with the splendid but ephemeral adornment or protection of the city—those things that could not ever be eternal, and that probably are confined to one city, at least in their manifestation. Is he like the *epistēmoni*, then, because of his attention to the gods? Even in his expenditure for the holy things, however, he is making votive offerings, sending sacred embassies, and providing sacrifices—each of which is probably peculiar to his city, and none of which is eternal. Does he then grasp the eternal character of the gods, and deduce the fitting offerings to make to them? This would seem to be a philosophic characteristic.[19]

The words Aristotle uses about the munificent might seem to some to point to a connection between the munificent and philosophy. Aristotle not only points to the knower in connection with the munificent, but also uses many words that can be translated, or are a compound of the word Aristotle in Book X of the *Nicomachean Ethics* uses to describe the activity of the philosopher: *theōria*, or contemplation. The munificent is like a knower because he is able to contemplate (*theōrēsai*) and spend great sums with care (*NE* 1122a35–36). He funds or leads sacred embassies (*architheōrōi*), and the sight (*theōria*) of his great and noble works "arouses wonder, and the munificent arouses wonder" (*thaumaston* [which can also be translated *admiration*], *NE* 1122b17). Readers of Aristotle are not only struck by the use of *theōria*, but by the connection Aristotle often makes between wonder and wisdom. The difficulty with the interpretation of the munificent as philosophic is that it does not take into account the necessary attachment between the munificent and his particular city. We have showed that attachment above, and insist upon it here, because of its connection with convention (*nomos*), whether of the tastes of the city or of the value of its currency (*nomos*).

There is an alternative explanation for the many times *theōria* appears in the discussion of the munificent. The munificent is more than he seems. It has been suggested that the magnanimous stands not only for the political actor, but also for the philosopher (*Post. Anal.* 97b8–26).[20] The munificent is like a knower, but at more than one place in his discussion of the magnanimous, Aristotle makes it clear that the magnanimous is like a *god* (*NE* 1123b17–20; 1124b13–16). The munificent "furnishes his private home splendidly, fitting to his wealth, for this is a sort of *kosmos*" (*NE* 1123a6–7). The magnanimous is *himself* a sort of *kosmos* (*NE* 1124a2). It is difficult to see how the munificent could be close to the philosopher when the magnanimous stands so clearly above him.

But as the magnanimous stands both for the political and the philosophical person, there is a similar duality in the munificent. The munificent stands for the discerning, wealthy citizen, but also for the poet. The word *theōria* is initially connected to words connoting sight and seeing. The spectacle (*theōrēma, theōria*) and its spectator (*theōros*) both contain the root *theōr-* in Greek. This would apply not only to the munificent, whose funded works must be spectacular, but also to the poet, who *creates* spectacles. In the *Poetics*, Aristotle says that "epic poetry [because of its greater number of parts than tragedy] has the good of *munificence*, and variety (*metaballon*) for the hearer, and diversity (*anomoios*) of episodes" (*Poetics* 1459b29; emphasis added). The good poet creates wonder (*thaumaston*) (*Poetics* 1452a3). Aristotle's discussion of munificence and magnanimity is a continuation of the quarrel between the philosopher and the poet that was begun by Plato.[21]

Unlike the poet, the philosopher is apart from the city and self-sufficient, as much as it is possible for human beings to be. His works do not depend on others—certainly not on others in his city—for their worth. He does not work for honor, although the political impact of his works might form and destroy cities. He has more than once been called the Legislator.[22] He is the craftsman of reason, both in the city and transcending it. The grasp of the first principles belongs not to *epistēmē* but to *nous*. Once the principles are intuited, *epistēmē* can deduce how they would unfold, how they would look. The work of *nous*, of grasping the first principles, belongs to the philosopher. The work that is "like" *epistēmē*, the applications of principles to the actual city here and now, belongs to the munificent and the poet. While the root for the word *theōria* occurs often in Aristotle's discussion of munificence, the word that is repeated often in the discussion of magnanimity is "truth."[23]

Nevertheless, the poet believes his understanding of the whole is truer than that of the philosopher.[24] The poet also emphasizes things about human beings that the philosopher looks at as secondary to reason, for example, emotions,[25] or a sense of the sacred. The poet, then, is determined "to make sense of the way the world is," and the place in it of human beings, from this point of view[26]—or he is following other poets who have done so.[27] "Tragedy confronted the deepest questions of human existence and challenged the spectators to make sense of human suffering" (JACT, 7.44 310). The poet is splendid because he gives to the spectators that which he believes humans need most: religion. The poet is a maker: of myths about the whole, and of the city's relation to the whole (cf. Euripides, *Bacchae*; Aristophanes, *Birds*). This reminds us of the munificent's expenditure on the realm of the divine. The first example Aristotle gave of the munificent's expenditures having to do with the gods was the votive offering (*NE* 1122b20). And Aristotle says that "his gifts have a certain resemblance to votive offerings" (*NE* 1123a5–7). In funding theater productions, the munificent introduces the people to the poets' works on how and what the gods are, perhaps the most influential public source of knowledge of the gods' nature from the time of Hesiod and Homer—or before.[28]

Aristotle thus points to an issue outside munificence that is always important to the political, the question of the place of religion in politics—even though this question might be answered by the insistence in modern times on the separation of religion and the state. Though some citizens may dispute that Providence plays a role in human affairs, others see religion as having vital importance in the course of the country's history and to the country's moral fiber. But whatever the two contending sides may believe, *they do not know.* (This is one reason why the secular age has not succeeded completely in silencing the sectarian.) The poet can give them the illusion that they do know—one way or the other—thus relieving many kinds of anxieties.

Aristotle has cited the works of the poets as examples of opportunities for the collective judgment by the many. The poet as well as the munificent reconciles equality and excellence, but the poet sometimes in comic or ironic ways. While the poet might elevate the many by introducing them to the gods, he might also, by the use of comedy, reduce great persons to a level of equality with the many.[29] He may even thus ridicule the philosopher (Aristophanes, *Clouds*)—perhaps a better way to have him step down than by giving him hemlock.[30] Although the comic character of the excess and deficiency in munificence might not be as laughable as the comedy of the poet, it could surely be used as comedy by the poet.

Like the munificent, the poet depends on the city as the philosopher does not: he needs his spectators and the city venue and its actors to perform his plays. He is dependent on the acclaim of the city, and vies with the other poets for its prizes.[31] The gods of the city are the subjects of or onlookers in the poet's work, which would be incomprehensible without the spectators' knowledge of these gods. The poet is the craftsman (*technos*) of the words to express the passions, and he depends on his deep knowledge of these passions to stir his audience. In presenting the passions, however, he must always keep in mind the conventions of the city. Even the laws of the city may be the source of the "religious festivities that include competitive artistic displays [which call for the] thought-provoking works of art and graceful wit."[32]

Thus, in both manifestations of munificence, we find the meeting of excellence and equality. It exists there in a way that also brings friendship to the community as a whole. Both the munificent and the poet, by the active operation of their excellence, provide the education to all that lifts up the many.[33]

Notes

1. *Aristotle's Nicomachean Ethics*, trans. Robert C. Bartlett and Susan Collins (Chicago: The University of Chicago Press, 2011). Aristotle, *Nicomachean Ethics*, trans. H. Rackham (Cambridge: Harvard University Press, 1999).

2. See A. Colmo, "Magnanimity: The Upper Limits of Reason" (Northeastern Political Science Association, 2004), and bibliography, for the great number of writings on magnanimity. Munificence, on the other hand, is the step-child of academic scholarship, and appears only fleetingly, if at all, in books about the *Nicomachean Ethics* as a whole.

3. *NE* 1122b2–8. The Greek word that I am translating as "munificence" (*megaloprepeia*) is often translated as "magnificence." "Magnificence," however, connotes more than an expenditure of funds, to which Aristotle confines his definition of the term. "Magnificent" can be used to describe a splendid speech, or an artistic or physical achievement. Moreover, "magnificence" also connotes the splendid trappings of the autocratic ruler. "Munificence" brings out both the monetary aspect of the virtue and its public or at least its philanthropic character.

4. For some other virtues, the translation "beautiful" for *to kalon* would not be appropriate. A death in battle, for example, may signify the nobility of the virtuous action, but it will not be beautiful. Just actions are often not beautiful, which is perhaps one reason why equity is necessary, where the just and the beautiful can coincide. See also the excellent discussion of the relation between moral virtue and *to kalon* in Gabriel Richardson Lear, *Happy Lives and the Highest Good: An Essay on Aristotle's Nicomachean Ethics* (Princeton: Princeton University Press, 2004), 123–46.

5. In *The Eudemian Ethics of Aristotle*, trans. Peter L. P. Simpson (New Brunswick, NJ: Transaction, 2013), Aristotle adds that the munificent cannot be a person "of low condition," such as Themistocles was (*EE* 1233b12–13). The *Nicomachean Ethics* is ambiguous on the necessity of high birth (*NE* 1122b30–34).

6. Cf. *NE* 1281a3–4: the political association must be set down for the sake of noble actions—for happiness—and not just for living together.

7. Thomas L. Pangle, *Aristotle's Teaching in the Politics* (Chicago: The University of Chicago Press, 2013), 12. Pangle uses the word *magnificence*, another translation of *megaloprepeia*.

8. Joint Association of Classical Teachers' Greek Course Background Book (JACT), *The World of Athens: An Introduction to Classical Athenian Culture* (Cambridge: Cambridge University Press, 1984) says that the *leitourgiai* were originally voluntary, "but under the Athenian democracy 'liturgies' were compulsory for those who owned a certain amount of property" (5.71 228). It quotes Lysias's speech *On a Bribery Charge* to indicate that liturgies were performed to defend the wealthy from accusations by the demos (5.72 228–29).

9. Those who reach for glory in conquest might also find it useful to have the wealthy citizens strive for the virtue of munificence. Aristotle is silent on whether cooperation with such a figure is a part of this virtue, and what expression of gratitude, still less wonder, might be, in terms of such a person.

10. The munificent not only funded triremes, but often were also the ship's commander, though it was the steersman (*kubernētēs*) who was, in fact, in charge (JACT, 6.41 272).

11. John R. Hale, *Lords of the Sea: The Epic Story of the Athenian Navy and the Birth of Democracy* (New York: Viking Penguin, 2009), xxvii–xxviii, 121, 208–209.

12. "The strong impulse to reciprocate is the only powerful motive to which Aristotle refers as a bond of common existence." Joseph Cropsey, "Justice and Friendship in the *Nicomachean Ethics*," in Joseph Cropsey, *Political Philosophy and the Issues of Politics* (Chicago: The University of Chicago Press, 1977), 262.

13. The sixth, judging of the advantageous and the just, is the province of the magnanimous. (See below, in text.)

14. JACT argues, however, that Athens was less prone to faction than other Greek cities of the time. This may be due in part to the munificent which could fund "less harmful outlets, e.g. festivals" for the passions leading to factions (3.16 146).

15. Jean-Jacques Rousseau, *Discourse on the Origins and Foundations of Inequality* (Second Discourse), in *The First and Second Discourses*, trans. Roger D. and Judith R. Masters (New York: St. Martin's Press, 1964), 177–81, makes it clear that the many have might on their side. Where the tendency for the many to believe itself weak comes from is an interesting question.

16. *Pol* 1309b14–17: The number of people wishing the regime to continue should be more than the number wishing to change it. Cf.: *all* the parts of the city must wish it to continue (1294b34–39). Fred D. Miller Jr., "Aristotle on Deviant

Constitutions," in *Aristotelian Political Philosophy*, Vol. II, ed. K. I. Boudouris (Athens: The International Center for Greek Philosophy and Culture, 1995), 112–14, explains this latter as the optimal desideratum for the city, and the former as the "fallback" when the optimal is not possible. He emphasizes, however, that the "fallback" is not just an argument of force.

17. Friendship, however, should include all the citizens in the city (*NE* 1155a23–29). Aristotle does not concern himself, in discussing politics or moral virtue, with the vexed question of self-love (which is discussed instead in the section on friendship). In order to be just or virtuous, a human being must act justly or virtuously to all in the community, *including himself*. As a citizen, he is also benefited by the physical results of his action, and it goes without saying that the action itself renders him more noble. The self-love of the munificent is implicated in his reciprocal relation to the community, especially to the many, or the equal.

18. In the *Nicomachean Ethics*, Book VI, Aristotle is largely silent, or at least ambiguous, about the relation between the moral and the intellectual virtues, with the exception of prudence (*phronēsis*). Thus, the relation of munificence to *epistēmē* in Book IV (though he says only that the munificent *resembles*—or *is like*—the *epistēmon*) is rather surprising.

19. By contrast, "Socrates . . . found the paradigm . . . of magnificence [munificence] in [the [philosopher's]] contemplation of all time and being." Ronna Burger, *Aristotle's Dialogue with Socrates: On the Nicomachean Ethics* (Chicago: The University of Chicago Press, 2008). In fn. 31, p. 251, Burger cites "Plato, *Republic* 486a; cf. 487a, 490c, 494b."

20. See also René Antoine Gauthier, O.P. and Jean Yves Jolif, O.P., *L'Éthique à Nicomaque: Introduction, Traduction et Commentaire* (Louvain: Publications Universitaires de Louvain, 1959), 289–96. Gauthier and Jolif, however, believe the magnanimous is *only* the philosopher, 289–90.

21. See *The Republic of Plato*, trans. Allan Bloom (New York: Basic Books, 1968), 386a–402b, but Plato's own poetry stands as the greatest challenge to the poets. Cf. Stanley Rosen, *The Quarrel Between Philosophy and Poetry: Studies in Ancient Thought* (London: Routledge, 1988), Preface; 3–11.

22. *NE* 1181b13–23. Cf. Jean-Jacques Rousseau, *Of the Social Contract*, ed. Christopher Bertram, trans. Quintin Hoare (London: Penguin Books, 2012), II.7, 42–45; Montesquieu, *The Spirit of the Laws*, ed. and trans. Anne M. Cohler, Basia Carolyn Miller, Harold Samuel Stone (Cambridge: Cambridge University Press, 1989), Part 6, ch. 19, 818.

23. The word *truth*, or an inflected form, occurs six times in Aristotle's discussion of magnanimity in *NE* IV.iii. It does not occur in the section on munificence, *NE* IV.ii.

24. A major cause of the quarrel between the philosopher and the poet. See Seth Benardete, trans. *Plato's Philebus: The Tragedy and Comedy of Life* (Chicago: The University of Chicago Press, 1993), ix–x.

25. "For all the desires pains, and pleasures in the soul that we say follow all our action, poetic imitation produces similar results in us. For it fosters and waters them when they ought to be dried up, and sets them up as rulers in us when they ought to be ruled" (Plato, *Republic* 606d). JACT, 7.72 334.

26. "The authority of tragedy stems from the conviction of the tragedian that he is handling topics which lie at the very heart of his own understanding of the human condition . . ." (JACT, 7.40 305–306). Hesiod's *Theogony* "is the earliest surviving attempt to impose order and definition on the shifting chaos of early Greek religious beliefs." J. W. Roberts, *City of Sokrates: An Introduction to Classical Athens* (London: Routledge and Kegan Paul, 1984), 111.

27. "Drawing on myth and legend relieved the playwright . . . if he wished to compete annually . . . of the problem of inventing plots." JACT, 7.38 304.

28. Roberts, *Sokrates*, 109–13.

29. "Aristophanes presented people and ideas in forms which made them laughable *in the eyes of the common man*" (JACT, 7.59 321; emphasis in original).

30. Socrates does, however, mention "a comic poet" as one of the accusers in his trial. Plato, *Apology of Socrates* 18d, in *Four Texts on Socrates*, trans. Thomas G. West and Grace Starry West (Ithaca: Cornell University Press, 1984). Aristophanes, *Clouds,* trans. Alan H. Sommerstein (Warminster, England: Aris and Phillips, 1982).

31. Roberts, *Sokrates*, 150–51.

32. Pangle, see above in text.

33. Plato, *Republic* 606e. "[Homer's] poems became the heart of Greek education" (JACT, P10 357).

Chapter 4

How Excellence Bows to Equality in Aristotle's *Politics*

Mary P. Nichols

It is commonly held that classical political thought privileged virtue, while modern political thought privileged equality and freedom. There is much truth to this view. As Aristotle says, "Virtue must be a care for every city, or at least every one that is named so in truth and not merely in a manner of speaking." Those distinguished by their virtue, or who can most contribute to this highest end of the city, therefore deserve a greater share in ruling (1280a7–81a9).[1] It is also true, however, that Aristotle gives a greater place to equality and freedom than he is given credit for. Indeed, he understood virtue or excellence to best flourish in political communities whose principles included equality and freedom as well as virtue. By the same token, he is not as aristocratic or elitist as he is often thought to be. My argument is divided into three parts. I begin with his treatment of the family in Book 1 of the *Politics*, whose component relationships with the male at the head—master and slave, husband and wife, and father and children—seems as inegalitarian a community as any could be. I shall nevertheless argue that by limiting the scope of despotism, literally the rule of a master (*despotēs*) over a slave, and by denying any despotic rule as appropriate between husband and wife or father and children, Aristotle prepares for his proposal of a form of rule that belongs to political life, a sharing in rule that he calls "political rule." Political rule, "sharing" or "taking part," is appropriate for human beings who are free and equal, in the sense that they are political by nature because they possess reason or speech. What they have in common allows their developing different contributions, and even different virtues, which political rule also requires.[2] Because Aristotle argues that the rule between husband and wife in the family is a sharing in rule based on their different contributions and virtues, he is able to trace the foundation for political life to the family.

In the second and third parts of my essay, I follow Aristotle's inquiry into the best regime in the *Politics*, first his treatment of the claims to rule in Book 3, especially the claims of equality or free birth, wealth, and virtue. His famous sixfold classification of regimes accords the rule of the many in the common interest (polity) a central place, and he claims that the rule of "a king over everything," an individual of preeminent virtue, deprives the others in the community of the honors they deserve. In the third and last section, I argue that his elaboration in Book 4 of a mixed regime, including a form based on a well-off middle class, and his treatment in Book 7 of a regime that "we would pray for," demonstrate his goal of forming good regimes by mixing the principles of equality and excellence. Excellence or virtue must bow to equality, in deference rather than submission, precisely because equality best allows excellence to flourish in the give and take of political life that requires citizens and statesmen to develop and exercise the virtues of moderation, justice, and prudence.

Rule within the Family

Aristotle begins Book 1 of the *Politics* by distinguishing the family from the city, objecting to those who think that the city is no more than a large household or family (*oikos*) and that there is no difference between political rule, kingship, family management, and mastery of slaves (1252a1–13). For them all communities are essentially the same, distinguished only on the basis of whether they are constituted from many or few. So too are rulers the same, distinguished only on the basis of the number over whom they rule. Aristotle, in contrast, finds communities and rulers who differ in kind or form (*eidos*). By implication, Aristotle has discovered politics, for he has discovered its specific difference. All communities aim at some good, but within that class communities differ in form. They can therefore be ranked. The political community is the highest or most authoritative community because the good at which it aims is highest, and because it can bring to greater fulfillment the purposes of other communities that it encompasses.

Aristotle's discovery of form or rank in politics has practical consequences for the way we live. If all rule were the same, political rule would not differ from mastery or despotism, and mastery serves the interest of the master. Justice would be nothing more than the advantage of the stronger, who rules in his own interest. The weak would in effect be his slaves. The unqualified principle of equality—all rule and all communities are fundamentally the same—paradoxically, leads to the greatest inequality, while Aristotle's discovery of form or difference allows him to distinguish political life from despotism and to connect it with excellence. The tyrant, who rules despotically, has no care for the virtue of the ruled and even protects his rule by suppressing the freedom in which virtue flourishes (see 1313b17–30). His subjects are truly slaves, if not in name. To conjoin excellence with equality, Aristotle must attack certain forms of inequality. Book I begins with an attack on slavery.

Most obviously, Aristotle distinguishes between slavery by nature and that by convention, denying that any conventional slave system that is not based on nature could be just. He observes, however, that nature wishes that those possessing the natures of slaves generate offspring with the natures of slaves, and similarly in the case of masters. But "the opposite often results" (1254b26–33). Even if we could identify some as natural slaves and others as natural masters, so as to justify slavery, it would be unlikely that its justification would outlast a generation. Moreover, if natural slaves can produce natural masters, and natural masters can generate natural slaves, masters and slaves share a common humanity. They are not separate species. This simple point plagues Aristotle's attempt to separate slaves by nature from masters by nature.

Aristotle describes the family as a coming together of master and slave for the sake of survival, and of man and woman for the sake of generation. In both cases, they are joined together (*sunduazesthai*) (literally, "are two together") and cannot exist without each other (1252a26–b1). Whereas man and woman are both necessary for human generation, whose survival is served by the conjunction of master and slave? Aristotle appears to mean the survival of both of them, for the master "can foresee with his mind" what is to be done while the latter can with the labor of his body carry out what the other foresees. Although the slave belongs to the master as a possession or part, he is also "separate" from him (*chōriston*) (1254a10–15).

Aristotle's account is puzzling. Perhaps master and slave are joined together, and cannot exist without each other, in the sense that there is no master without a slave, or slave without a master, just as there is no father unless he has a son, nor friend unless he has a friend. That a master does not exist until he masters another, and that a slave comes into being only when he is enslaved, does not mean that there are human beings who are by nature masters and slaves. Poor men, of course, cannot afford slaves, Aristotle soon points out, and for them, "a house, a wife, and an ox for ploughing" might constitute a household (1252b10–12). A master (in theory) cannot exist without a slave, but a human being can do so. Indeed, a poor one must, and one who is better off would not need slaves if he can afford many oxen. Aristotle thus lets creep into his discussion of slavery households or families without slaves. In any case, master and slave do not "go together" in the way that friends do. When Aristotle describes friends as "two going together," he explains that as a result they are "more able to think and to act" (*NE* 1155a16). It is thinking and acting that go together for a human being, while the coming together of master and slave unnaturally separates the two.

When Aristotle associates mind with the master, and body with the slave, he seems to be describing not two different human beings, but one composite being, who has both a mind or soul and a body, and who therefore can think and act. Indeed, in other works, Aristotle says that "the soul is the form of a body that has the potential for life" and that living for a human being involves perception and thought (*De Anima* 412a20, *NE* 1170a16–19). It is body and soul (and matter and form) that cannot exist apart from the other. When Aristotle refers to the "naturally ruling" as what is able to foresee with its mind, and to the "naturally ruled" as what is able to labor, he uses neuter forms rather than masculine ones (1252a31–32).[3] Aristotle has separated soul and body, which are joined together in a human being, to show what would be required for a natural and just despotism. Natural slaves, Aristotle says, are "those who differ from other human beings as a body does from a soul" (1254b16–17). A body without a soul would not be able to labor, of course, to say nothing of being able to execute the commands of a master, nor could a soul without a body have need of another's labor, to say nothing of being able to issue commands to a slave.

Since despotism is just only in the case of slaves by nature, if they exist, it should not come into other relations within the family. Barbarians, a word used to refer to non-Greeks, treat women and slaves as if they were the same, although "a woman differs by nature from a slave" (1252b1–6).

So too in the *Ethics*, Aristotle points out that among the Persians fathers treat their children as slaves. Such tyrannical rule, Aristotle says, is "in error: for those who differ, rule should differ" (*NE* 1160b28–30). His reproach applies to Greeks as well as barbarians. Far from describing the superiority of the Greek family to that of the despotic barbarians, he is appealing to the Greek prejudice against barbarians to move families and political communities away from despotic relations.[4]

Aristotle reminds us of that prejudice when he observes what "poets say": on the ground that the barbarian and the slave are the same in nature, it is said that "it is fitting that Greeks rule barbarians" (*Politics* 1252b8–9; Euripides, *Iphigeneia in Aulis* 1400–01). But it is a woman, Iphigeneia, who voices this prejudice that identifies rule with despotism. It is a prejudice from which women themselves suffer, for Iphigeneia's father, the Greek king Agamemnon, is about to sacrifice her to propitiate the gods so that the Greeks can proceed to Troy to conquer barbarians.[5] Her words appear to justify her sacrifice. The word she uses for what is "fitting" (*eikos*), however, also means what is "likely." She might be describing not what is just or fitting, but rather voicing a complaint about what is likely to happen to the Trojans, and what is about to happen to her. "Silence" might be "a woman's grace," as Aristotle quotes Ajax reproaching Tecmessa when she speaks up, but Ajax does so when she questions his actions (1260a30; Sophocles, *Ajax* 293). By speaking in favor of Greek despotism, Iphigeneia calls attention to her father's despotic treatment of herself. She is not entirely silent.[6] Aristotle lets her speak a second time by quoting her. He confirms the irony in her statement when in Book 2 he includes Carthage, a non-Greek regime, among the most highly reputed regimes he discusses (1272b24–25). And he offers support for her complaint against Agamemnon when he maintains that the forms sof rule differ: marital—and paternal—rule differ fundamentally from despotic rule, for a wife and children are "free persons" (1259a38–b2). It is among the flesh-eating Cyclops whom Homer describes that one finds true barbarism, where each "enacts divine law for their children and wives" and hence assumes the power of a god in his household (1252b23; *Odyssey* 9.112–15).

In describing the relations within the household, Aristotle encounters a quandary. Whereas Greek has a word for the rule of slaves, *despotikē*, and a word for the father's authority over his children, *patrikē*, the relation between the husband and wife is "without a name" (1253b9–10). Of course, if the man's rule of his wife were no different from the rule of his children or of his slaves, it would not need a name of its own. Aristotle is attempting to specify what has not been previously specified. He calls the relation between husband and wife *gamikē*, using a word that typically refers to arrangements for a marriage or wedding (*gamos*) (e.g., 1304a15; 1306a34; 1334b34). In Homer's *Iliad*, for example, Hera reminds the gods that they attended Thetis's wedding feast (*gamos*) (24.62). Aristotle is stretching the meaning of the wedding celebration, as it were, to apply it to the relation between the man and the woman throughout their marriage. Unlike the despotic and paternal relations with which he contrasts *gamikē*, and which refer to the master (*despotēs*) and father (*patēr*) respectively, *gamikē* does not refer to anyone as ruler, but rather to the wedding (*gamos*), almost as if the wedding celebration might rule the relations between husband and wife.

Male and female "go together" for the sake of generation, Aristotle says, for there is "a natural striving to leave another like oneself behind" (1252a26–31). Although this natural striving also exists for plants and animals, the conjunction of male and female in the family has other ends as well. The family might come into being for the sake of generation, but it continues to exist for the sake of cultivating the virtue of its members. By the end of Book 1, Aristotle says that household management is more concerned with the virtue of its members that with its property (1259b19–22). He states that humans alone perceive good and bad and just and unjust, and that sharing in these things constitutes not only a city *but also a family* (1253a8–19).

More specifically, the rule between husband and wife is "political," just as the father's rule of his children is kingly. Although he distinguished political rule at the outset of Book 1, he does not explain what political rule means (other than what it is not, namely, despotism) until he turns to the relation between a man and a woman in marriage. Although in most cases of political rule, when ruler and ruled "wish to be on an equal footing and to differ in nothing," and "the ruler and ruled change [places] (*metaballei*)," Aristotle says, this does not happen in marriage (1259b4–9). In other places, Aristotle refers to political rule as ruling and being ruled "in turn" (*en merei*), and while this might mean that ruler and ruled change places, it can also mean that each rules "in part" or that there is a sharing in rule (e.g., 1261b1–5; 1179a9–13; 1317b3, 16, 20; 1325b8; *NE* 1161a28–29). This latter is the way in which political rule belongs to husband and wife, for as Aristotle puts it in the *Ethics*, "The man rules according to worth [or merit] in regard to those things he ought to rule, while yielding to his wife the rule over those things suited to her" (*NE* 1160b33–35). "Changing places" or "alternating" would be neither just nor beneficial in such a case, whereas sharing in rule is. As to what is suited to each, Aristotle observes that the work of the man is to acquire, that of the woman to guard [or protect]" (*phulattein*) (1177b25). Whatever Aristotle means to suggest by attributing to women the work of the *Republic*'s "guardians," he also makes clear that household management involves "use" of household goods rather than their acquisition or protection (1256a11–12). He does not say who is best suited to the task of "using" them. Presumably, a task of this sort has many forms and is shared by husband and wife as merit or capacity warrants.

Aristotle also mentions that while both man and woman possess ethical virtues, "the moderation of a woman and of a man is not the same, nor their courage or justice," for "there is a ruling and a serving courage, and similarly with the other virtues" (1259a20–24; 1277b20–24). But does the ruling virtue belong to the man and the serving virtue to the woman? We tend to assume so since the male is "more inclined to lead" (1259b3), but Aristotle does not say so. Moreover, it is difficult to separate ruling and serving, except in despotism (see 1279a18–22). In other cases, the ruler serves the ruled, and in correct forms of rule as Aristotle will later describe them the ruler rules for the benefit of the city rather than only for his own benefit (1279a26–39). The one possessing the virtue of greatness of soul, Aristotle says in the *Ethics*, is eager "to serve" (1124b18–19). Serving, for its part, could entail ruling, as would have been the case for Tecmessa had Ajax heeded her speech. In discussing friendship in the *Ethics*, Aristotle claims that there might be a friendship between husband and wife, not only on the basis of utility and pleasure, but also on the basis of their virtue: "For there is a virtue belonging to each, in which they would delight" (1162a24–27). It is such delight in each other's virtues that keeps alive the wedding celebration. In this case of "political rule," those who share in rule not only do not change places, but they also do not wish to eradicate difference. Paradoxical would it be if the highest form of "political rule" (and perhaps the most successful) were found in the family rather than in political life as such; however much the family needs the city both to protect it and to foster the virtues of its members, this highest end of the city first comes to light in the family itself.

Aristotle can therefore call the ruling and being ruled in turn found in family life "political rule" without its involving "alternation" or "changing places." Although he mentions "political rule" on numerous occasions, he does not refer to it again in Greek as "changing places." In fact, Aristotle uses the latter word (*metabolē*) to mean a change or revolution in regimes, such as a change from tyranny or oligarchy to democracy (1276b10; 1276a8–17). The word is often translated as "revolution." In cases of revolution, if some rule "in turn" they do so by overturning the regime. In discussing political revolution, Aristotle uses the word or its derivatives almost forty times (1302a17–1307b25). As the result of a revolution, or change of regime, rulers and ruled change places, precisely because ruling is not shared. Democrats and oligarchs, for example, do not want "to be on an equal footing" with each other, as Aristotle describes political rule, but to rule the other. Although Aristotle's discussion of the family in Book 1 may serve more than one purpose, at the very least it suggests that political reform begins with family reform. Only then will the human desire to acquire be moderated by the desire to guard or to protect, and political stability follow from shared rule, in which "two together" use the goods they share. Political life, like household management, would then focus on putting human capacities to "use" or to "work" rather than merely "acquiring" and "guarding."

Aristotle's last word in Book 1 connects household management to virtue, for household management concerns human beings more than possession of inanimate things (*apsuchōn*), the excellence or virtue of the former more than of the latter, and the virtue of its free persons rather than of its slaves (1259b19–22). Even the slave, Aristotle points out, should possess the ethical virtues, at least in some form, and the master must instill them in him as well as instructing him about his work. Those who "deny reason (*logou*) to a slave" are in error; Aristotle says even that admonishing rather than commanding is more appropriate to a slave than to children (1260b3–5; cf. *NE*, 1102b35–1103a1). As to the virtue of husband and wife and father and children, since the family is part of the city, "both women and children must be educated with a view to the regime." For in a city, "women are half of the free persons, and children will one day share in the regime" (1260b9–20; see also 1269b16–20). Aristotle moves beyond Book I and the family to regimes, just as the city develops out of the family. He does not say that the head of the household "educates" the women and children in virtue in so many words, as he said the master did the slave. After all, the mother along with the father has the task of educating their children (NE 1162a5–8). Moreover, the father's education is at issue as much as that of his family members, for he is among the other half of the free and therefore on whom as in the case of women and children the excellence of the regime depends.

Examining Regimes and Claims to Rule

After examining in Book 2 what others have proposed about the best regime and praised in existing cities, Aristotle undertakes in Book 3 to investigate regimes, "what sort each is and what is its quality" (1274a33). Regimes are defined by the number of those who rule, one, few, or many, and by whether they rule in the common interest or in their own interest. These two criteria produce six regimes. He distinguishes king and tyrant by the end of their rule, as he does rule by the few, aristocracy and oligarchy, and rule by the many, polity and democracy. The former regimes in each group are correct (*orthai*) regimes "according to what is simply just," the latter are erring (*hēmartēmenai*) regimes, deviations (*parekbaseis*) from correct ones (1279a18–21; 1275b5).

A curious feature of Aristotle's classification of regimes is his giving the name *politeia* to the correct form of the rule by the many, the very word for regime that he is differentiating into its forms. Using *politeia* to name a form of *politeia* is like calling one kind of dog "dog." Following the sensible translation of Carnes Lord, I will use the traditional "regime" when speaking of regimes of which there are many forms, and "polity," the English word closest to the Greek *politeia,* to refer to the specific regime. Aristotle's usage is unique to him. When in the Plato's *Statesman* the Eleatic Stranger presents a similar sixfold classification, better and worse forms of the rule of one, few, or many, he points out that there is no distinct name for the better form of the rule of the many, and uses democracy for both better and worse forms (302d-e). Aristotle elevates the correct form of the rule of the many by giving it not only a name of its own, but also a name that is not entirely its own since it belongs to its class. Just as he says that tyranny is "least a regime" (1293b30–31), polity may be "most a regime."[7]

Aristotle admits that his simple classification requires qualification. Oligarchy, for example, occurs when the wealthy have authority, and yet the name means literally "rule by the few" (*oligoi*). By the same token, democracy occurs when the poor have authority, for it means literally "rule by the demos" and hence by a particular class in the city distinct from the wealthy. It is "only accidental," however, that the wealthy are few and the poor are many. If oligarchy is rule by the few rich and democracy by the many poor, we are left with no names in which either many well off or few poor rule. "Are there no other regimes besides those we have spoken of," Aristotle asks, warning us from the outset that his classification is not as comprehensive as it might appear (1279b21–1280a4). As in his naming of polity, Aristotle is looking for regimes not captured by the common names we have for them. When Aristotle proceeds to discuss how democrats and oligarchs speak of justice, we see that he is looking for regime possibilities that go beyond the claims of democrats and oligarchs, while giving both a share in governing.

Democrats claim that justice is equality, assuming that those who are equal in freedom (being born free rather than as slaves) should have an equal share in ruling the city, whereas oligarchs claim that those who are unequal in wealth should have an unequal share in ruling. Although Aristotle admits that both are correct up to a point, he does not merely advocate combining their claims for a more comprehensive understanding of justice. Rather, there is a third claim that both democrats and oligarchs neglect—the claim of virtue. The city does not exist primarily for the sake of preserving life or safety, or for the sake of wealth, but for the sake of living well, and nobly. Those with virtue that supports this end—those with "political virtue"—should have a part in the community, even a greater part than those who "are equal in freedom or descent" or "those who outdo them in wealth but are outdone in virtue" (1280a7–1281b10). Even more radically, if there were one person with "an excess of virtue," like a god among human beings, "a law unto himself," "what remains—and it seems like the natural course—is for everyone to obey him gladly, so that persons of this sort will be kings in their cities forever" (1284a5–14; 1284b32–34). Aristotle uses the word *forever* to refer to their rule, although he elsewhere refers to an office without term limits only as lasting for life (*dia biou*) (cf. 1271a42, 1285a8, and 1285b28 with 1285a15 and 1285a30), thus letting their rule resonate with the immortality that a god would possess. Like a god, the king who rules forever does not have to bow to time, or death.

Although this seems like an endorsement by Aristotle of the rule of the one virtuous person, Aristotle's claim that should he exist, "everyone would obey him gladly" might give us pause,[8] especially when we remember Aristotle's criticism of the rule of the wise in the *Republic*: it is hazardous to have the same persons ruling always, for "this will cause faction," Aristotle says, pointing to the spirited and warlike guardians of the *Republic* who are excluded from rule (1264b7–10). There is also a question of justice. Aristotle's observation about the rule of the few virtuous applies even more forcefully against the one most excellent of all: "When the same persons always rule, the others are necessarily deprived of their honors or prerogatives" (1281a29–34). Aristotle approaches the problem through a list of kingships and its varieties, culminating in a "king overall" (*pambasileus*), whose rule might be justified only if his virtue outdid the virtue of all the others (see 1283b15–26).

Although "we assert that [kingship] is one of the correct regimes," Aristotle begins with the question of "whether a city or territory that is to be well administered should be under a kingship." Of kingships, he lists "four in number." There is the kingship "based on law," such as the king in Sparta, whose limited tasks include leading the army in foreign territory. Aristotle appeals to Homer for evidence: when King Agamemnon commanded at Troy, Homer has him say that "whomever I find far from battle . . . will not escape from the dogs and vultures, for death is in my power" (*Iliad* 2. 291–93). Aristotle not only quotes especially brutal words spoken by the so-called king "by law"—for they do not respect the Greek custom of burial—but he adds the last line to the Homeric text that has come down to us. That is, he makes Agamemnon assert authority over who lives and who dies (1285b20; 1285a4–16).[9]

Next, there are the kingships that exist among some of the barbarians, which are close to tyrannies in power, but their rule is accepted by the people since they are more slavish in their characters than the Greeks. When Aristotle says that such kingships are hereditary and based on laws, he presumably means that transitions to power are lawful because hereditary. The third type of monarchy (Aristotle slips into using the generic name that includes tyrannies) is that of the dictator or "elected tyranny," which differs from the barbarian kingship only in its not being hereditary. Aristotle questions the advantage of such a kingship indirectly by quoting the drinking song of a poet who criticized the Mytileneans for electing such a tyrant. Finally, the fourth "in number" is a kingship that existed in ancient times, held by those who benefited the people by bringing them together in cities or in some other way. They too "arose over willing subjects" and were "according to law," but eventually yielded their powers to others (1285a1–b19).

Aristotle's description of these types of kingship blurs kingship with tyranny, the correct regime with the deviant one—the kingship under the law illustrated by Agamemnon, the kingship among the barbarians, who are too slavelike to resist the rule of the master or despot, and the dictatorship or "elected tyranny."[10] Later, when Aristotle lists kinds of tyrannies, he includes this barbarian kingship and dictatorship among them (1295a1–16). To be sure, he does not call the fourth kingship tyrannical, but over time it yields to a more inclusive political order. His enumeration of these kingships as "correct regimes," does not bode well for the last kingship he describes, "a fifth" in addition to the four, "when one person has authority over all matters, just as each nation or city has authority over common matters, with an arrangement that resembles household management. For just as the rule of the household manager is a kind of kingship over the household, this kind of kingship is household management for a city or nation (or several nations)" (1285b29–34).

Such a kingship, presumably, finds a place for the individual who is like a god among human beings, and whose virtue is so excessive that it warrants his ruling forever. And yet this "king overall" is less a ruler in a regime than a household manager. His rule does not belong to a city as such, for it might extend over a nation, or even several nations. The search for the best regime that moves Aristotle's politics culminates in a rule that reduces the city to a household, and perhaps even to an individual, and hence destroys the city (see 1261a15–22). Aristotle's description of this king as a household manager, justified only if he were like a god among humans, has an ominous ring in light of the brutal Cyclops, a household manager without the restraint of any political community of which his family is a part, who "enacts divine law for his wives and children" (1252b23–24).

Whereas Book 3 of the *Politics* begins with the citizen, especially the democratic citizen, it ends with the king overall. That citizen is the one who participates in deliberating and judging, the offices of the assembly that deliberates and the courts that judge. Participating in the assembly and the courts in a democracy does not require any definite property qualifications nor is it limited to a specific term. Although there is no name that characterizes these offices—Aristotle gives it one, "undefined" (*aoristos*) office (1275a32). He does so, he says, "for the sake of defining" (*diorismou charin*) (1275a29–32). Democracy breaks down boundaries (*horoi*) or limits, whereas Aristotle defines terms that have no name. So too the king overall is undefined, Aristotle says nothing about his appointment, nor is his term limited since he will be king "forever." Whereas Agamemnon claims no one far from the battle will escape death at his hands, this king seems to escape his own death. When Aristotle refers to the "excess of virtue" belonging to an outstanding individual, he chooses a word that he uses in the *Ethics* to describe one of the extremes of which virtue is a mean (*NE* 1106b5–7; 16–18). He mentions no specific virtues or skills or knowledge that define him, and surely no citizen could call him to account. He rules "according to wish" (1287a11), rather than according to law, since he is himself a law.

Earlier in Book 3, Aristotle was much more specific about the virtues of the statesman or the political ruler and even about how those virtues come to be. In regimes in which there is political rule rather than despotism, that is, in those regimes that Aristotle defines as correct rather than deviations, the ruler learns to rule by being ruled. The virtue of a citizen is "to know and to be capable of the rule of free persons from both sides" (1277b7–18). That is, he knows how to be ruled as a free person (rather than as a slave), and how to rule as a free person (rather than as a master), and he learns the latter from his learning the former. To be ruled as a free person requires moderation and justice; to rule as a free person requires prudence in addition (1277b19–20). To prudence belongs deliberation and judgment, the work with which Aristotle initially defined citizenship (1275b18–20), to which he now adds prudence, since it allows its possessor to deliberate and judge well. It is in this context that Aristotle responds to the question of education that he raised and left open at the end of Book 1—the education in the virtues required by the regime, which no doubt is fostered by the political rule between a man and his wife and reinforces it in turn.

Unlike "the king overall," the political ruler rules over those who are similar to himself, those who are free. So too, his rule is bound by law, for law regulates the manner in which he shares rule with others (1287a17–19). He does not possess "an excess" of virtue, because he is moderate and just as well as prudent. His rule is situated in time, for he comes to rule by established law, and looks forward to the rule of others in turn. Unlike the king overall, he does not rule "forever."

Aristotle thus moves to the question whether it is better for law to rule rather than human beings. It would seem better that law were to rule, for law is like god and intellect, while a human being is moved by desire and spiritedness, which perverts even the best human beings. But laws themselves are universal, cannot deal with particular cases, and hand over what they are not able to determine to the rulers (1286a24–35). But should the rulers be many or one? Aristotle observes that one person alone cannot see everything that needs to be taken into account, so that a single ruler requires the help of others. After all, if a good person should rule because he is better than others, "two good persons are better than one." He refers to Diomedes's wish in the *Iliad* that "two go together," as well as Agamemnon's prayer" that "ten such counselors be mine" (*Iliad* 10.224; 2.372). Aristotle's discussion of the overall king has moved back to Agamemnon, a man who was surely in need of counselors, as he himself recognizes in the words that Aristotle quotes. "Monarchs" thus seek out those friendly to their rule as "co-rulers" (*sunarchous*), Aristotle says with Agamemnon as his authority, using a word joining "ruling with" or "ruling together," that is found only here in classical

Greek literature (1287b8–35). Aristotle, once again, is trying to persuade his readers of a new sort of rule, not found in the Greek world, both in its thinking and practice about politics. Rather than a king overall, who does not have co-rulers, Aristotle sides with "co-rulers," which is a way of describing ruling and being ruled in turn.

These arguments are given by those who dispute against kingship, Aristotle says, leaving us to infer that he himself is among them. They make a persuasive case. He does say in his own name that they hold against kingship in some ways, although perhaps not in others. "One people may be apt for kingship," while "another is political," which is in such cases "both just and advantageous" (1287b37–40). In bringing his discussion of kingship to a close he reminds us of his argument in Book 1 that "human beings are by nature political," sharing in reason or speech about the advantageous and the just (1253a9–15). If a people is apt for kingship, they have not yet developed their full potential as political beings. Kingship is best for them, but it is not the best simply. The early Greeks were ruled by kings, but when "many arose who were alike in virtue," they "no longer tolerated kingship "and "established a polity" (1286b1–13).

Aristotle gives a final statement on the rule by one, few, and many, with respect to the sort of "multitude" (*plēthos*) in the city. The multitude apt for kingship can support "a family (*genos*) preeminent in the virtue that exercises political leadership." A multitude apt for aristocratic rule is one able to be ruled as free persons by those engaging in political rule. A multitude apt for a polity is one "capable of ruling and being ruled in accordance with law that distributes rule on the basis of merit to those who have resources (1288a8–15). In each case, Aristotle's formulations expand the role of "political rule" or statesmanship. He even reminds us that the education that makes a man excellent is the same as that which makes him "a *political* and kingly ruler" (1288b1–2; emphasis added). He therefore can speak of the individual of outstanding virtue not merely as one alone, but along with a "whole family" of such individuals. He is no longer one alone, incommensurate with no other human being.

Aristotle leaves Book 3 in midsentence, claiming that it is now time to speak about the best regime. Some scholars argue that there is a corruption in the manuscripts that have come to us, and that the last two books of the *Politics* on the best regime were meant to follow. But just as "kingship overall" gives way to political rule or statesmanship, the "best regime" gives way to the topics of Book 4 such as which regime is the best in the circumstances, which is the best possible, and which is more attainable by everyone

(1288b38–39). Aristotle's concluding remarks in Book 3 about multitudes apt for different regimes prepare us for this discussion in Book 4, as does the prominence of political rule as an alternative to kingship overall prepare for the prominence of polity in Book 4. Aristotle's discussion of polity and its many forms, as we shall see, makes feasible our prayers for what is possible.

Equality and Excellence "Going Together" in Political Life

In Book 4, Aristotle reminds us of his sixfold classification of regimes, claiming that he has already spoken of aristocracy and kingship—the best regimes in that they "wish to be established on the basis of virtue" (1289a28–36). Aristotle has given an extensive treatment of kingship, to be sure, but the first four of the five kings he describes are established on the basis of law rather than of virtue. Aristotle says that they can exist in any regime (1286a4–5). The fifth, the "king overall," may possess an "excess of virtue," but he rules a city or a nation as if it were his household. In examining kingship, Aristotle has not found the best *regime*. The first four are not regimes, and the household management of the fifth renders it apolitical. As to aristocracy, he has not given it similar attention, mentioning only in passing that the aristocrats' claim to rule on the basis of their virtue might be surpassed by the collective virtue of the many or the superlative virtue of a single individual (1281a40–b16; 1283b30–35). The search for the best regime is still ongoing. It remains to speak of polity, he says, and the three erring regimes, oligarchy, democracy, and tyranny (1289a36–38). Of tyranny Aristotle is dismissive—it does not leave room for "much argument" (*polulogia*), both because tyrants do not permit arguments against their rule and because it would be difficult for one investigating regimes to say anything in favor of it. Moreover, it turns out that he has already discussed two forms of tyranny in discussing kingships, the barbarian monarch who rules a slavish people and the elected dictator. The third is the tyrant who is the counterpart to the "king overall" (1295a1–24). Aristotle's emphasis, instead, will be on the other three regimes, democracy, oligarchy, and polity, which allow "mixtures" of elements characteristic of the pure forms. There are four kinds of democracies and four kinds of oligarchies, some of which have elements of the other. Some polities, which he calls mixtures of democracy and oligarchy, recognize virtue as well as freedom and wealth. And in the course of describing polities, Aristotle lets aristocracy reappear as a mixed form.

Aristotle begins with several forms of democracy and oligarchy, depending on the character of those ruling, and the extent to which law holds sway. Some democracies, for example, restrict participation to those possessing a moderate amount of property and govern themselves in accordance with law, while at the other extreme the many poor have authority and not the laws. Similarly, oligarchies range from those in which a larger number of persons moderately well off have authority to those with very restrictive property qualifications for office. Democracies and oligarchies first appeared in Aristotle's schema as deviations in which those ruling do so for their own advantage rather than for the common advantage, and therefore are despotic, but now we see that there are better and worse forms of each, more or less despotic, whose rule more or less serves the common interest under the restraint of law. We also see that the better forms of each approach each other, oligarchies expanding those with authority, and democracies restricting them to more moderate elements under law. By doing so, Aristotle prepares us for a new formulation of the regime he calls polity.

Although, in the original scheme, polity held the place of the correct form of the rule of the many, Aristotle now describes polity as "a combination (*mixis*) of democracy and oligarchy" (1293b34). The many still rule, but they are no longer the poor, as Aristotle first characterized the democratic multitude (1279b20). Rather, the many include those who are well off. As a mixture of democratic and oligarchic elements—in the mode of election, for example, or in qualifications to rule (1294a36–b35)—polities have many forms, some inclining to oligarchy, others to democracy (1293b34–37). Indeed, "polities that incline toward oligarchy are customarily called aristocracies, since education and good birth especially accompany those with resources," Aristotle observes (1293b35–37).

Aristotle singles out Carthage and Sparta as aristocratic forms of polity, precisely because of their recognition of virtue, Carthage because it offers a place in its regime to the wealthy, the virtuous, and the demos, while Sparta does the same with regard to virtue and the people (1293b15–19). These were two of the regimes (along with Crete) that he discussed in Book 2 when he examined the most highly reputed regimes that had come into existence. There he took note as well of a "monarchic" element, the kings, contrasting their election in Carthage with their hereditary character in Sparta, and preferring the former to the latter (1272b38–41). In Book 4, he does not mention the kings in these regimes. They appear to have become inconsequential, mere officials for limited roles within the regimes. In a good mixture, Aristotle explains, "the same polity can be spoken of either as a democracy or an oligarchy." The democrats call it a democracy, and the wealthy call it an oligarchy, and thus the regime is preserved "because none of the parts of the city would wish to have another regime" (1294b14–19; 35–39). The ambiguity preserves the regime. Aristotle's naming the regime "polity" allows numerous mixtures, not only of demoracacy and oligarchy but of these elements with virtue. An aristocratic polity finds a place for virtue without restricting rule simply to the virtuous (1293b2–8). One feature of the Carthaginian polity that Aristotle mentions in Book 2 is that proposals are presented to the people not simply for their approval but for their judgment or decision (*krinein*), and "whoever wishes is permitted to speak against the proposals—something which does not exist in other regimes" (1273a9–13).

Moreover, Aristotle now describes a regime where neither the rich nor the poor predominate but those of middling wealth, which we would call the middle class.[11] He has recourse to the *Ethics* for his argument that "the happy life is one of virtue" and that "virtue is a mean." So too he locates a mean with regard to wealth: "a middling possession is best" for it militates against the hubris and contempt of the rich and against the envy and malice of the poor. It is difficult for either the rich or the poor "to obey reason." The former do not know how to be ruled, and hence they know how to rule only like a master over slaves. The latter do not know how to rule, and hence they know how to be ruled only like a slave. The middle class are not so wealthy that others plot against them, nor so poor that they plot against the possessions of the others. They are therefore best able to share ruling and being ruled that belongs to free individuals, to be party to political rule rather than despotism (1295a25–1296a34).

Of course, cities do not necessarily have a large middle class, and Aristotle is looking for the regime and a way of life in which "most can share" (1295a29–30). He therefore has recourse to political reform. Although it is "the greatest good fortune" when there exists a large middle class, "the legislator should add the middle to the dominant part of the regime (1295b40; 1296a35–36). He might require a property assessment for office in a democracy, or raise one that exists, or lower one in an oligarchy. The richest of the poor, in other words, should be included among the wealthy, while the poorest of the rich should be included among the poor. In both cases, the predominant part is expanded and moderated. There would not be an absolute difference between poor and rich. The poor, being only more or less poor, would approach the middle, as would the rich, being only more or less rich. As a newly expanded group, the former would have less cause for envy, the latter less cause for arrogance. Whichever is the predominant class in the regime would by mixing come closer to the middle. The many would not want to deprive the rich of their resources, for they too would have something to lose. The rich could not view the many as "no better than beasts" (see 1281b19–20), because they include those with property.

Although Aristotle began his discussion of the middle-class polity by insisting that he is looking not for the best regime simply, but for one that most can share in, as he proceeds he speaks of this regime as simply the best. He refers to "the political community that depends on the middle class," for example, as "the best of all" (1295b35–37). As he concludes his discussion of the middle-class polity, he says it is clear "what the best regime is and why" (1296b3). He also uses the middle-class polity as a standard for judging other regimes: "Once the best is defined, it is not difficult to see which is to be regarded first, which second, and so on." Although other regimes may be more advantageous under the circumstances, Aristotle nevertheless concludes that the regime "closest to the middle must of necessity always be better, the one more removed from the middle worse" (1296b3–10).

There is nothing inconsistent with this conclusion and Aristotle's turn to the best regime in Books 7. It is true that in Book 4, just before introducing the middle-class polity, Aristotle distinguished "the regime one would pray for" from a regime and way of life "possible (*dunatos*) for most to share in" (1295a25–30). In Book 7, when he considers how a regime "is to be constituted on the basis of what one would pray for," he includes such things as an appropriate size for the territory, a good quality of soil, a natural seaport for commerce, and even a people of suitable character. But "like persons offering prayer, we should not ask for the impossible" (*adunaton*) (1325b35–1326a9). The best regime has become the best possible regime. The thinkers he discussed such as Plato are those who propose the impossible (see e.g., 1264b19; 1265a18–19).

The regime of Book 7 that we would pray for is indebted to what Aristotle has brought to light in considering the middle-class regime earlier. The territory, for example, should be large enough so that "those living there are able to live at leisure in the manner of free persons and at the same time with moderation," avoiding "the excesses of both poverty and luxury" (1326b30–32; 38–39). Aristotle seems to have in mind a well-off middle class, without the conflict we find in oligarchies and democracies between the rich and the poor. Like a legislator who inclines an oligarchy or a democracy to a middle, this legislator establishes a regime in which the middle replaces the extremes. In listing the elements from which a city must of necessity be constituted, he includes "the well-off" (*euporon*), or the "well-provided," not the wealthy (1328b20–21).

As to the sort of persons composing "the political multitude," they too should be a mean, between those peoples so filled with spiritedness that they remain free but are unable to live a political life, and those people endowed with thought and art but so lacking in spiritedness that they remain enslaved. They must be a people, in other words, apt for political rule, who "remains free and governs itself in the best manner" (1327b19–34). Unlike the *Republic*, spiritedness is not found in one class in the city, intelligence or thought in another. Indeed, both belong to the citizen body, the political multitude. And both together make possible a self-governing people.

Aristotle now uses *plēthos*, the word that he used earlier to refer to "the many" as opposed to "the few" and "the one" who rule in the different regimes (1279a27–31; 39) to refer to the citizen body (*to men plēthos tōn politōn*) in the regime according to prayer (1331a20). This multitude performs the three tasks Aristotle assigns to the citizens, depending on their age—the work of soldiers, who at a certain age take their turn in deliberating and judging, and when elderly become the priests. The members of the citizen body have households of their own, although some property is reserved for the city, to host common meals and temples for worship (1329a3–34; 1330a10–12). Aristotle responds to his earlier complaint about the *Republic*'s spirited guardians who would not tolerate being excluded from rule (1264b7–10). Here there is no separate ruling class, as in the *Republic*; rather, "all the citizens take part in the regime," and thus possess not only the moderation and justice belonging to both rulers and ruled but also the prudence belonging to the rulers. Nor do they take their turn from ruling like the *Republic*'s philosopher-kings to dwell in the light of the sun outside the cave of political life; rather, they are released from ruling to lead the religious ceremonies in which the citizens participate.

Aristotle observes that the city is not any chance multitude but one "self-sufficient with a view to life." When discussing what one would pray for, Aristotle never forgets that the city must contend with foreign affairs—as when he considers the appropriate size of the territory, the city's need for walls, to say nothing of the city's military, which protects the city against disobedience from within and against those who threaten injustice from without. The city is not self-sufficient, even with a view to life, because it exists in a world of other cities. Aristotle insists that the city's streets be laid down not simply in straight lines producing beauty and order, but in patterns that would make it difficult for an invading force to find its way around (1330b21–32). If it is not self-sufficient with a view to life, it is not self-sufficient with a view to "living well"—the second and higher end Aristotle attributed to the city at the outset (1252b30).

Among the elements needed by any city, Aristotle includes sustenance and therefore those who farm. Compromises not only with beauty (street patterns) but also with justice become apparent when Aristotle speaks of the need for slaves to farm the land and the threat of subversion they pose. "How they should be treated," he says, and "why it is better to hold out freedom as a reward for them, we will speak of later" (1330a24–34). Aristotle never does in the works that have come down to us. But he is not shy about bringing up the problem soon again. He reminds us that justice requires sharing in rule unless human beings are as different from one another as gods and heroes [semi-divine offspring of gods] differ from human beings (1332b16–24; see also 1254b17–18), and he warns that those "on the land" will want to subvert the regime. Whether they will "take part in ruling and being ruled is necessary for the legislator to investigate" (1332b30–34). That he leaves this problem for the legislator, indeed one of this magnitude, would be almost funny if it were not so sad. He has called attention to the city's gross injustice: slaves who could assume freedom (as a reward) are capable of freedom. They are not natural slaves. Their slavery is not just.

In describing what we would pray for, Aristotle reveals his own prayer—and hope—that he can succeed in educating future legislators who will aspire to the sort of political rule that conjoins excellence and equality as much as possible and who will understand that compromises with despotism should be avoided as much as possible. Such rule would be the best possible. In the *Politics*, Aristotle directs equality to excellence, as when he insists that the city's end is not mere life but living well, when he includes virtue among the claims to rule, even designating it as the weightiest, and when he shows that the many have a claim to rule on the basis of their collective virtue. He also directs excellence to equality. In speaking to the few, Aristotle questions whether human beings could differ from one other as much as a god could from a human being, and therefore insists that similar human beings should share in ruling. "Among similar persons nobility and justice are found in ruling and being ruled in turn, for this is something equal and similar" (1325b7–10). It is the more virtuous, such as Aristotle himself, and the legislators and statesmen he attempts to educate, who bear the greatest responsibility for reform and therefore encounter the greatest challenges.

Notes

1. Citations in parentheses, unless otherwise noted, are to Aristotle's *Politics*. Translations are my own, although I have consulted the translation of *Aristotle's Politics*, by Carnes Lord, with an Introduction, Notes, and Glossary, 2d ed. (Chicago: University of Chicago Press, 2013).

2. For further discussion of these and other issues in this essay, see Mary P. Nichols, *Citizen and Statesman: A Study of Aristotle's* Politics (Lanham, MD: Rowman and Littlefield, 1992).

3. Lord captures this in his translation: "the naturally ruling and naturally mastering element is that which can foresee with the mind" and "the naturally ruled is that which can do these with its body." *Aristotle's Politics*, 2. He is not referring to persons. The naturally mastering element is the soul, and the naturally ruled one is the body. Aristotle soon gives the soul's rule of the body as an example of despotic rule (1254b6).

4. See Stephen G. Salkever, *Finding the Mean Theory and Practice in Aristotelian Political Philosophy* (Princeton: Princeton University Press, 1990), 184, n50.

5. Michael Davis asks whether Agamemnon's sacrifice of his daughter is "less barbaric than treating women as slaves?" Michael Davis, *The Politics of Philosophy: A Commentary on Aristotle's* Politics (Lanham, MD: Rowman and Littlefield, 1996), 17.

6. Nor is Iphigeneia's mother Clytemnestra silent, whose unctuous words lure Agamemnon to his death upon his arrival home from Troy. See Aeschylus, *Agamemnon* 895–974.

7. The Stranger presents his six forms of regime, although dividing them into better and worse, as all deviations that occur when the best regime proves impossible, the rule of the virtuous individual possessing knowledge and therefore with no need for law (301a–302e). Only this one is "correct," the Stranger says, using the word Aristotle uses for three forms of regime that are in the common interest (cf. *Statesman* 297d, 302b, and 302c with *Politics* 1270a18). The Stranger has only one correct regime, whereas Aristotle has three. Plato presents too radical a difference, Aristotle implies, between one correct regime and all the others and between the one knowledgeable and virtuous ruler and those he rules.

8. When Aristotle repeats this thought later, using similar language ("all that remains is for a person of [preeminent virtue] to be obeyed and to have authority simply and not by turns"), he leaves out that his subjects are ruled "gladly." He no longer mentions that such obedience "seems like a natural course" (cf. 1284b32–34 with 1288a28–30).

9. Since the *Iliad* is the story of a deserter, who remains far from the battle to great detriment to the Achaean cause, Agamemnon's claim about the fate of deserters proves false. So too does Aristotle's addition of the line not found in

our texts of the *Iliad*. Achilles, of course, did not desert out of cowardice, nor did Agamemnon have any power over his life and death.

10. In examining his predecessors in Book 2, Aristotle claims that "it is said in the *Laws* that the best regime should be composed out of democracy and tyranny," but this is not a proper mix, for "democracy and tyranny are not regimes at all or at least the worst of them all" (1266a1–3). Although Aristotle is not entirely fair to Plato's *Laws*—at least the Athenian Stranger maintains in that work that democracy and *monarchy* are the principles of all regimes, that a wellgoverned regime must partake of both if it is to have freedom, friendship, and prudence [or wisdom]" (693d-e)—his misrepresentation allows him to express his reservation against monarchy by identifying it with tyranny.

11. For a persuasive exposition of Aristotle's middle-class regime and its similarities to the American republic, see Leslie G. Rubin, *America, Aristotle, and the Politics of a Middle Class* (Waco: Baylor University Press, 2018).

Chapter 5

First among Equals

Philosophers, Statesmen, and Citizens in Spinoza's Democracy

STEVEN FRANKEL

In chapter 16 of his *Theological-Political Treatise*, Spinoza develops his doctrine of equality in terms of natural rights and argues that such rights are rooted in God, as an extension of his power.[1] He then argues that democracy is the best and "most natural" regime because it best preserves these rights. This argument appears at first glance to be a forerunner to John Locke's argument that the purpose of government is to protect our natural rights. More recently, Spinoza scholars have found Spinoza's metaphysical and political arguments to be compatible with the contemporary version of liberalism, including ideas such as empowerment, inclusivity, and equal access.[2]

However attractive it may be to enlist Spinoza's authority to support such ideas, there are a number of obstacles to presenting him as an advocate of liberal, not to say radical, egalitarianism. For one thing, Spinoza insists that we are not equal, that is, he maintains a strict distinction between the few, who are wise and rational, and the many, who are driven by their passions (cf. V, 77–80). He continually decries the multitude in blunt terms: "And those who have experienced the fast-change mentality of the masses are almost in despair about it, because the masses aren't governed by reason but only by affects. They rush headlong in all directions, and are very easily corrupted by greed or by extravagant living. Each person thinks that he alone knows everything" (XVII, 203).

This pessimistic view of the overwhelming power of irrationality might be mitigated by the hope of educating people so that reason can overcome vanity and superstition. Unfortunately, Spinoza rarely suggests that education will have such effect, particularly on mitigating the passions of most people. To the contrary, he argues that our passions, particularly our desire for self-preservation, are far stronger than our reason, such that even a lifetime of education is likely to have little effect:

> You may like the thought that all people are naturally led to act according to the rules and laws of reason; but that is just wrong. In fact, all people are born ignorant of everything, and even those who have been well brought up reach a relatively advanced age before they come to know the true principle of living and acquire a virtuous disposition. Until that happens—if indeed it does happen—they have to live and take care of themselves as best they can by their own power, i.e., by the prompting of appetite alone. Why? Because nature has given them no alternative, having denied them the power to live according to sound reason. They aren't obliged to live according to the laws of a sound mind, any more than a cat is bound to live according to the laws of a lion's nature! (XVI, 190, tr. Bennett)

We could easily add many similar passages that reiterate Spinoza's skepticism about making people more rational in light of the power of passions and superstitions.

Indeed, Spinoza recounts several attempts by philosophers to enlighten Jews, Christians, and Muslims and catalogues their failures. In the case of Christianity, philosophy was incorporated into the faith by unscrupulous theologians, who used it to appear wise and thereby attract and control followers. Soon, Christian theologians began to quarrel fiercely over "the theories of Aristotelians and Platonists" (TTP preface, XIX; see also XIII, 156). Rather than strengthen reason, the invocation of philosophy undermined Christianity's salutary teachings, such as *caritas,* and earned the hatred of the multitude who treat it as a "source of impiety" (TTP preface, XX). Most attempts at educating the multitude are, in reality, thinly disguised strategies for gaining power and influence over the multitude.[3]

Even when the reformers remained focused on promoting reason and philosophy, the results have been equally dismal. Their efforts at checking the passions succeeded only in strengthening them and increasing the hostility toward reason. Spinoza describes the case of Maimonides, who attempted to enlighten the multitude by taking into account their reliance on images and poetry. He believed that he could import reason covertly into theology by suggesting that the contradictions in the Biblical account could be explained by recourse to reason and philosophy.[4] Spinoza observes that this effort failed because it foolishly believed that philosophy might resolve conflicts among irrational people: "The vulgar, having generally no comprehension of, nor leisure for, demonstrations, would be reduced to receiving all their knowledge of Scripture on the authority and testimony of those who philosophize, and consequently, would be compelled to suppose that the interpretations given by philosophers were infallible. Truly this would be a new form of ecclesiastical authority, and a new sort of priests or pontiffs, which the vulgar would ridicule rather than venerate."[5] Instead of making people more rational, the attempt to import philosophy into theology to elevate the status of philosophers backfired and led to ever more intense bouts of irrational hostility.[6]

The purpose of this essay is to examine how Spinoza manages to reconcile his strong support for equality and natural rights with his insistence on the radical inequality of human beings. We shall also seek to understand how Spinoza's endorsement of democracy as the best regime might be understood in light of his emphasis on the distinction between the few who are rational and the many who are superstitious. Resolving the theological-political problem requires coming to terms with superstition and seeking strategies to mitigate it that do not rely on increasing the rationality of the multitude. Spinoza's doctrine of natural rights, and his argument for equality, reflects the limitations of politics rather than the highest possibilities of humanity.

The Theological-Political Problem

Spinoza's analysis of natural rights is presented as a solution to what he describes as the "theological-political problem." Before turning to his doctrine of natural rights, therefore, it is necessary to examine more carefully the problem which he seeks to solve.[7] Spinoza makes several statements about aspects of this problem, but the most comprehensive analyses are in the preface, chapter 5, and chapter 16. Spinoza does not simply repeat himself in restating the problem, but adds important new information with each iteration. His first statement in the preface focuses on the problem of superstition and the imagination of the multitude. Most people interpret the world by imagining a series of causal relations based on their partial observations and experiences. Because they are driven by their passions and do not have adequate knowledge of the causes of their fortune, they are susceptible to despair and manipulation. Ambitious theologians and politicians offer novel superstitious explanations in order to enthrall the multitude. The result is even more instability and violent passion.[8]

Spinoza suggests that the competition among theologians and politicians benefits no one, least of all the citizens. Rather than propose education and scientific literacy as a solution to the problem of superstition, Spinoza suggests instead discovering the original teaching of the Bible which has been lost amid all the competition among theologians. The first fifteen chapters of the TTP therefore focus mainly on rediscovering the essential teachings of the Bible, especially *caritas* and justice. Despite later additions, multiple authors, and faulty manuscripts, the main teachings of Scripture are ultimately easy to identify because they are taught consistently throughout the text and confirmed by the internal testimony of our hearts. These teachings emphasize the practice of charity and justice.[9] Theologically, he shows that certain beliefs—his seven dogmas of universal faith—are necessary to support the practice of justice and charity including the belief in a providential God who rewards and punishes. The Bible's true teaching, then, not only checks the tendency of theologians and politicians to make contrary claims about the text or to add extraneous teachings, but also provides a "salutary and necessary" teaching for a republic. In other words, the Bible furnishes a civil religion that allows citizens to live "peacefully and harmoniously" together (XIV, 179).

The explicit suggestion of the first fifteen chapters is that the theological-political problem is largely a problem of theology and can be resolved by clarifying the teachings of Scripture. The TTP leaves the reader with the impression that Spinoza's political claims are secondary and follow largely from his theological analysis. Such an argument is clearly aimed at Spinoza's pious readers, those who accept the authority of Scripture, who are the largest part of his audience. However, there are suggestions throughout that he is simultaneously addressing a different audience. He observes in his discussion of prophecy, for example, that "those who are very powerful in imagination are less capable of understanding things" (II, 29). Subsequently, when considering the notion that the Jews have been chosen by God, he remarks that the acquisition of intellectual and moral virtue "depends chiefly on our power alone. And because of this . . . these gifts have been peculiar to no nation" (III, 46). Such virtues, in other words, are the province of extraordinary individuals and not of cities or nations in general. In short, Spinoza consistently—if less directly—addresses individuals who seek intellectual virtue through their own efforts rather than through revelation. Perhaps with this audience in mind, Spinoza presents an additional political teaching, one that is not based directly on Scripture.

Spinoza restates the theological-political problem briefly in chapter 5 without referring to theology or Scripture. There, he shifts his focus from theology and the problem of superstition to politics and the problem of resentment as the most serious and enduring threat to political stability. He explains that we form society to avoid living in misery and poverty in nature. The problem is that most people are irrational and perceive only their own interests while ignoring the interests of others; inevitably, conflict emerges and undermines the society. Following Hobbes, Spinoza argues that to leave the state of nature and maintain the peace, men need a sovereign to enforce a law with some degree of compulsion. But, for Spinoza, the social contract brings with it a problem that Hobbes had obscured: although the sovereign may through compulsion prevent some conflicts, the use of force generates a new source of conflict.[10] Thus, even after the establishment of the sovereign, the situation remains volatile with simmering resentment at the sovereign's authority which must often oppose self-interest. The problem of politics comes to light as a problem of organizing interests so that resentment does not undermine obedience to law.[11]

These initial statements of the theological-political problem suggest that Spinoza's argument develops simultaneously in two directions: one aimed at pious readers, which claims that the problem can be resolved by rescuing the Bible's true teaching from superstition, and the other aimed at philosophical readers, which claims that politics is a problem of managing interests and directing passions. One version of the theological-political problem urges us to take our bearings from theology while the other approaches the problem from the perspective of natural rights. This discrepancy, according to Spinoza, is more apparent than real. He argues that these distinct views complement each other. The solution to the political problem, especially unifying irrational individuals and alleviating resentment, can be found in his natural rights teaching which in turn supports a civil religion rooted in Scripture.[12]

Spinoza's State of Nature

Spinoza begins chapter 16 by alerting readers to the shift from the perspective of theology to a philosophical perspective, which only considers the laws of nature without reference to Scripture:[13] "So far, we have taken care to separate Philosophy from Theology and show the freedom of philosophizing which Theology grants to each. Therefore it is time for us to inquire how far this freedom . . . extends in the best Republic" (XVI, 189). This sudden transition has led some interpreters to suggest that Spinoza simply appended a separate text that he had written earlier (perhaps after his excommunication) to the TTP. The problem with such claims is that they suggest the work as a whole was hastily thrown together and is therefore largely incoherent. As Leo Strauss observes, "No author who deserves the name will incorporate into a book parts of an earlier writing which do not make sense in the new book."[14]

This combination of such divergent views suggests that reason and revelation need not undermine each other, and that at least in politics, reason and revelation complement each other. A closer inspection of Spinoza's account of natural right shows that the relation is more complicated. After announcing the shift to studying politics from the point of "the whole of nature," Spinoza begins his account with the *ius institutum naturae* or the right which is established by nature. This right depends on two natural facts: first, that everything is striving to "persevere in its state," and second, that the effort to preserve depends on one's capacity and power. Spinoza emphasizes that these are universal considerations by beginning his discussion with animals rather than man. He says that "fish are by nature determined for swimming and the big ones for eating the small ones; and so fish take possession of water, and large ones eat small ones, with the highest natural right" (XVI, 189). Natural right describes the power and capacity of an individual thing to pursue its own self-preservation, or in the case of an inanimate object, to preserve its internal structure.[15]

Unlike Hobbes, who introduces the idea of natural law as a check, albeit a weak one, on natural right, Spinoza avoids mention of natural law altogether. This distinction is even more pronounced since Spinoza has already discussed natural and divine law in chapters 4 and 12. In the first fifteen chapters of the TTP, the divine law plays a central role because it contains the central commandment of Scripture, namely *caritas*. Now we learn that from the point of view of nature "[t]he highest law . . . is that each thing endeavor, as much as is in it, to persevere in its state—and do so without regard to anything but itself" (XVI, 189). *Caritas* and moral law have no place in nature and cannot check our natural striving to preserve ourselves. In this way, Spinoza emphasizes the strength of natural right, which is the basis for his political teaching and alerts us to the fact that checking natural right will require an equally powerful force: "Whatsoever, therefore, an individual (considered as under the sway of nature) thinks useful for himself, whether led by sound reason or impelled by the passions, that he has a sovereign right to seek and to take for himself as he best can, whether by force, cunning, entreaty, or any other means; consequently he may regard as an enemy anyone who hinders the accomplishment of his purpose" (XVI, 190). Natural right permits unlimited selfishness in the pursuit of self-preservation and respects no moral limits.

Spinoza's explanation of natural right takes additional complexity when we move from big fish to people. Our striving to preserve ourselves is mediated by our consciousness and our greater awareness of our role in preserving ourselves. In contrast to fish, we believe that we are free to choose different strategies to preserve ourselves. "Everyone will, of two goods, choose that which he thinks the greatest; and, of two evils, that which he thinks the least, for it does not necessarily follow that he judges right. This law is so deeply implanted in the human mind that it ought to be counted among eternal truths and axioms" (XVI, 191–92). In reality, we do not see that our choices themselves as well as our perception of our choices are themselves determined by prior causes. Our freedom to choose is illusory as is our confidence that we have correctly identified the good. In fact, such beliefs are the result of passions and erroneous beliefs, that is, they are natural superstitions.

As with the belief in our freedom, the belief in equality rests on an illusory account of our situation in nature. However, it is not simply an arbitrary belief but reflects the primacy of our desires, the centrality of our concern for ourselves, and the fact that we are not subject to the authority of others in nature. Our narrow focus on our own well-being reflects well the situation in nature in that no one is more concerned with my well-being than I am. Others may claim to have my best interests in mind, but they may deceive me to further their own well-being.[16] These elements persist in political life: "Each deems that he alone knows everything, and wants everything to be modified on the basis of his own mental cast, and figures something is equitable or inequitable . . . insofar as he judges it to fall to his profit or harm."[17]

Spinoza's use of the term *natural right* describes our pursuit of self-preservation as mediated through our belief in freedom and equality as well as our tendency to rely on our own evaluation of the best strategies for self-preservation. Spinoza shows us simultaneously why such beliefs are illusory and, at the same time, form a solid and reliable basis for a political teaching. Since Spinoza takes a dim view of superstition, one might expect that he would turn next to curing these superstitions and eliminating them from political life. Instead, he suggests that some form of superstition is inevitable because among passionate individuals, reason does not have any special authority:

> The wise man has sovereign right to do all that reason dictates, or to live according to the laws of reason, so also the ignorant and foolish man has sovereign right to do all that desire dictates, or to live according to the laws of desire . . . .Nature has given them no other guide, and has denied them the present power of living according to sound reason; so that they are not more bound to live by the dictates of an enlightened mind, than a cat is bound to live by the laws of the nature of a lion. (XVI, 190)

The belief in equality reflects the irrelevance in politics of the distinction between the wise and the unwise. The unwise do not recognize or defer to the wisdom of their more rational and less superstition companions. Nor should they be blamed for this misplaced confidence. Just as big fish (and lions) are determined by nature to hunt and consume their smaller prey, so too are irrational and unwise individuals determined to act according to their desires. Neither education nor preaching can do much to enlighten them (cf. PT II. 2).

The argument in chapter 16 culminates in Spinoza's claim that democracy is the best regime because it is the "most natural" regime in the sense that it best preserves the belief in freedom and equality (195).[18] The natural rights doctrine further elevates these beliefs by assigning them the authority of nature. Spinoza begins his defense by referring to chapter 5, where he argued that the main obstacle to leaving the state of nature is finding some basis of agreement for nonrational individuals to live together (cf. 191). The Hobbesian solution of having a sovereign impose a social contract on the citizens is problematic because the subjects resent such authority.[19] Any effort to suppress irrational desires or violate the belief in freedom and equality will undermine the stability of the regime. Spinoza emphasizes the belief in equality as particularly critical in political life: "Least of all can human beings abide serving their equals and being regulated by them"

(74). Democracy is more successful than other regimes because it accepts equality and freedom, and thereby minimizes destabilizing resentment. It is, Spinoza suggests, "a society whose imperium is in the possession of all and whose laws are sanctioned on the basis of common consent" (74). In this sense, democracy is the "most natural" regime because it preserves our natural beliefs in equality and freedom.[20]

Thus, the TTP recognizes and explains the political relevance and efficacy of equality by locating its basis in our perceptual world in nature. At the same time, Spinoza shows the limitations of democracy by providing grounds for challenging its widely held beliefs.[21] The surprising thing about Spinoza's argument is that rather than suggest philosophers enlighten the public, he insists to the contrary that philosophy has little to offer to the stability and security of democracy. For example, in permitting freedom of speech and thought, liberal democracy permits the proliferation of superstitious beliefs. In response, philosophers might be sorely tempted to check or eliminate such freedoms (cf. XX, 244–45). That philosophers perceive the limitations of democracy, particularly its dogmatic adherence to equality and freedom, may render them opponents or critics of such a regime.

The challenge that Spinoza confronts in the TTP is to celebrate philosophy's superiority to superstition while checking its understandable temptation to rule. In short, he must teach philosophy moderation in order for his political solution to succeed. To that end, he employs a variety of strategies. As we have already seen, he shows repeatedly that the best attempts to enlighten citizens, or to install philosophers as rulers, have failed miserably. Even the subtle approach of Maimonides, who used the authority of Scripture to install covertly the rule of reason, was met with ridicule and inadvertently succeeded only in strengthening superstition. Rather than correct or guide superstitions, philosophers must learn to live with them. Fortunately, the beliefs in equality and freedom can provide a basis for a stable and humane regime, especially when enshrined in natural rights that limit the authority of the rulers and prevent more excessive superstitions such as theocracy.

But Spinoza does not leave things here with a regime that provides a workable solution to the theological-political problem and a history lesson in the failure of philosophy to reform politics. The temptation for philosophers to become statesmen can easily generate arguments to overcome such claims. So Spinoza presents philosophy as a way of life that is wholly opposed to politics. First, he shows that the distance between the philosophical and political interpretations of the world is so vast that it cannot be bridged.

Our commonsense views of the good and the beneficial are incompatible with knowledge of nature. "Whatever seems to us ridiculous, absurd, or evil in nature comes from the fact that we know things only in part and are for the most part ignorant of the order and coherence of nature; and we want everything to be directed on the basis of the use of our reason (191)."

The ascent of the philosopher alienates him from the affairs of the multitude. The philosophical perspective views "human affects—like love, hate, anger, envy, love of esteem, compassion, and the other emotions—not as vices of human nature but as properties that it has, in the same way that heat, cold, storms, thunder, etc., are properties of the air" (PT I. 4). "Philosophy liberates us to see the true good, but from that perspective, human beings appear as little more than 'specks' in a vast whole determined by an infinite set of laws" (XVI, 191).[22] The notion of law, which depends on the necessity of nature rather than the willingness of human beings, is "obvious only to a few; most human beings are more or less incapable of perceiving it" (IV, 58–59). Lawgivers and statesmen, he continues, have cleverly redefined law so that it is consistent with our experience of "willingness" to obey. They have also discovered effective ways to persuade their subjects by using the passions, especially hope and fear. Philosophy looks to a different law, that of the necessity underlying all of nature. To grasp such a law points to knowledge and freedom from the passions which are stirred by ignorance.

In short, Spinoza resolves the theological-political problem by separating politics from philosophy. Politics addresses superstitious individuals by enlisting the passions, especially hope and fear, and with superstitions. Spinoza shows how freedom and equality are durable superstitions, when enshrined in natural rights and supported by democracy. In sharp contrast, Spinoza presents philosophy as pursuing true excellence and intellectual virtue. As part of its understanding of the whole, philosophy can in turn grasp why some statesmen are more successful than others; however, this same wisdom causes philosophers to eschew politics as inferior to the pursuit of virtue and true happiness. Joseph Cropsey characterizes this solution as follows: "The highest task of political philosophy is to understand, as the highest task of statesmanship is to govern, the relation of political life to thought."[23] While this characterizes the strategy of the work, it does not exhaust it. The *Theological-Political Treatise* is nothing less than an attempt to found a new political order and it is carried out by a philosopher. For this order to succeed, philosophy must impose a kind of moderation upon itself by paying homage to Spinoza.

Notes

1. *Tractatus Theologico-Politicus* (henceforth TTP), in *Spinoza Opera*, ed. Carl Gebhardt (Heidelberg: Carl Winters Verlag, 1925), 3:1–267. TTP references are given according to chapter number and Gebhardt page number. As for the translations into English, I have mainly used Martin D. Yaffe's outstanding translation in Spinoza's *Theologico-Political Treatise*, ed. Martin D. Yaffe (Newburyport: Focus, 2004), which incorporates the Gebhardt pagination. I have also consulted Edwin Curley's translation in *A Spinoza Reader: The Ethics and Other Works*, ed. E. Curley (Princeton: Princeton University Press, 1994), as well as Jonathan Bennett's more fluid and provocative translation, which has the advantage of being available on line: https://www.earlymoderntexts.com/authors/spinoza (2017).

2. See, for example, Andrew Youpa who argues that "Spinoza's moral philosophy is egalitarian. It is not the case that there is a standard for a certain type of person, a standard that does not hold for the rest of us. The freedom as empowerment model applies to all human beings equally. Nevertheless, the empowered life is not accessible to everyone equally." *The Ethics of Joy: Spinoza on the Empowered Life* (Oxford: Oxford University Press, 2020), 183. See also *Feminist Interpretations of Benedict Spinoza*, ed., Moira Gatens (University Park: Pennsylvania State University Press, 2009). Edward Halper argues that Spinoza's theological argument is a tool, a means for pulling citizens willy-nilly closer to philosophical freedom: "Spinoza views freedom of religion as a tool that the sovereign can use—cynically perhaps, but not necessarily so—to entice citizens to still or mold their passions voluntarily and, thereby, to exercise, through politics a semblance of the freedom that the philosopher enjoys through thought." Edward C. Halper, "Spinoza on the Political Value of Freedom of Religion," *History of Philosophy Quarterly* 21, no. 2 (2004): 167–68. Another version of this view was developed by Alan Donagan who refers to Spinoza's view as a "naturalized theology," by which he means (in Edwin Curley's reconstruction) that "nature has sufficiently many of the characteristics traditionally ascribed to God to make it reasonable to identify nature with God" (Curley, "Donagan's Spinoza," *Ethics* 104, no. 1 [1993]: 117). See Alan Donagan, *Spinoza* (Chicago: University of Chicago Press, 1989). Most recently, Lee Ward has made an interesting and useful case on behalf of the superiority of democracy on the grounds of its greater rationality in *Modern Democracy and the Theological-Political Problem in Spinoza, Rousseau, and Jefferson* (London: Palgrave Macmillan, 2014), 35–82.

3. Cf. Machiavelli, *Discourses on Livy*, III.1.

4. I've explored Spinoza's critique of Maimonides in "Spinoza's Response to Maimonides: A Practical Strategy for Resolving the Tension between Reason and Revelation," *International Philosophical Quarterly* 45, no. 3 (2005): 309–25 and in "Spinoza's Rejection of Maimonideanism," in *Spinoza and Medieval Jewish Philosophy* (Cambridge: Cambridge University Press, 2015), ch. four.

5. TTP VII, 99.

6. TTP VII, 100; see also XIII, 159. The TTP argues that it is far better to separate philosophy from religion and allow religion to guide men (see ch. XV). Several scholars have elaborated on this argument, rejecting the view that Spinoza prefers democracy because it fosters greater rationality. See, for example, Douglas Den Uyl: "Political action is never active in Spinoza's sense, and the effort to make it such carries with it confusions that can translate into social conflict. Politics for Spinoza has a simple limited function that in itself has nothing to do with perfection, activity, or blessedness. . . . The best we could say is that 'democracy' does not contradict the perfected active life—not that it fosters it. To foster it would mean we would have some clear conception of how to bring activity about through political means." *God, Man, and Well Being* (Bern: Peter Lang, 2009, 12–13). See also F. Mignini, "Theology as the Work and Instrument of Fortune," in *Spinoza's Political and Theological Thought*, ed., C. De Deugd (Amsterdam: North-Holland, 1984), 130. Mignini argues that reason can never have very much control over the passions and therefore religion is always necessary, even for rational men: "The imagination is the instrument and impassable limit of fortune; if it is founded upon the relation between the human body and other bodies, as the representative structure of *affectiones*, one can understand why Spinoza affirmed that reason, considered as true knowledge, has no power of the imagination and can do nothing against the course of fortune and the emotions which it produces" (ibid.). See also Wolfgang Bartuschat, "The Ontological Basis of Spinoza's Theory of Politics," in the same volume. Bartuschat argues that, for Spinoza, the state "fits into an ontological structure which is independent of all human projects, without being based on a knowledge of this ontological structure" (35).

7. See Hilail Gildin, "Notes on Spinoza's Critique of Religion," in *The Philosophy of Baruch Spinoza*, ed., Richard Kennington (Washington, DC: Catholic University of America Press, 1980), 155–71, and Gildin, "Spinoza and the Political Problem," in Marjorie Grene, ed., *Spinoza. A Collection of Critical Essays* (Norwell: Anchor Books, 1973), 377–87.

8. I've examined Spinoza's presentation in the preface in "Politics and Rhetoric: The Intended Audience of Spinoza's *Tractatus Theologico-Politicus*," *The Review of Metaphysics* 52 (June 1999): 897–924.

9. This solution is provisional because, as Spinoza argues in chapter 16, justice and charity can rule only where one finds just and charitable rulers. In short, Spinoza suggests that the problem of superstition can be solved, not primarily by reason, but by political means.

10. Hobbes emphasizes the fear of violent death as the ultimate keeper of peace in society. Spinoza agrees but, like Locke, places more emphasis on the desire for comfortable self-preservation.

11. This is the first mention of democracy in the TTP, which Spinoza suggests provides the best solution because it maintains a clear connection between individual interest and the state. The alternative solution is theocracy, but that requires convincing people of a divine mandate. The problem is that men believe

they are equal, and once the illusion of divine authority wanes, they have greater resentment from their equals.

12. Both natural right and Scripture present a doctrine of equality, one in terms of nature; the other in terms of dignity.

13. He describes the view of nature as "the thought that all things happen according to laws common to the whole of nature" (XIX, 229).

14. Leo Strauss, *Persecution and the Art of Writing* (Chicago: University of Chicago Press, 1988), 165, cf. 193–97.

15. This doctrine is consistent with Spinoza's metaphysical account in the *Ethics,* where he argues that in nature "each thing, as far as it can by its own power, strives to persevere in its being" (E III 6) and that this striving to preserve one's being, *conatus,* is "nothing but the actual essence of the thing" (E III 7).

16. The fact that desire and imagination dominate our self-perception is not necessarily a disadvantage. Unfortunately, theologians and political leaders have found a way to mitigate our self-concern by using our very irrationality to imagine a hierarchy and authority in (or above) nature. By imagining God above nature, or a natural law as a standard, these ambitious individuals can pose as spokesmen or prophets for this higher law (cf. VI, 82). In this way, our very notions of will, freedom, and equality are used to bolster the authority of political leaders.

17. TTP XVII, 193; cf. PT II, 12. Spinoza's account of human action is developed in E III, especially propositions 28–39. For a more detailed commentary, see Harold Skulsky, *Staring into the Void* (Newark: University of Delaware Press, 2009), 121–29. For an alternative view, see Ursula Renz, "Spinozism as Radical Anti-Nihilism: Spinoza on Being and the Valuableness of Being," *In Circolo,* no. 10 (December 2020): 391–406.

18. I've dealt with the meaning of freedom in Spinoza's argument in "Determined to be Free: The Meaning of Freedom in Spinoza's TTP," in *The Review of Politics,* 73, No. 1 (Winter 2011), 55–76.

19. For a fuller treatment of Hobbes's account, see Peter Zagorin's *Hobbes and the Law of Nature* (Princeton: Princeton University Press 2010).

20. Spinoza also suggests theocracy as alternative in chapter 5 because it can achieve stability if the leadership can convince people that they have access to a superior source of wisdom, which is recognized by all. See also chapter XVII: "For the sake of making themselves secure, kings who seized the throne in ancient times used to try to spread the idea that they were descended from the immortal gods, thinking that if their subjects and the rest of mankind did not look on them as equals, but believed them to be gods, they would willingly submit to their rule, and obey their commands" (217). By endorsing democracy, Spinoza advances the cause of freedom and equality, noting that once people believe such concepts, it is very difficult to reverse such beliefs (cf. V, 74).

21. For more on the consistency of the TTP and the *Ethics,* see Edwin Curley, "Notes on a Neglected Masterpiece: the TTP as Prolegomenon to the *Ethics,*"

in Cover and Kulstad, *Central Themes in Early Modern Philosophy* (Indianapolis: Hackett, 1990).

22. "Nature is not bounded by the laws of human reason, which aims only at man's true benefit and preservation; her limits are infinitely wider, and have reference to the eternal order of nature, wherein man is but a speck" (XVI, 19x).

23. See Joseph Cropsey, "Introduction: The United States as Regime and the Sources of the American Way of Life," in *Political Philosophy and the Issues of Politics* (Chicago; University of Chicago Press, 1977), 1–15.

Chapter 6

Excellence and Equality in Fénelon's *Telemachus*

Ryan Patrick Hanley

Montesquieu's famous account of the Troglodytes in the beginning of his *Persian Letters* provided the eighteenth century with one of its most important studies of political growth and decay. The story is, at its heart, a simple one. A wicked people, having among them "no principles of either equity or justice," abandons itself to the pursuit of self-interest.[1] Devolving into a chaotic state of nature and war of all against all, the society collapses. Only two men—indeed remarkable men—escape: "They had humanity, they knew justice, they loved virtue."[2] On these virtuous foundations these two men built a new social order that was the antithesis of the old failed order: a "new union" founded on "a common solicitude for the common interest."[3] This new order flourished and grew, and indeed in time grew to a point that the Troglodytes "believed it was proper to choose a king for themselves."[4] But in this story, the transition from a prepolitical social state into an elective monarchy is not a moment to be celebrated but to be lamented. Not because the Troglodytes choose poorly: "They agreed that it was necessary to bestow the crown on the one who was the most just," and this led them to select "an old man venerable for his age and his extensive virtue." But the old man clearly sees that to which the rest of the Troglodytes are blind: that to sacrifice self-rule for rule by another, however virtuous, is voluntarily to place around one's neck a new and terrible "yoke."[5]

103

Montesquieu's story of the Troglodytes and their choosing of a king, of course, has its literary antecedents going back to Hebrew scripture.[6] But its most proximate antecedent is to be found in the book Montesquieu himself called "the divine work of this century."[7] The book to which Montesquieu here refers is Fénelon's *Telemachus*, and in it we find the story of the inhabitants of the island of Crete and their own choice of a king. Like Montesquieu's Troglodytes, Fénelon's Cretans are simple and virtuous. Like Montesquieu's Troglodytes, Fénelon's Cretans seek the best man for their king. And like Montesquieu's Troglodytes, Fénelon's Cretans choose an old and wise man who laments rather than welcomes his new appointment. But Montesquieu's and Fénelon's accounts part ways on an important detail. For where the wise old man elected king of the Troglodytes is unnamed, the wise old man elected king of the Cretans is give a name: Aristodemos.

Fénelon's choice of this name that so consciously combines high and low, elite and popular, affords us an important glimpse into his project as a political philosopher as well as his unique standing in the quarrel between the ancients and the moderns. For Fénelon was ultimately neither strictly modern nor strictly ancient. Rejecting this binary, Fénelon rather sought to combine the best of the ancient with the best of the modern.[8] In terms of the question at the heart of this volume, Fénelon sought to preserve a reverence for virtue and nobility in an age that was moving ever closer to acceptance of universal equality and popular rule. The result is that, writing in this crucial transitional period of the end of the seventeenth century and the dawn of the eighteenth, Fénelon developed a novel synthetic concept of moral and political virtue, one that sought to preserve greatness even within an ever more egalitarian world.

What follows aims to document Fénelon's attachments to both ancient excellence and to modern equality, and to open up the question of whether and how these seemingly competing attachments might be reconciled. On the former front, it specifically focuses on Fénelon's treatment of two types of virtue: the warrior virtue characteristic of the ancients, and the philanthropic virtue characteristic of the moderns. As I hope to show, Fénelon has genuine reverence for both types of virtue, and believes that each has its place in modern moral and political life. But Fénelon was also keenly aware that the quarrel of the ancients and the moderns—in the first and most famous iteration of which he was himself a direct and very prominent participant—was not a simple binary struggle.[9] Indeed, in his efforts to reconcile ancient and modern, Fénelon, like his contemporaries Hobbes and Spinoza and Locke, was constantly governed by a deep consciousness that in fact "there is an antiquity that is not Greek."[10] Yet, unlike Hobbes and Spinoza and Locke, Fénelon thought that it was precisely in this non-Greek antiquity that the path toward reconciliation of ancient and modern, excellence and equality, lies.

I

To say the very least: Fénelon today does not enjoy the same name recognition as his three famous philosophical contemporaries mentioned above. The reasons for this are many and complex. But the fact that Fénelon is today less known in the English-speaking world than Hobbes and Spinoza and Locke is one that no eighteenth-century reader could have predicted. The best-selling book in all of eighteenth-century France after the Bible in fact was none other than *Telemachus*, and Montesquieu's praise of the work quoted above was hardly an outlier.[11] *Telemachus* captured the imagination of the Enlightenment, and in light of the relative unfamiliarity of the text and its author to Anglophone audiences today, we do well to say a few very brief words about them at the outset.[12]

Fénelon was born in 1651 and died in 1715—only months before the death of Louis XIV, with whose life his own was so intimately bound. His many accomplishments make his relative obscurity today perplexing. Among these, we might note that Fénelon was at once a pioneering educational theorist, a leading participant in the key theological quarrel of his age (over pure love), a leading participant in the main literary quarrel of his age (over the ancients and the moderns), and of course a best-selling author. But for our purposes his most important contributions were political. For at the same time that he was engaged in the disputes noted above, he was also a trail-blazing economist (especially important for an early defense of free trade) and theorist of international relations (especially important for an early articulation of a balance of European powers). And Fénelon also led the aristocratic resistance to Louis XIV and his monarchical absolutism, and it is to his work in this capacity that we owe the composition of his masterwork *Telemachus*.

First published in 1699, *Telemachus* was written by Fénelon during the period of his service in the Sun King's royal household. Here, he held the position of preceptor or tutor to the Duke of Burgundy, grandson of Louis XIV and expected heir to the throne. This was a delicate position, to say the least: enamored with the ideal of pure love and critical of the original sin of self-love, Fénelon was appalled by the excesses of Versailles and the costs that the French people were compelled to bear as a result of the love of glory and vanity of Louis XIV. Fénelon thus dedicated his energies in educating the Duke of Burgundy to make his charge a lover of virtue and a lover of his people in the hopes that he would in time rule France in a way diametrically opposed to the methods of his grandfather. A central piece in this education was *Telemachus*.

Fénelon described *Telemachus* in a memoir as "a fictional narration in the form of an epic poem, like those of Homer and Vergil, in which I put the key teachings appropriate by birth to reign," including "all the truths necessary for government, and all the faults that sovereign power can have."[13] For his part, Louis XIV was appalled by the text; when it was published (an accident that happened only because the manuscript seems to have been leaked by a valet to a bookseller), Louis took it as a personal attack and promptly stripped its author of his court position and banished him to the provinces. Fénelon himself, in this same memoir, professed his intentions were innocent, and that he sought "only to entertain the Duke of Burgundy with these adventures, and to instruct him while entertaining him, without ever wishing to give this work to the public."[14] However this may be, *Telemachus* is indeed a modern novel in the form of an ancient epic. It explicitly presents itself as a direct continuation of the fourth book of the Odyssey, chronicling the adventures of the son of Odysseus as he travels across the Mediterranean in search of his lost father. Guided by the goddess Minerva disguised as Mentor, Telemachus in the course of these travels is given a series of lessons in moral virtue and political rule that the young Duke of Burgundy (who would have likely been in his early teens when the manuscript was written) was meant to take to heart. The result was a publishing phenomenon that would captivate the eighteenth century. But for us what matters is that Telemachus is at its core a novel written by an aristocratic Catholic archbishop about ancient heroes who evince modern virtues. And it is this synthesis—which we might provisionally and perhaps perversely call Fénelon's ancient Catholic Enlightenment—that we need to unpack by attending to the text and its teachings on excellence and equality.

II

To this end we do well to begin with one of the most prominent elements of the text, its emphasis on the heroic ancient virtues. Two such virtues are especially prominent. One is self-command; throughout the text Telemachus is admonished to cultivate a capacity for austere self-denial. This self-denial is indeed the theme of Mentor's very first speech in the book, which serves as an initial sounding of a note that will be repeated again and again over the course of the story. The speech comes in the context of the arrival of Telemachus and Mentor on Calypso's island. In a reprise of her role in Homer's epic Calypso here again plays the role of enchantress, now concerned not to lose her chance to trap the son of the father who had previously escaped her. To this end she does her best to tempt Telemachus to submit to her captivity with promises of ease and luxury, even going so far as to present the heir to the throne of Ithaca with a fine purple robe embroidered with gold trim. These calculated gifts succeed at entrancing Telemachus when he is first presented with them. But then Mentor issues his warning: "O Telemachus: are these then the thoughts that ought to occupy the heart of the son of Ulysses? Think instead of upholding the reputation of your father and of vanquishing the fortune that afflicts you. A young man whose vanity leads him to love decking himself out like a woman is unworthy of wisdom and glory: glory is proper only to a heart which knows how to withstand pain and trample pleasures underfoot."[15] Mentor's speech is itself calculated; reminding Telemachus of his royal lineage, the tutor artfully reminds his charge of his duty and his destiny. But it is the moral substance of his reminder that is of most concern to us here. For here, in this first invocation of themes of virtue and vice in this book so centrally concerned with virtue and vice, Fénelon lays out the essential ethical struggle at the heart of the book: the conflict between vanity on the one hand, and wisdom and glory on the other. The former is the result of a debased form of self-love to which lovers of ease and comfort and external goods are prone. The latter is a noble form of self-denial and self-transcendence that demands renunciation of vulgar self-love.

In time, this contrast between debased self-love and noble self-denial will manifest itself in almost all of Fénelon's political teachings in *Telemachus*, extending beyond those related specifically to the ethical virtues into the realms of economics, statecraft, and civic education. Emblematic on this last front is the education prescribed by Minos, the lawgiver of Crete, who is presented as the epitome of the supremely wise legislator:

> Men want to have everything, and they render themselves unhappy by the desire for the superfluous. If they had wanted to live simply and content themselves with satisfying their true

> needs, then abundance, joy, peace, and union would be seen everywhere. This is what Minos, the wisest and best of all kings, understood. All the most wonderful things that you see on this island are the fruit of his laws. The education that he gave the children renders the body healthy and robust. They are accustomed thereby to a simple, frugal, and industrious life. It is assumed that all pleasure weakens the body and the mind. No other pleasure is ever proposed to them than that of being invincible by virtue, and of acquiring great glory.[16]

Minos, like Mentor, pointedly criticizes the desire for material finery and luxury, and insists rigorously on the distinction between the necessary and the superfluous, true needs versus false needs.[17] Fénelon's decision to use the text's exemplars of wisdom as the vehicles for developing this claim attests to the strength of his conviction—contra Hobbes and Spinoza and Locke—that this low form of self-love is an insufficient foundation for stable political orders.

A second ancient virtue on prominent display in *Telemachus* is courage in war. To a degree perhaps surprising for an ostensibly pacifistic Catholic archbishop—though hardly out of place in an imitation of a Homeric epic—*Telemachus* conspicuously emphasizes both the place of war in politics, and the capacity to wage war as an indispensable part of virtue. A great number of Mentor's lessons focus on this theme, and Mentor even goes so far as to lead by example on this front. At the end of the first of the eighteen books of *Telemachus* we are given a striking image of Mentor waging war in defense of the city of Acestes: "Death rang out on every side under his blows. Like a Numidian lion overcome by cruel hunger coming upon a flock of weak lambs, he tears, he slits their throats, he swims in the blood, and the shepherds, abandoning their flock, flee trembling in order to escape his fury."[18] Moments like this are not rare in *Telemachus*, and reading them it seems difficult to see how Fénelon could be regarded as pacifistic.[19]

In time, Telemachus proves himself a worthy student of Mentor on this front. Later in the book Mentor, giving advice to another king, counsels that even in times of peace, "in order to prevent the entire nation from going soft and falling into a forgetfulness of war, it is necessary to send the young nobility into foreign wars," as this serves to "stimulate in the nation as a whole emulation of glory, love of arms, indifference to fatigue and death itself, and finally experience in the military arts."[20] Mentor goes on to practice what he preaches, arranging for Telemachus to fight in foreign battles in which, we are told, he "showed his courage amidst the perils of war."[21] And it is not only in military combat that Telemachus shows his strength and courage. One important contest comes in Crete. Telemachus and Mentor arrive at Crete at the very moment at which the Cretans are holding competitions to determine a worthy successor to their exiled king. Telemachus enrolls in the games in his own right, excelling not just in the debates over law and ethics but also in wrestling and chariot racing and battling with the cestus. Telemachus in fact succeeds so well that the Cretans award him the crown: a crown that he ultimately passes to Aristodemos in a scene to which we will need to return. But here what matters is that these Cretan competitions serve as important training opportunities that later prove useful to Telemachus in two higher-stakes episodes of hand-to-hand combat.

In the first of these, Telemachus does battle with Hippias, who seeks to punish the young prince for an affront to his brother. Telemachus bravely and perhaps rashly decides to take on this formidable rival, ultimately succeeding in besting him with Minerva's help. But at the moment that he stands over his fallen rival, knowing that he could dispatch him with a blow, he chooses to show mercy and moderation. Letting Hippias go, Telemachus then returns back to his tent and concludes that in fact "true greatness is to be found only in moderation, justice, modesty, and humanity."[22] This important episode is later reprised in another instance of hand-to-hand combat in which Telemachus bests a second rival, this time Adrastus. And once again, at the moment at which he holds his opponent beneath him "with his sword raised ready to pierce his neck," Telemachus frees him, stating he takes no pleasure in spilling blood. This story plays out a bit differently from that of Hippias: where Hippias accepts his defeat, Adrastus repays Telemachus's mercy and moderation by trying to kill him, with the result that Telemachus is ultimately compelled to finish off Adrastus in the name of justice. All the same, both stories work to the same end, and serve to show the reader another side of courage in war: though necessary it is not sufficient, and must be supplemented by a very different sort of virtue.

III

The stories of Telemachus's encounters with Hippias and Adrastus are crucial to understanding Fénelon's position vis-à-vis the ancient virtues and the modern virtues. As we have seen, Fénelon clearly admires the valor and courage of the ancient military hero. But he also insists that this valor, in order to be genuinely noble, has to be tempered by other virtues. And in explicating these virtues, Fénelon makes his case for supplementing the virtues of the ancient hero with the virtues of the modern philanthropist.

Two specific instances are especially revealing on this front. One comes again at Crete in the course of their search for a new king. As noted above, this search began with physical competitions. But it then proceeded to an examination of the candidates focused on three questions, each of which was intended to help discern the candidate who stood in closest accord with the original position of Minos. The third question asked the candidates to explain "which the gods prefer: a conquering king, invincible in war; or a king without experience of war, but fit to govern the people wisely in peace." Most of the candidates chose the conquering warlike king. But Telemachus himself answers that neither of these kings is sufficient in themselves: "A king who knows how to govern only in peace or in war and who is not capable of conducting his people in both of these two states is only half a king."[23] In continuing, he explains that a king incapable or fearful of waging war stands open to the depredations of his enemies, where the king too eager for war will often sacrifice the well-being of his nation to his personal glory. What is needed, it is suggested, is rather a disposition that inclines the king toward peace in ways that temper and supplement the courage kings need to sustain defensive wars that preserve and protect their people.

Telemachus's lessons here also speak to another main theme of the text, one that parallels a distinction noted above. For not only does Fénelon distinguish true needs from false needs, but he likewise distinguishes true glory from false glory.[24] Throughout the text Mentor calls attention to the dangers of being misled by glory: "A king who spills the blood of so many men and who causes so many evils in order to acquire a little glory or to extend the limits of his kingdom is unworthy of the glory he seeks and deserves to lose that which he possesses."[25] But his fullest and most important explication of this point comes in a key speech Mentor delivers before two warring camps on the field of battle at the end of book 9:

> From this point forward, though under different names and different leaders, you will be only a single people. It is thus that the just gods, lovers of men whom they have created, want to be the eternal bond of their perfect concord. All the human race is only one family dispersed over the face of all the earth. All peoples are brothers and must love themselves as such. Woe

to those impious who seek a cruel glory in the blood of their brothers, which is their own blood! It is true: war is sometimes necessary. But it is the shame of the human race that it is on certain occasions unavoidable. O kings, do not say that one must desire it in order to acquire glory. True glory is not to be found outside of humanity. Whoever prefers his own glory to the sentiments of humanity is a monster of pride, and not a man. He achieves only a false glory even, because the true is found only in moderation and goodness.[26]

This is an arresting claim. It is arresting first insofar as it attests to Fénelon's belief, even as an admirer of Homer's heroes, that there exists a glory superior to that of Homer's heroes. This point is made explicitly when Telemachus visits the underworld in book fourteen. On witnessing the happiness of the good kings in the Elysian Fields, he is told: "Take note, my son, that their glory surpasses that of Achilles and of other heroes who merely excelled in combat, as much as a gentle spring is superior to a frozen winter, and sunlight is more radiant than moonlight."[27] But especially important for us is the particular virtue that we are here told the man of true glory adds to the virtues of the Homeric hero. For this virtue, as Fénelon now twice has explicitly emphasized, consists in the specifically modern virtue of "humanity."[28]

Humanity in fact plays a prominent role in Fénelon's account, and is often presented in the context of its utility in tempering the courageous hero's ardor for war. At times, this humanity is described in ways that anticipate the sentimental other-directedness that later Enlightenment thinkers would name pity or compassion or sympathy. And indeed Fénelon himself uses these terms: take for example his account of Telemachus's reflections on seeing the dead and wounded lying on that same battlefield to which he had been sent in order to gain experience of war: "On returning to the camp, [he] saw the saddest sights of war: the sick and the injured, unable to drag themselves out of their tents, were unable to escape the conflagration. They seemed half burnt, calling out to heaven their cries of pain with a plaintive and agonized voice. Telemachus's heart was pierced by them, and he was unable to hold back his tears. Several times he turned away his eyes, seized by horror and compassion."[29] The spectacle provides Fénelon with an opportunity to voice an extended lament that is at once an excoriation of the disastrous foreign wars of Louis XIV and a plea to his grandchild to be governed by the sentiments of humanity unknown to the Sun King himself: "What monstrous glory! Can one too greatly abhor and too greatly despise men who have thus forgotten humanity? No, no: far from being demigods, they are not even men."[30]

Fénelon's reflections on the need to combine the modern virtue of humanity with the ancient virtues of courage and valor reach their peak in his study of a specific and oft-overlooked people, the Mandurians, the peoples native to the Italian coast on which the Cretan refugee Idomeneus comes to build his new city of Salente. Alternately described as "savages" and "barbarians," Fénelon's Mandurians are worth study for their anticipation of similar accounts in the later French Enlightenment, from Montesquieu's Troglodytes to Rousseau's natural savage to Diderot's Tahitians. But for our purposes they are important for their self-conscious combination of the warlike virtues of the ancients with the peaceful virtues of the moderns. Fénelon calls attention to this combination in the speech he has them deliver to the Cretan refugees on their initial arrival:

> "We abandoned these pleasant seashores in order to cede them to you. There remain to us only the almost inaccessible mountains. At the very least it is just that you leave us there in peace and freedom. We find you wandering, dispersed, and weaker than us. It would be easy for us to slit your throats, and thereby deprive your companions of even the knowledge of your ill fate. But we do not want to dip our hands in the blood of those who are men just as much as we are. Go, and remember that you owe your lives to our sentiments of humanity. Never forget that it is from a people that you call crude and savage that you receive this lesson of moderation and generosity."[31]

The Mandurians have achieved precisely the synthesis to which Mentor calls Telemachus, bringing together both a capacity for heroic valor and a capacity for sentimental humanity. In holding forth this ideal, Fénelon here specifically anticipates the efforts of several other later Enlightenment thinkers who would also seek to effect this synthesis. Thus, Hume—who interestingly and explicitly contrasts "the ethics of Homer" with "those of Fénelon"—would later speak of the distinction between what he called the "amiable" and the "awful" virtues.[32] And Hume's friend Adam Smith would further develop this distinction in the course of his effort to trace the origins of both of these virtues, explaining that "the soft, the gentle, the amiable virtues, the virtues of candid condescension and indulgent humanity" exist alongside another sort of virtues: "the great, the awful and respectable, the virtues of self-denial, of self-government, of that command of the passions which subjects all the movements of our nature to what our own dignity and honour, and the propriety of our own conduct require."[33] In this vein, Hume and Smith share Fénelon's admiration for the virtues of both the ancients and the moderns. Yet Hume's and Smith's efforts to reconcile these different virtues took very different forms from that taken by Fénelon. In particular, Fénelon's route to this reconciliation led him precisely back to the Christianity that Hume in particular sought to move beyond.

IV

The role of Christianity in effecting Fénelon's synthesis of ancient and modern virtue is felt in a number of different ways. Two deserve particular mention here. One concerns the foundations or origins of the virtue of humanity examined in the section above. There, we saw that Fénelon often speaks of humanity as a sentimentalized other-directedness in ways characteristic of later Enlightenment theorists. But this point needs to be handled with care. For Fénelon is not calling for anything so simple as a turn away from reason to sentiment. His turn to the modern virtues that would later come to be sentimentalized by others is in fact not itself founded in sentimentalism but in a very different commitment: namely, an awareness of human equality built on a particular foundation.

Mentor designs much of Telemachus's education to instill in him a sense of concern for others that would be capable of tempering his self-love, and specifically his predilection to value himself above others. The text blames this on his mother: "His mother Penelope, despite Mentor, had encouraged in him a haughtiness and a pride which tarnished all that was most endearing in his character. He regarded himself as being of a different nature than the rest of men, the others seemed to him out on the earth by the gods only in order to please him, to serve him, to anticipate his every desire and to treat him in every way as a sort of divinity."[34] Fénelon himself, having witnessed firsthand in the court of Louis XIV the practical consequences of such royal self-deification, sought to take pains to instill in the potential heir to the throne a keen appreciation of both his own ungodlike humanity as well as the humanity of others. To this end, Mentor exposes Telemachus to a long series of sufferings and misfortunes that teach him just how ungodlike he in fact is. Ultimately, as Mentor himself proclaims, these had their desired effect: "I am very pleased to see you so changed. You were born hard and haughty; your heart allowed itself only to be touched by your goods and your interests. But in the end you have become a man, and you begin, owing to the experience of your sufferings, to sympathize with those of others. Without this compassion, there is neither goodness, nor virtue, nor an ability to govern men."[35] Telemachus develops sympathy, and specifically, a sympathy capable of tempering his pride, which in turn allows him to govern effectively. Yet this sympathy is hardly the product of a sentiment separated from reason, but rather the result of long experience of suffering and conscious reflection on the meaning of this suffering for himself and for others.

In this way Fénelon points to a route to modern virtue quite different from the route taken by many of his successors. And interestingly, this route points not only to the virtues of humanity and sympathy, but to equality. Fénelon was indeed committed to equality, but in fact to an equality of a very specific sort. For though he would come to be embraced by the later French revolutionaries as a hero—his figure graces the pediment of the Panthéon, the Revolution's temple—Fénelon was neither a democrat nor a leveling egalitarian of the sort that his latter-day revolutionary admirers sought to become. Fénelon himself was keenly conscious of his own aristocratic lineage, and though his practical writings for the reform of French institutions places great weight on the import of the Estates-General,[36] among other institutions, Fénelon was yet committed to the belief that a robust aristocracy might serve as a mediating force capable of tempering the potential excesses of both strong monarchy and popular democracy. This is especially evident in *Telemachus*. "Regulate ranks by birth," Mentor tells Idomeneus, and on such grounds goes on to reform Salente by dividing the citizenry into seven hierarchical classes.[37] All of this marks Fénelon as distant from the sort of egalitarianism that would much later come to be associated with political liberalism. Even so, Fénelon anticipates a certain side of these concerns in insisting on the necessity of preserving a reverence for equality, albeit of a particular sort: specifically, the equal capacity of human beings to suffer.

Fénelon goes on to show that this foundational concept not only serves to shape our idea of equality in specific ways, but also shapes the practice of political rule. Specifically, the sympathy that Telemachus came to know as a result of reflecting on his suffering was intended to shape his approach to practical policy in ways that might benefit the common good. Mentor makes this lesson especially clear: "When you will become the master of other men, remember that you were once weak, poor, and suffered like them. Take pleasure in succoring them: love your people, detest flattery, and seek only that you might be good insofar as you are moderate and courageous in vanquishing your passions."[38] Mentor's exhortation once again reminds us of the depth of Fénelon's commitment to combining harshness to the self with indulgence toward others. But to this he now also joins a new lesson: that this moral disposition is important for specifically political reasons insofar as it is what enables the king to rule in ways that are salutary to the whole, and specifically enables him to rule in a way governed not by love of self but by love of others.

With this we come closer to the core of Fénelon's distinctive and original reflections on the ways in which the virtues of the ancients and the moderns might be synthesized. To see this, we might remind ourselves of the general contours of this debate. On one side of it stand those seventeenth-century contemporaries and predecessors of Fénelon who were less concerned to recover the ancient virtues than to move beyond them; on this side we might place the aforementioned Hobbes and Spinoza and Locke. On the other side stand those eighteenth-century successors of Fénelon who were indeed concerned to synthesize the ancient virtues and the modern virtues, but sought to do so on specifically secular grounds; on this side we might place the aforementioned Montesquieu and Hume and Smith. But Fénelon's position is distinct from both of these, and his efforts to synthesize ancient excellence and modern equality reach their peak in the image of the good king, an image he often presents through the metaphor of the king as the shepherd or pastor of his people. Early in *Telemachus*, Mentor explains what animates this metaphor: "'Happy the people led by a wise king! They enjoy abundance, they live happily, and they love the one to whom they owe their own happiness. It is thus, O Telemachus that you must reign and bring joy to our people, if ever the gods allow you to possess the kingdom of your father. Love your people as your children: savor the pleasure of being loved by them, and make it such that they can never feel peace and joy without remembering that it is a good king who made them these rich presents.'"[39] Mentor's admonition is first and foremost a rebuke of the Machiavellian politics of fear in favor of a politics of love, and indeed *Telemachus* itself is very explicitly crafted as an anti-Machiavellian mirror-for-princes.[40] But it is also a call for a politics of love—the love of a king expressed in the first place as the father of his people, and ultimately, and in its most explicitly Christian formulation, as the shepherd and pastor of his people. It is a point that Fénelon took particular pains to develop in an important letter:

> By this conduct, a king truly fulfills the duties of a king—that is to say, the father and pastor of the people. He works to render them just, wise, and happy. He must believe that he merely does his duty, when he takes the crook in hand to lead his flock to pasture, safe from wolves. He must believe his people to be well-governed only when everyone is employed, is fed, and obedient to the laws. He must obey the laws himself because it is necessary to set an example, and he is only a simple man like the others, charged with dedicating himself to their tranquility and happiness.[41]

V

With this, Fénelon's synthesis comes full circle. The reconciliation of greatness and goodness, of excellence and equality, is ultimately achieved only via a love that aspires to emulate the love exhibited by Jesus; Fénelon's key statement of the necessity of the king's adherence to the rule of law indeed ends with the insistence that the king is in fact called to "sacrifice" himself for the public good.[42] But what then of the figure with whom we began, Aristodemos? Aristodemos was ultimately given the crown of Crete at Telemachus's own recommendation. Telemachus tells us that Aristodemos deserved the crown specifically because he "is already the father of the people," and he goes on to give a brief précis of his virtues: Aristodemos knows war and has courage but prefers peace and quiet, he likes work and scorns excessive wealth, he is generous with his possessions and succors the sick, he reveres virtues and loves his family in proportion as they exhibit virtue.[43] But his true greatness is ultimately revealed in what he says in his own words. In his public speech accepting the crown, he outlines three conditions for his acceptance: that he be allowed to resign after two years if the people do not believe they are better off, that he be free to live simply and frugally without the pomp of office; and "that my children would have no rank, and that after my death they will be treated without distinction, according to their merit, like the rest of the citizens."[44] These last words elicit a cry of joy from the people: they revere his reverence for equality. But Fénelon also gives his reader reason to admire Aristodemos as much or more for what he says in private as for what he says in public. As he prepares to take leave of Telemachus and Mentor, he reminds them that they have made him king. On such grounds he asks them: "Beg of the gods that they might inspire me with true wisdom and that I might surpass other men in moderation as much as I surpass them in authority. For my part, I shall pray to them to convey you happily to your fatherland."[45] If the people revere Aristodemos for his public praises of equality, Fénelon himself admires Aristodemos for his private expressions of piety.

Notes

1. Montesquieu, *Persian Letters*, in *Œuvres complètes*, ed. Roger Callois (Paris: Gallimard, 1949), vol. 1, 146 (letter 11).

2. Montesquieu, *Persian Letters*, vol. 1, 149 (letter 12).

3. Montesquieu, *Persian Letters*, vol. 1, 149 (letter 12).

4. Montesquieu, *Persian Letters*, vol. 1, 152 (letter 14).

5. Montesquieu, *Persian Letters*, vol. 1, 152–53 (letter 14).

6. See e.g. 1 Samuel 8:6, as noted by Stuart Warner in a note in his excellent translation of the *Persian Letters* (South Bend, IN: St. Augustine's Press, 2017), 26, n. 24.

7. Montesquieu, *Pensées*, ed. Louis Desgraves (Paris: Robert Laffont, 1991), 215 (*pensée* 115).

8. I am anticipated in this synthetic approach by Henk Hillenaar, though his substantive areas of focus are very different from those I focus on below; see Hillenaar, "Fénelon ancien et moderne," *Studies on Voltaire and the Eighteenth Century* 265 (1989): 1232–38.

9. On Fénelon's role on this quarrel see, e.g., Patrick Riley, "Rousseau, Fénelon, and the Quarrel Between the Ancients and the Moderns," in *The Cambridge Companion to Rousseau*, ed. Riley (Cambridge: Cambridge University Press, 2001), 78–93.

10. Joseph Cropsey, "On Ancients and Moderns," *Interpretation* 18 (1990): 32.

11. Among other eighteenth-century thinkers enamored with Fénelon, Rousseau deserves particular notice. I treat their relationship in "Rousseau and Fénelon," in *The Rousseauian Mind*, ed. Eve Grace and Christopher Kelly (London: Routledge, 2019).

12. I provide more complete introductions to Fénelon's life and writings in *The Political Philosophy of Fénelon* (Oxford: Oxford University Press, 2020), 1–15; and *Fénelon: Moral and Political Writings* (Oxford: Oxford University Press, 2020), 1–10).

13. This memoir is reproduced in the *Œuvres complètes de Fénelon*, ed. Jean-Edmé-Auguste Gosselin (Paris: J. Leroux et Jouby, 1848–1852), vol. 7, 665.

14. *Œuvres complètes de Fénelon*, ed. Jean-Edmé-Auguste Gosselin, vol. 7, 665.

15. Fénelon, *Telemachus*, in *Oeuvres*, ed. Jacques Le Brun (Paris: Gallimard, 1997), vol. 2, 6 [Hereafter *O*]. All subsequent citations to Telemachus are to this edition; translations are my own and wherever possible are drawn from those published in *Fénelon: Moral and Political Writings* [hereafter *MPW*].

16. Fénelon, *Telemachus*, *O* 2:58, *MPW* 78.

17. I develop this point in more detail in *The Political Philosophy of Fénelon*, 51–58 and passim.

18. Fénelon, *Telemachus*, *O* 2:13.

19. See, e.g., Paul Schuurman, "Fenelon on Luxury, War and Trade in the *Telemachus*," *History of European Ideas* 38 (2012): 182. I treat Fénelon's views on war and peace much more comprehensively in ch. 3 of *The Political Philosophy of Fénelon*.

20. Fénelon, *Telemachus*, *O* 2:152.

21. Fénelon, *Telemachus*, *O* 2:195.

22. Fénelon, *Telemachus*, *O* 2:214.

23. Fénelon, *Telemachus*, *O* 2:67; *MPW* 81.

24. See Hanley, *The Political Philosophy of Fénelon*, 26–27 and passim.

25. Fénelon, *Telemachus*, *O* 2:193.

26. Fénelon, *Telemachus*, *O* 2:145–46.

27. Fénelon, *Telemachus*, *O* 2:255.

28. On Fénelon's transformation of the ancient conception of heroism, see also esp. Riley, "Rousseau, Fénelon, and the Quarrel," 84–85.

29. Fénelon, *Telemachus*, *O* 2:225.

30. Fénelon, *Telemachus*, *O* 2:225–26.

31. Fénelon, *Telemachus*, *O* 2:128; *MPW* 89.

32. Hume, *Enquiry Concerning the Principles of Morals*, 7.15 and Appendix 4.6.

33. Smith, *The Theory of Moral Sentiments*, 1.1.5.1. And in this context see also esp. Clifford Orwin, "Montesquieu's *Humanité* and Rousseau's *Pitié*," in *Montesquieu and His Legacy*, ed. Rebecca Kingston (Albany: State University of New York Press, 2009).

34. Fénelon, *Telemachus*, *O* 2:210.

35. Fénelon, *Telemachus*, *O* 2:305.

36. See, e.g., Fénelon, *Plans of Government*, in *MPW* 189–91, 203–205.

37. Fénelon, *Telemachus*, *O* 2:160; *MPW* 92.

38. Fénelon, *Telemachus*, *O* 2:21.

39. Fénelon, *Telemachus*, *O* 2:16; *MPW* 72.

40. I explore this aspect of the text and how it can help inform our reading of other texts of Fénelon's in "L'éducation du prince selon Fénelon: de l'amour-propre à la justice," *Revue française d'histoire des idées politiques* 53 (2021), 113–24.

41. Fénelon" to the Marquis de Louville, in *MPW* 116.

42. Fénelon, *Telemachus*, O 2:59.
43. Fénelon, *Telemachus*, O 2:74.
44. Fénelon, *Telemachus*, O 2:75.
45. Fénelon, *Telemachus*, O 2:75.

Chapter 7

The Seductive Dangers of Equality and Excellence

The Moderating Wisdom of Montesquieu's Science of Ovidian Metamorphosis

Frank J. Rohmer

Celebrated as the author of the principle of separation of powers so frequently cited by Federalists and Anti-Federalists in the American constitutional ratification debate, Montesquieu (1689–1755) remained for more than two centuries a writer more often quoted than carefully read. Such persistent neglect can be traced to both the style of his writing and the substance of his teaching in his great works *Persian Letters* (1721), *Considerations on the Causes of the Greatness of the Romans and Their Decline* (1734), and *Spirit of the Laws* (1748). That the deepest significance of Montesquieu's novel political science would escape the grasp of luminaries including Voltaire, Helvetius, Condorcet, Thomas Jefferson, John Adams, and Destutt de Tracy can partly be attributed to what D'Alembert perceived as the "purposeful obscurity" underlying Montesquieu's work.[1] Those patient enough to enter into the labyrinthine structure of Montesquieu's works and find the Ariadne's thread connecting the disconnected parts begin to understand how his style of juxtaposition, ambiguity, paradox, and multiple perspectives involves a deliberate attempt to convey a substance revealing the complexity of the human situation; Montesquieu's reflections on that complexity recommend to humanity an appreciation of moderate government and existing customs as a shelter against radical calls for a return to the equality established by nature or for a noble transcendence of an uninspiring life for a civic excellence reminiscent of ancient Sparta and Rome.[2] The close interrelation of Montesquieu's style and substance also exposes the complexity of the author himself, a man at once engaged and detached, a cosmopolitan in search of knowledge and social success and a Bordeaux baron comfortable in the enjoyment of his estate, a man fully aware of the imperfections and injustices of the human condition yet finding enchantment in every moment of life's unfolding diversity.[3]

Montesquieu's desire for social success and literary acclaim was achieved in his erotically charged *Persian Letters*, where he employed epistolary style and reversal of perspectives, tragic events and comic wit, European freedom versus Persian despotism, literary novel and philosophic discourse, religious faith and rational knowledge, enlightened science and self-misunderstanding. The reversal of perspective and epistolary style employed by Montesquieu unveil how much our familiar lives are molded by custom formed by a particular history often in conflict with truth and justice.[4] Juxtaposed throughout the *Persian Letters* are the comparative stories of the tragic collapse of the fictional character Usbek's Persian harem and the corruption of the French monarchy during the long reign of Louis XIV (r. 1643–1715), the disintegrating changes in both regimes revealing a Heraclitean world of motion tending to chaos without the ordering art of politics. Montesquieu's purpose here and in his later works was to provide an enlightened science to understand the human condition and to provide prudent counsel to guide political life. The tormented condition of the confined women of Usbek's harem, the denatured condition of the eunuchs who guard them, the oppressive rule of a despot whose tyrannical rule threatens Usbek's own security, and a moral world inspired by the Islamic religion all coalesce to form a political order infused with the spirit of radical inequality and despotic fear resulting in an ever-present unhappiness.[5] Much freer, happier, and livelier is the situation in France, where women's greater freedom and relative equality compared to Persia increase their power to shape the sociability of a nation given to fashion, to taste, and to change.[6] Despite this far better condition in which human beings enjoy a happiness rooted in freedom, the French monarchy depicted by Montesquieu in 1721 was already a regime impoverished by constant wars, drained by high taxation, corrupted by despotic tendencies, and ultimately awaiting the deluge. Louis

XIV in his desire for greatness had impelled the French monarchy in the direction of despotism by the reduction of the intermediary powers—the nobility, parlements, and the church—weakening the nation as he glorified himself. The sun shining over the late Roi Soleil and the kingdom of France was clearly, for Montesquieu, a setting, not a rising, sun.[7]

Given Montesquieu's pessimistic account of the French monarchy's life expectancy, scholars differ in their assessment of his preference for actual monarchy or for a commercial republicanism with the appearance of monarchy modeled on England.[8] Preservation of monarchy or any other regime, for Montesquieu, depends on a clear understanding of the elements and causes constituting that form and the artful implementation of appropriate remedies—a realism lacking in French statecraft as presented by Montesquieu in the *Persian Letters*.[9] Such artful preservation requires not only a correct perception of the complex parts composing each body politic but also the self-understanding on the part of the statesman to grasp his own place within the particular order needing its own prescriptive remedy. Perhaps the most powerful lesson conveyed through Montesquieu's comic depiction of the gravest of issues is the opaqueness of the human situation owing to the complexity of the surrounding world and the tendency of human beings to misperceive the world and their true place in it. The *Persian Letters* depict Usbek as deeply perceptive about the maladies of France while being self-blinded about the real causes of his harem's disorder, a disorder rooted in the miseries created by the radical inequality of men and women.[10] Usbek's distorted desire for honor shaped by the cultural contours of Islamic Persia generates a conflict with his burning desire for erotic love, which together lead him to prefer his newest wife, the apparently virtuous Roxanne, and to allow a degree of freedom inconsistent with the despotic rule essential to the harem's order. Usbek's lack of self-knowledge and his misperception of the elements necessary to the harem's order delude him into restraining the despotic hand when it is most necessary.[11] The tragedy that engulfs Usbek, Roxanne, and the harem, when compared to the morally corrupt happiness of France, demonstrates how the greater freedom and equality of women can create the social dynamic of a lively and satisfying order in which human happiness is generated by pleasure.[12]

Montesquieu presents this tragic misunderstanding as a blindness rooted in a psychological self-blinding requiring a retrospective turn from how humans have formed themselves distinctively and unequally in society to how they stand as equals in nature. This return to the natural condition of human beings claims little space in Montesquieu's works and involves no universal standard by which to judge the justice or injustice of existing regimes. Nevertheless, the brief attention Montesquieu gives to the natural condition of human beings reveals much about the importance of the escape from pure nature and the need for the artful creation and preservation of governments, even those far from perfect in their justice, which he presents as standing between humanity and the extremes of chaos and despotism. Most unsettling here is Montesquieu's revelation in the Troglodyte story in the *Persian Letters* and in the early part of the *Spirit of the Laws* that enlightenment itself unveils the precariousness and potential demoralization of the human position in nature.[13] Montesquieu follows Hobbes in presenting the truth of humanity's natural condition as one of equality in which human beings find themselves inferior to the threatening surroundings of a strictly material world devoid of divine logos. Enlightenment knowledge thus strips from the human psyche the aesthetic elevation of the human within the artful contrivances of various civilizations and political orders.[14] Hobbes's understanding of the precariousness of humanity's natural condition correctly identified how desperately far the human prospect was from survival much less excellence.[15] So equally dangerous was the natural condition of human beings that the invention of civil society was necessary to escape this unhealthy situation.[16] However, where Hobbes saw in natural man a rational faculty capable of a calculus of self-interested salvation,[17] Montesquieu, anticipating Rousseau, finds such providential reasoning a far less likely explanation than a sentient feeling, including sexual attraction, for the emergence of civil society.[18] With the growth of civil society, argues Montesquieu, came a new human confidence in the face of nature and the development of human inequality at the foundation of human vanity, a passion eventuating in personal and political rivalry, the origins of the state of war Hobbes had mistakenly attached to humanity's natural condition. Montesquieu thus attributes humanity's violent competition for dominance as rooted in the inequality generated by the growth of human confidence as humans rise above the severe necessity imposed by inhospitable nature.[19]

As depressing as the prospect of physical survival of human beings in nature was before the invention of civil society, modern enlightenment had dealt a devastating blow to the psychic confidence of humanity in society by depicting the human being as having a strictly earthly existence in a purely physical world of matter in motion. Thus, the enlightenment journey on which Montesquieu takes us through his Persian travelers and his comparative empirical exploration of times long ago and places far away in his more mature works uncovers the awful truth of a human existence naturally devoid of moral purpose and spiritual protection.[20] The exchange of letters between Usbek and his Persian friend Mirza raises the question whether a life of virtue or pleasure leads to human happiness.[21] Usbek's response to Mirza's perplexity suggests the doubtful rational ground of virtue and the consequent need for moral truths to be inspired by feeling.[22] The human growth occurring in civil society leads to human concern with ultimate causes and purposes eventuating in the origin of religious belief, elevating the place of human beings within the surrounding world to such an extent that the material world no longer fully encompasses them. The invention of religion introduces the spiritual into a world without spirits, the developed imagination of social man giving distinct existence to what is not.[23] The metaphysical longings of mortal human beings and the vivid presence of religion in their lives explain Montesquieu's preoccupation with the subject of religion in his political science and his own skeptical acceptance of a Catholic faith that he did not believe as true, and which he so ungraciously ridiculed in the *Persian Letters*.[24]

The pursuit of truth and security were Usbek's objects in the *Persian Letters*, and these concerns remained Montesquieu's in his later works.[25] Human self-preservation depended on a correct understanding of the human condition, and this understanding depended on an accurate grasp of causes rather than an abstract consideration of sovereignty and political legitimacy as starting points for the science of politics.[26] To understand the real causes underlying the growth, development, and decay of political orders became the focus of Montesquieu's too often neglected *Considerations on the Causes of the Greatness of the Romans and Their Decline*.[27] Here, Montesquieu begins not with natural man but with men as they were formed by a political order within their own specific circumstances. The *Considerations* and the *Spirit of the Laws* awaken the reader's imagination to a grandeur that astonishes the small modern soul busied with finance and commerce, while simultaneously these works evoke a sense of horror at the human cost of such political excellence.[28] The *Considerations* explores the causes behind the formation of a particular polity dependent on a unique refraction of common human nature to be infused with a spirit uncompromisingly virtuous in its devotion to the res publica, which required unnatural self-denial consummated through military conquest of surrounding peoples destroyed one after another.[29] Montesquieu's descriptive study of the Romans draws the reader into the hard-to-believe alternate reality of a people who even in their ruins leave us stunned by the magnificence of their accomplishment and unnerved by the painful realization of what we are not.[30] Nevertheless, Montesquieu's descriptive work, in which history serves as the laboratory of his empirical investigation of causes, purposely leaves in this dazzling vision of Roman political excellence the disturbing awareness of virtue practiced without happiness and glory acquired through misery.[31] Constant wars to destroy actual and potential external threats presented a stage for the externalization of Rome's violent virtue and suppressed for centuries the internal volcano of plebeian resentment of painful and insulting inequalities imposed under patrician rule; by venting its potentially destructive violence upon alien peoples, Rome devoured other nations without devouring itself.[32] Centuries of Roman expansion indeed brought Roman greatness, but only through the slaughter and degradation of the surrounding peoples of the Mediterranean world.[33] The Roman achievement was a glorious prospect to behold, but such greatness meant a despotism not only external but also internal. The towering greatness of Roman political virtue denied the possibility of true excellence of soul. Might, not right, prevailed. Human nature was violated by the very virtue that defined Rome's civic excellence.[34]

When the military conquests of Pompey reached geographical finality, the martial valor once earning the coveted reward of a triumph, so long the spring of Roman expansion, could no longer express itself outwardly;[35] it was then that Roman cruelty turned inward, consuming the Roman people themselves until the spirit of Roman liberty gave way to the spirit of Caesar.[36] Rome's historical trajectory had reached its humanly as opposed to divinely defined telos. Once the embryonic greatness of early Roman virtue had reached its mature development, the metamorphosis of Rome began. The spirit of great Caesar triumphed even before the body of Caesar, and this corrupt spirit the residue of Roman excellence embodied in the virtuous Brutus could not kill.[37] The republic was dead.

Rome's greatness, however, did not die immediately with the republic. With the change in Rome's spirit came a metamorphosis of its form under imperial rule, where greatness survived as long as some martial virtue remained in the increasingly degenerate Romans.[38] Once that virtue had vanished and the Romans employed the Germanic peoples to protect the frontiers of the empire, the gates were left open for the invasion of those nations that would transform Europe.[39] The conquest of Rome by the Germanic peoples completed the chain of causation Montesquieu examines in the *Considerations* and reveals the impulse that propelled Rome to its greatness and the physical and moral causes of its decline and ultimate death.

The death of Rome marked a cataclysmic end but also a surprising beginning. This remarkable story Montesquieu unfolds through the empirical, historical science he first outlined in the *Considerations* and perfected in the *Spirit of the Laws*, especially in the much-neglected sixth part, sometimes mistakenly described as a mere addendum to his masterpiece of twenty years' labor.[40] What immediately strikes the reader is the desultory appearance of the work made even more impenetrable by Montesquieu's frequent use of epigrammatic expression, repeating the puzzling juxtaposition and ambiguity employed in the *Persian Letters*. Equally daunting for the reader who attempts to fully digest the work is its lengthy and broad historical detail, the roughly two pages given to the equality of human beings in their natural condition being dwarfed by more than seven hundred devoted to a comparative study of their unequal lives as refracted in civil societies formed by custom, law, geography, and climate. Montesquieu's inductively descriptive approach to various peoples leads eventually to deductive principles about various ideal forms of government, demonstrating how each is formed by a nature and a principle unique to that government.[41] This comparative approach into the causes maintaining the form and life of various governments provides the data of Montesquieu's descriptive science, the novelty that he proclaims in the epigraph to *The Spirit of the Laws* taken from Ovid's *Metamorphosis*, "*Prolem sine matre creatum*" (Offspring begot without mother).[42] This dedication to the discovery of a comprehensive political and social science of causes of the life and death of various forms of government was the distinct purpose of Montesquieu's life, a purpose that would intrigue careful readers but moderate his prescriptive counsels and thereby cool the ardor of those philosophes more optimistic about the prospects of transformational reform or radical revolution.[43] Far from Rousseau's cry in the *Social Contract* that "Man is born free yet everywhere in chains,"[44] Montesquieu describes human beings as they are in history and reveals himself frequently charmed by their variety and generally tolerant of their imperfections. Far from Rousseau's insistence in the *Second Discourse* that we set the facts aside and proceed by an imagination of what ought to be, Montesquieu's plea "may we be left alone" expresses a moderation that recognizes that "even virtue hath need of limits."[45]

Critical to Montesquieu's novel science was his shift from natural right to history to reveal the real stuff out of which human life was made.[46] This shift from universal human nature to human nature refracted by historical experience displays Montesquieu's detached cosmopolitan fascination with the complex unfolding of diverse human possibilities and his engaged attachment as a good citizen of the monarchical France he so loved for the space it gave to individual freedom and for the encouragement it gave to the achievement of human excellence.[47] This alternating current running through the *Spirit of the Laws* has understandably led scholars to characterize Montesquieu as a liberal advocate of commercial republicanism or as a conservative defender of the French monarchy.[48] Such divergent interpretations have strong foundations in the structure of the work and the enigmatic style of his writing. Consistent with the critical perspective presented in the *Persian Letters*, the *Spirit of the Laws* depicts a French monarchy headed like a Cartesian vector without countervailing viscosity into its own self-annihilation. Despite this bleak picture of one Ovidian form metamorphosing into another in a world in which all human things come to an end, Montesquieu will not let the reader forget the three centuries of greatness France experienced under the monarchy beginning with Charles VII (r. 1422–1461).[49] This sympathetic treatment of the historical excellence of the French monarchy was reinforced by Montesquieu's empirical science, which required the study of the origins of the French monarchy and Kingdom of France in the Germanic conquests of the Roman Empire. The monarchical France disintegrating into some other form during Montesquieu's time was itself the product of more than one Ovidian metamorphosis. Motion and change were the story of France's past and would be the story of its future. The principal concern of Montesquieu was to describe scientifically the causes of political and social change; his secondary concern was to counsel moderate and humane statesmanship in response.[50]

The France Montesquieu sought to understand and to preserve was the result of the Germanic conquests of the Gallo-Romans and the metamorphosis of the King of the Franks into the Kingdom of France.[51] The spirit or spring giving life to the Frankish constitution under the Merovingian and Carolingian dynasties was the love of honor and the desire for plunder among independent, warlike men.[52] The constitutional health of the Merovingian kingdom depended on the warriors' fealty to the king, the greatest of the various warlords, who was constantly challenged to display an unequalled valor in war and an unequalled generosity in the reward of fiefs to his faithful followers.[53] For as long as the Merovingian kings displayed their excellence as warriors, they commanded the loyalty of their simple but violent compatriots. However, as the Merovingian monarchs abandoned the art of war, the inequality that sustained Merovingian rule eroded. Effectual power passed into the hands of mayors of the palace, first merely subordinate managers of the royal household, who grew by the time of Pepin to join the most powerful office (mayor) to all authority but the most prestigious title (king).[54] Building on the foundation laid by

Pepin (mayor, 623–29,639–40), Charles Martel (r. 718–741) and Charlemagne (r. 768–814), Pepin's greatest descendants, assumed the title of king and restored the Franks' political greatness based on a renewed inequality between crown and nobility.[55] To maintain their kingly supremacy against rivals for power, the two great Carolingians had to realistically assess the elements compounding their regime and extract the inequality necessary to kingly authority while not overly offending the two great rival powers of their time, the nobility and the Church. With a cynical realism worthy of Machiavelli, Montesquieu presents an admiring account of both Charles Martel and Charlemagne, the former oppressing the Church to satisfy the nobility, the latter patronizing the Church to restrain the nobility. Amid the unrelenting motion of all earthly things, these great kings realized the need for an equilibrium appropriate to the constitution of the Frankish monarchy. The constitution of the Franks could not exist without monarchical greatness, and that greatness could not prevail where either the nobility or the Church rose to equality with the king.

Montesquieu's insightful treatment of the force of Christianity in Carolingian Europe opens a window to an issue boldly raised earlier by Machiavelli and later by Rousseau: whether the political-military greatness of classical antiquity could be replicated in Christendom.[56] The divergent educations impressing those living in the Christian era reflected conflicting claims on the human conscience and made the complete civic devotion so formative in ancient Sparta and Rome no longer possible,[57] but the public-spirited virtue of classical republicanism Montesquieu repeatedly presents as unnatural and unhappy.[58] Christianity substituted its own self-denying virtue demanding a spiritual perfection at odds with worldly desires and civic loyalties,[59] and Montesquieu treats this new transcendent demand on human life as undeniably real even though of human invention.[60] Departing from Machiavelli and Bayle, Montesquieu presents a view of Christianity's influence on French and European civilization as not without positive contributions. In the corrupt and disintegrating world of the late Western Roman Empire, Christianity offered consolation and hope. Christianity also elevated the status of women, slaves, and conquered peoples by proclaiming all human beings created equally in the image of God—the age of Saturn had returned.[61] From its foundation in a Roman world becoming increasingly cruel, dissolute, and disordered, Christianity inspired the customs and morality of a new European civilization, making direct assaults on this religion a potential threat to the mystic inspiration necessary to the moral claim of custom providing the common bonds of a particular society.[62]

Even as it presented a heavenly challenge to the authority of the earthly kingdom, Christianity anointed the earthly power of kings with spiritual legitimacy, rescued multitudes of conquered people from the degradation of servitude, and taught the people of God a humility consistent with the obedience of subjects.[63]

Charlemagne, the greatest king of the Franks as Montesquieu presents him, clearly understood religion as part of the complex and competing elements both giving life to and potentially disintegrating the Frankish constitution. Charlemagne achieved greatness as a king by balancing without destroying the vital forces forming the Franks as a nation. This equilibrium he maintained by channeling the nobility's violence into expansionist wars rewarded by attractive plunder, by protecting the Church with generous benefices, and by preserving domestic peace with the fitting practice of judicial combat, a violent method of preserving peace among a nation formed in blood and conquest.[64] In a style so characteristic of Montesquieu, the author writes of the challenge facing the Frankish kings: "The Franks . . . tolerated murderous kings because they were murderous themselves; they were not struck by the injustice and pillaging of their kings because they too plundered and were unjust."[65] Faced with the reality of ruling a brutal and warlike people, Charlemagne exercised the fearful power and astute calculation required to increase and maintain his kingdom.[66] The reader cannot help but be struck by the author's admiration for his subject. The imposing character of Charlemagne reigns in Montesquieu's laconic language: "The Empire was maintained by the greatness of the leader; the prince was great, the man was greater."[67]

Nevertheless, one king's surpassing excellence does not necessarily constitute a great nation. On the contrary, the very greatness of Charlemagne exposed the weakness of monarchy in general and of the Frankish constitution in particular. Where "[e]verything was united by the force of his [Charlemagne's] genius," the Frankish kingdom rapidly disintegrated following the death of the great leader whose magnificence sustained its fragile form.[68] Charlemagne enjoyed the support of nobility and Church while checking both; his son Louis the Pious, proving himself unequal to the task, succeeded at making enemies of both.[69] Within the space of only two generations, the Carolingian monarchs had so dissipated their domains that they could no longer support even the expenses of the royal household.[70] A nation that under Charlemagne had appeared to rival the greatness of ancient Rome had declined to "a spectacle worthy of pity" under his successors.[71] The transition from the Carolingian to the Capetian dynasty, as Montesquieu presents it, was far more than a change in rulers; it represented a profound change in the constitution of the Frankish kingdom. In the person of Hugh Capet, the highest title was joined to the greatest fief.[72] Civil law, especially involving the relations of property, replaced the political law defining the relation between king and subjects.[73] As the lords won their demand for irrevocable fiefs to replace revocable ones, the nobility established greater independence from the king and the foundation of fealty from their own larger number of vassals. In the age where "[t]he one who had the fief had the justice," the feudal age of largely independent local rule was born.[74]

This metamorphosis of the centralized Frankish constitution of Charlemagne into the decentralized constitution of feudalism provides perhaps the clearest view of Montesquieu's empirical scientific method, which many scholars have mistakenly understood as a deductive approach based on Cartesian principles of motion.[75] Montesquieu's depiction of the Romans and the Franks, however, does not merely trace an example of a theory of motion he had formulated long before; rather, his deductive principles take shape only after many years of historical immersion in the distant times and places of his intellectual journeys. Like natural science, Montesquieu's political science gathers historical data from which he forms hypotheses, which then lead to further investigations resulting in revisions to the original hypotheses, laboriously drawing the boundaries of a sea seemingly without any shores.[76] Comparing himself to the painter Correggio, Montesquieu depicts with an inspired sensuality an Ovidian world of metamorphosis where universe is always tending to chaos amid the inescapable reality of change.[77] In the absence of divine logos, only human art guided by human wisdom can provide form and a degree of permanence. Only human beings of unequaled intelligence could provide this godlike science and governance. Montesquieu offers himself as the inspired founder of political science and St. Louis as the consummate artist of politics, each towering in their godlike excellence over the mass of humanity needing their providential care.

As the caring Christian shepherd of his people, St. Louis (Louis IX, r. 1226–1270) exercised the wisdom of the true legislator, adapting specific legislative reforms to the distinctive constitution of his nation. Wise, patient, and moderate, St. Louis avoided the imposition of a masterpiece of legislation and, following the practice of Solon, gave to his imperfect people not the best laws, but the "best they could endure."[78] St. Louis brought about desperately needed change not by commanding and forcing change, but by insinuating and encouraging voluntary reform.[79] With deft sensitivity to the needs of the Church and to the martial inclinations of a crude and warlike nobility, St. Louis brought about change gradually, increasing the power of the monarchy while giving life to a new intermediate body, the provincial parlements composed of legal scholars versed in Roman law, who increasingly substituted the rule of a complex, written law for the violent nobility's preference for judicial combat.[80] The subtle and caring statesmanship of St. Louis began the transformation of the feudal world of the Frankish monarchy into the modern kingdom of France, laying the political foundation for centuries of French greatness under a balanced monarchical constitution, so praised by Machiavelli in *The Prince* and *The Discourses*, with the spirit of honor as its animating principle.[81]

The French constitution formed by St. Louis testified to the historical possibility of the coexistence of Christian humility and human equality before God and the magnificent actions of a nobility founded in social inequality and driven by the lust for honor. However spiritually inconsistent, the two spirits existed simultaneously and contributed to the equilibrium of the French constitution, checking and balancing one another while restraining the monarchy.[82] The unintended resultant of these balanced and contending forces was political moderation, for Montesquieu the sine qua non of wise, stable, and humane government.[83] This moderation Montesquieu thought more likely to prevail under monarchy than under the cruel virtue of democratic republics or under the imperious tendency of aristocratic republics to destroy the equality necessary to their survival. How moderation could result from the monarchical form of government in which, as Montesquieu makes clear, the monarch need not be moderate and the spring of honor animating the regime was a false honor has remained for scholars a troubling and doubtful foundation for the maintenance of such a regime against the destructive tendency to despotism presented in the *Persian Letters*.[84] When the Roi Soleil at the height of French greatness propelled the monarchy toward the Oriental despotism he so admired, did this not reveal the inevitable tendency of monarchy to its own destruction amid the degradation of the nation? Could the balanced monarchical constitution so celebrated by Montesquieu, and by Machiavelli before him, contain within itself sufficient corrective forces to preserve the moderate equilibrium Montesquieu considered necessary to a humane life?[85] Montesquieu to our distress provides no clear answer to this unavoidable question, but in his treatment of monarchy's capacity for self-correction he more than suggests that the monarchy could survive and prosper; such rejuvenation, however, would depend on a prudently realistic monarchical statesmanship guiding the nation back to its own unique, balanced constitution, though with adaptive changes reflecting the rapidly changing world of the time. Critically important was a reinvigorated nobility, a flourishing commerce of luxury, a tax policy supporting the needs of the state while not burdening the people, and an independent judiciary creating a sense of security based upon the rule of law.[86]

Might France find this corrective course based on the model of the commercial republic with the semblance of monarchy Montesquieu had painted, perhaps as aspirational as it was realistic, about England?[87] While Montesquieu's provides extensive treatment of this modern model of a republic not requiring the denaturing excellence of the classical republic, this alluring prospect of a moderate and humane commercial republic was no simple palliative. The modern commercial regime presented its own problems, and the surrounding world in which that commerce occurred should not be assumed to be always defined by a moderating and enlightening commerce.[88] Reflecting on ancient and modern commercial regimes, Montesquieu offers a powerful defense of commerce as productive of luxury, luxury the perfection of the arts, and the perfection of the arts as productive of the greatest human excellence.[89] The dazzling brilliance of Hellenic civilization, a civilization, for Montesquieu, whose excellence has never been equaled, depended heavily on its commercial wealth.[90] Tyre, Marseilles, Venice, and the Netherlands all demonstrate how geographically disadvantaged peoples have been invigorated, not enervated, by commerce.[91] Nations more favored by geography, such as ancient Carthage and modern England, provide examples of commercial peoples whose economies propelled their rise not merely to economic prosperity but to political prominence among nations.[92] This optimistic treatment of ancient and modern commercial regimes, however, proves to be less than the whole story of Montesquieu's treatment of commerce. While commerce might bring nations closer through reciprocal dependence,[93] commerce, even as it thrives on equality within a nation, divides people within that same nation, generating inequality with luxury and creating a civil society characterized more by rivalrous, lonely confederates than by fellow citizens.[94] Montesquieu, on the one hand, expresses revulsion at the prosaic and unsociable prospects of such a life[95] and, on the other, displays in anticipation of Tocqueville a clear understanding of the inexhaustible productivity of a dynamic nation whose restiveness is restrained by its rigorous legalism.[96] Among such a people "continually striving for small gains," ambitious enterprises are possible, but few great spirited human beings are to be found; magnanimous characters, Montesquieu scornfully remarks, are more frequently found among pirates.[97]

Small-souled peoples, though lacking in excellence owing to their concentration upon immediate objects of gain, can accomplish bold projects if given the hope of acquiring more.[98] While a nation can internally regulate this commercial spiritedness by a complex system of laws, its laws cannot restrain the aggressive external actions of other nations; here the right of nations prevails.[99] Montesquieu first presents the right of nations in a favorable light: in peace, each nation rationally should do as much good to other nations as possible without harming itself; in war, each nation should rationally do as little harm to other nations as possible without jeopardizing its own preservation.[100] International law is the logical derivative of this equal right of nations rationally construed.[101] Having presented the right of nations so rationally and optimistically, Montesquieu then follows with a much harsher picture: the object of nations in war is victory; the object of victory is conquest; and the object of conquest is preservation.[102] International law, based in reason, limits the exercise of belligerent might to what is necessary to self-preservation—each nation, however, equally retaining the right of nations to judge rightfully or wrongfully what is reasonable to its security.[103] Here Hobbes's condition of "meer" nature reemerges in the fullness of its inescapably bleak reality, made even worse by the massively unequal power advantage acquired by some nations over others.

The more Montesquieu brings historical examples to bear upon his theoretical statement of the right of nations, the more his rational principles come to be devoured, sometimes literally, by harsh realities—the inequality of slavery, a product of the right of nations, by no means being the harshest. The Iroquois exercise the right of nations, but this right includes eating their prisoners.[104] In their faithful practice of the right of nations, the commercial Carthaginians increased their commercial and political power by a ruthless treatment of all nations they conquered. By this faithful and brutal exercise of the right of nations, Carthage "increased its power by its wealth, and its wealth by its power."[105] Carthage's expanding empire propelled by its unequalled commercial excellence did not escape the notice of a Mediterranean rival, which acted upon its equal right of nations, displaying a hatred of the Carthaginians that lasted even beyond Carthage's destruction.[106] Perceiving the relation between Carthage's unparalleled commercial excellence and its potential political preeminence, Rome waged three wars on Carthage as a political not a commercial rival,[107] with Rome, driven by its civic and military excellence, ultimately emerging as the unequaled master of the Mediterranean world. In the world of equal right among nations, Rome acted from its own internal constitution to violently conquer and destroy all peoples within its reach.[108] To see the Romans as anything other than a people driven by their own internal dynamic to destroy the equality and independence of other nations was to misunderstand the danger Rome posed by its own constitutional excellence. After their corruption and decline, the once excellent Romans received a taste of their own medicine when the conquering Germanic tribes overran Rome and what remained of commerce in the western empire. Caring little for commerce, the invading Germanic tribes, exercising their equal right of nations, seized Roman lands most suitable for the herding of animals.[109] The modern examples of commercial power Montesquieu brings into view only reinforce this dismal picture. The Portuguese and Spanish trading systems, far from bringing enlightenment and peace, were built upon brutal conquests and maintained by trading monopolies highly unfavorable to their colonial acquisitions and to rival commercial powers.[110] Once the leader in maritime exploration, the Portuguese would eventually discover the right of nations to be a scourge as the Dutch in their greed would displace the Portuguese through a mightier exercise of their equal right.[111] Repeatedly, Montesquieu presents an Ovidian world of metamorphosis in which an equal Hobbesian right of nations prevails to the advantage of those of unequaled excellence in military prowess and political statecraft. Commercial nations cannot presume a restraining benevolence or legalism in the actions of other commercial nations; even worse, a commercial nation might encounter a power such as the Romans, the Germanic tribes, or the Tartars unconcerned about commerce but driven by a glorious lust for conquest and plunder.[112]

The impending danger of the universe disintegrating into the extremes of chaos or despotism pervades Montesquieu's political science from the *Persian Letters* through *The Spirit of the Laws*. Neither the natural equality of human beings nor the civic excellence of the ancient Romans presents a desirable guidepost for the human escape from the fundamental precariousness of the human condition. Enlightened science had revealed by Montesquieu's time a world devoid of divine logos, leaving man dependent on his own artful contrivances productive of a humane life within a naturally hostile world.[113] Montesquieu's great achievement was the founding of a novel science of politics—the long sought "*Italiam, Italiam*"[114] of his extensive intellectual travels—which sought to reveal the chain of causation descriptive of the birth, growth, and death of political bodies, all the while marveling at the variety of human experience in history as forms changed into other forms in an impermanent Ovidian world of metamorphosis. In this world of relentless motion tending to unravel the equilibrium necessary to civilized life, Montesquieu subordinated prescriptive counsels of progressive reform to the descriptive science that he begot without a mother. To steer the divine chariot of statesmanship too high or too low in the pursuit of excellence or equality would, for Montesquieu, abandon the prudent moderation his realistic science of politics counseled.[115] Like the good astronomer, the wise statesman and the scientific scholar should find the sun's position and take their bearings amid the motion of all things from the existing imperfect constitutions of political life.[116]

Notes

1. Thomas L. Pangle, *Montesquieu's Philosophy of Liberalism* (Chicago: University of Chicago Press), 17, 20–21; Judith Shklar, *Montesquieu* (Oxford: Oxford University Press, 1987), 69; Isaiah Berlin, *Against the Current* (Princeton: Princeton University Press, 2001), 131; Anne M. Cohler, *Montesquieu's Comparative Politics and the Spirit of American Constitutionalism* (Lawrence: University of Kansas Press, 1988), 1, 5; David Carrithers, "Introduction," in *Montesquieu's Science of Politics*, ed. David W. Carrithers, Michael A. Mosher, and Paul A. Rahe (Lanham, MD: Rowman and Littlefield, 2001), 7; George Sabine, *A History of Political Theory* (New York: Holt, Rinehart, and Winston, 1961), 551; J. Robert Loy, *Montesquieu* (New York: Twayne, 1968), 130, 135, 147; Diana J. Schaub, *Erotic Liberalism: Women and Revolution in Montesquieu's Persian Letters* (Lanham, MD: Rowman and Littlefield, 1995), 144–45; Paul Rahe, *Montesquieu and the Logic of Liberty* (New Haven: Yale University Press, 2009), 88.

2. *De L'Esprit Des Lois*, VI, 30.2 in *Oeuvres Completes* (Paris: Gallimard, 1956); Peter V. Conroy Jr., *Montesquieu Revisited* (New York: Twayne, 1992), 14–16, 82.

3. *Lettres Persanes* in *Oeuvres Completes*, XLVIII; Loy, 17, 26, 29; Robert Shackleton, *Montesquieu* (Oxford: Oxford University Press), 1961, 46, 55–57, 68–9, 82–5, 171, 178–90, 193–96; Conroy, 85; Rahe, *Logic of Liberty*, 94.

4. *Lettres Persanes*, VIII, XX, XXII, XXVI, XXVII, XXXI–XXXII, XXXV, LXXVIII, LXX–LXXI; Conroy, 13, 29, 31, 36, 40–41, 63–64; Cohler, 3; Loy, 55; Schaub, 134; Rahe, *Logic of Liberty*, 90.

5. *Lettres Persanes*, II–VII, IX, XV, XIX–XXII, CIII, CXIV, CXV, CXLI, CL; Schaub, 19.

6. *Lettres Persanes*, XXIII, XXVI, XXXIV, XXXVIII, XLVIII, LV, LXIII, LXX, LXXI, LXXXVII, XCIX, C, CVII, CX; Catherine Larrere, "Montesquieu on Economy and Commerce," in *Montesquieu's Science of Politics*, ed. Carrithers, Mosher, and Rahe, 345; Andrea Radasanu, "Montesquieu on Moderation, Monarchy, and Reform," *History of Political Thought*, 31, no. 2 (Summer 2010): 289.

7. *Lettres Persanes*, XXIII, XXVI, XXXIV, XXXVIII, XLVIII, LV, LXIII, LV, LXIII, LXX, LXXI, LXXXVII–VIII, XCII, XCIX, C, CVII, CX; Rahe, *Logic of Liberty*, 16–18; Schaub, 124.

8. Loy, 110; Rahe, *Forms of Government*, 85, 96–97; Rahe, *Logic of Liberty*, 41, 5; Schaub, 60–61.

9. *Lettres Persanes*, XXIV, XXXVI–VII, XLVIII, LIV, LVIII, LXIII, LXXIII–IV, LXXXIII, LXXXVII–VIII, XCII, XCVIII–IX, LVC, CVII, CIX, CXI, CXXVII, CXXXII, CXXXVIII, CXL, CXLV, CXLIX.

10. *Lettres Persanes*, II–IV, VII, LXII, LXIV, LXV.

11. *Lettres Persanes*, XXVI, LXIV–LXV, XCVI, CXLVII–CLXI; Conroy, 34–35; Thomas L. Pangle, *The Theological Basis of Liberal Modernity* (Chicago: University of Chicago Press, 2010), 33

12. Loy, 20; Schaub, 9, 41, 60–61, 122; Larrere, "Montesquieu on Economy and Commerce," 345.

13. *Lettres Persanes*, XII–XIV, XVI, LXIX, LXXVI; Conroy, 25; Pangle, *Theological Basis*, 13.

14. *Lettres Persanes*, XXXV.

15. Thomas Hobbes, *Leviathan*, Part I: Of Man, chs. 13–14, Part II: Of Commonwealth, ch. 20; Mosher, "Monarchy's Paradox," in *Montesquieu's Science of Politics*, ed. Carrithers, Mosher, and Rahe, 217.

16. *Lettres Persanes*, LXXXIII; *De L'Esprit Des Lois*, I.1.3.

17. Hobbes, *Leviathan*, Part II: Of Commonwealth, chs. 17–18.

18. *De L'Esprit Des Lois*, I.1.2; *Lettres Persanes*, XII; Loy, 60–61; Schaub, X–XI, 22; Cohler, 44, 48.

19. *De L'Esprit Des Lois*, I.2–3; Schaub, 93–99; Pangle, *Theological Basis*, 21–22; C. P. Courtney, "Natural Law," in *Montesquieu's Science of Politics*, ed. Carrithers, Mosher, and Rahe, 51–52.

20. *Lettres Persanes*, XVII–XVIII; Conroy, 12; Schaub, 46; Mosher, "Monarchy's Paradox," 170.

21. *Lettres Persanes*, X.

22. *Lettres Persanes*, XI; Cohler, 26–27; Pangle, *Theological Basis*, 34.

23. *Lettres Persanes*, XVI, CXLIII; Cohler, 8; Pangle, *Theological Basis*, 5,44, 66; Rebecca Kingston, "Montesquieu on Religion and the Question of Toleration," in *Montesquieu's Science of Politics*, ed. Carrithers, Mosher, and Rahe 378, 386.

24. *Lettres Persanes*, XXIV, XXIX, XXXV, XLVI, XLIX, LVII, LX–LXI, LXXV, LXXXV, CI, CXV–CXXI, CXXXIV; Loy, 15–16; Conroy, 20–22, 73, 101; Schaub, 41–44.

25. Pierre Manent, *An Intellectual History of Liberalism* (Princeton: Princeton University Press, 1994), 52.

26. Manent, 52; Andrea Radasanu, "Montesquieu on Monarchy, Moderation, and Reform," *History of Political Thought* 31, No. 2: 288.

27. *Considerations Sur Les Causes De Les Grandeur Des Romans Et De Leur Decadence*, I, III, VI; David Lowenthal, trans., *Considerations on the Causes of the Greatness of the Romans and Their Decline*, "Introduction," (Ithaca: Free Press), 13; Courtney, "Natural Law," 49; Schaub, 28.

28. *Considerations*, II, III, VI; Esprit, II, 10.14; Pangle, *Theological Basis*, 71; David Carrithers, "Democratic and Aristocratic Republics," in *Montesquieu's Science of Politics*, 135; Rahe, "Forms of Government" in David W. Carrithers, Michael A. Mosher, and Paul A. Rahe, *Montesquieu's Science of Politics*, ed. Carrithers, Mosher, and Rahe, 74–75, 92; Rahe, *Logic of Liberty*, 31, 73.

29. *Considerations*, I, V–VI, IX; *De L'Esprit Des Lois*, II, 10.14; Conroy, 65–66.

30. *De L'Esprit Des Lois*, II.11.15; Pangle, *Theological Basis*, 83–84, 139–40; Rahe, "Forms of Government," 75; Rahe, *Logic of Liberty*, 29.

31. *Considerations*, VIII; Rahe, *Logic of Liberty*, 92; Carrithers, "Democratic and Aristocratic Republics," 112; Schaub, 19; Pangle, *Theological Basis*, 70–71.

32. *Considerations*, I–II, IX; Conroy, 67; Loy, 65; Mosher, 201.

33. *Considerations*, V–VI; *De L'Esprit Des Lois*, II.11.19.

34. *Considerations*, XI; *De L'Esprit Des Lois*, III.19.25, VI. 27 (only chapter); Pangle, *Spirit of Modern Liberalism*, 5; Pangle, *Theological* Basis, 70; Carrithers, "Democratic and Aristocratic Republics," 121; Rahe, "Forms of Government," 73–75.

35. *Considerations*, I, II, VII, IX, XI.

36. *Considerations*, XI–XII.

37. *Considerations*, XII; Loy, 67.

38. *Considerations*, X, XVIII.

39. *Considerations*, XVIII–XIX; *De L'Esprit Des Lois*, IV.23.23; VI.30.5–8.

40. *De L'Esprit Des Lois*, Tome II, Preface, 231; Conroy, 71, 103; Loy, 25, 64.

41. *De L'Esprit Des Lois*, I.3.1, II.2.5, III.14.1, III.14.10, VI.28.28; Carrithers, 113; Courtney, "Natural Law," 49, 53–54; Courtney, "English Liberty," 279; Cohler, 5, 38, 68; Conroy, 101; Rahe, *Logic of Liberty*, 36.

42. *De L'Esprit Des Lois*, 227 (my translation); Courtney, 41; Cohler, 33; Conroy, 61.

43. *De L'Esprit Des Lois*, II.11.6; Courtney, "Natural Law," 60; Loy, 132–35; Schaub, 134; Rahe, *Forms of Government*, 77.

44. Jean-Jacques Rousseau, *Du Contract Social*, in *Oeuvres Completes* (Paris: Gallimard, 1964), Tome III, 351 (my translation).

45. Rousseau, *Discours Sur L'Origine Et Les Fondemens De L'Inegalite Parmi Les Hommes* in *Oeuvres Completes*, Tome III, 123, 132; *De L'Esprit Des Lois*, II. 11.4; III.19.6 (my translations); VI.29.1; Loy, 29, 118–119; Pangle, *Theological Basis*, 23, 82; Carrithers, "Democratic and Aristocratic Republics," 112, 135–36; Mosher, "Monarchy's Paradox," 161.

46. *De L'Esprit Des Lois*, I.1.3; III. 14.10; III.19.14; Berlin, 138; Shklar, 72; Courtney, "Natural Law," 51, 55; Pangle, *Philosophy of Liberalism*, 6–7, 9; Pangle, *Theological Basis*, 23–24; Rahe, *Forms of Government*, 70.

47. Conroy, 91; Mosher, 205–207.

48. Loy, 110; Carrithers, "Democratic and Aristocratic Republics," 109–11, 115, 134; Mosher, "Monarchy's Paradox," 162–63, 176; Pangle, *Theological Basis*, 66, 135–36; Manent, 52.

49. *Lettres Persanes*, C, CXXXI; *De L'Esprit Des Lois*, VI.28.45.

50. *Lettres Persanes*, XIX, LI, LXI, CXXII; *De L 'Esprit Des Lois*, I.6.9;,II.11.6; Rahe, "Forms of Government," 77; Cohler, 5–7; Pangle, *Theological Basis*, 77, 81.

51. *De L 'Esprit Des Lois*, VI. 30.2–6,14,24; VI.31.4.

52. *De L 'Esprit Des Lois*, III.18.24.

53. *De L 'Esprit Des Lois*, VI.24.30; VI.31.4–5,9; Cohler, 32.

54. *De L 'Esprit Des Lois*, VI.31.5–7.

55. *De L 'Esprit Des Lois*, VI.31.21.

56. Machiavelli, *The Prince*, chs. VI, XII, XV, XVII–VIII, XXVI; Rousseau, *Emile, Oeuvres Completes*, Tome IV, Book I, 249–51; Rahe, *Logic of Liberty*, 94.

57. *De L 'Esprit Des Lois, I.4.4*; Carrithers, "Democratic and Aristocratic Republics," 136; Rahe, *Logic of Liberty*, 92–93.

58. *De L 'Esprit Des Lois*, III.15.7; III.15.19; Carrithers, "Democratic and Aristocratic Republics," 116–17, 138; Shklar, 36–37, 62.

59. *Lettres Persanes*, XCIII, CXVI, CXVII; Cohler, 24; Schaub, 57; Pangle, *Theological Basis*, 56–57.

60. *Lettres Persanes*, LXXV; *De L 'Esprit Des Lois,* I.1.3, V.24.1–2; Pangle, *Theological Basis*, 44–47, 59, 64, 76; Kingston, 379; Cohler, 50.

61. *Lettres Persanes*, LXXXV; *De L' Esprit Des Lois*, III.15.7; Cohler, 9, 24, 55; Conroy, 73, 94; Pangle, *Theological Basis*, 25, 34, 64; Kingston, 378, 391.

62. *De L 'Esprit Des Lois,* III. 19.4–5,10,14; VI.30.11, VI.31.2,9; Cohler, 9, 24.

63. *De L 'Esprit Des Lois*, VI.30.3–4,11,19,24; VI.31.4; Cohler, 32.

64. *De L 'Esprit Des Lois*, VI.30.3–4,12,19; VI.31.2,4,6.

65. *De L 'Esprit Des Lois*, VI.31.2 (Translations to all quotations, except notes 42 and 45, from Montesquieu *De L 'Esprit Des Lois* are taken from Montesquieu, *The Spirit of the Laws*, ed. and trans. Anne Cohler, Basia Miller, and Harold Stone (Cambridge: Cambridge University Press, 1989).

66. *De L 'Esprit Des Lois*, VI.31.18, Tome II, 968; Cohler, 62.

67. *De L 'Esprit Des Lois*, VI.31.18.

68. *De L 'Esprit Des Lois*, VI.31.20–21.

69. *De L 'Esprit Des Lois*, VI.31.20–21.

70. *De L 'Esprit Des Lois*, VI.31.23, Tome II, 975.

71. *De L 'Esprit Des Lois*, VI.31.23.

72. *De L 'Esprit Des Lois*, VI.30.20; VI,31.25; VI.31.32; Cohler, 61.

73. *De L 'Esprit Des Lois*, VI.30.20; VI.31.25; VI.31.28; VI.31.32; Cohler, 32.

74. *Lettres Persanes*, XCVII; Conroy, 45, 101; Loy, 52–54; Sharon Krause, "Despotism," in *Montesquieu's Science of Politics*, ed. Carrithers, Mosher, and Rahe, 252.

140 | Frank J. Rohmer

75. *De L'Esprit Des Lois*, VI.28.28; VI.28.38; VI.30.1; VI.30.14; Conroy, 12; Loy, 25, 64.
76. *De L'Esprit Des Lois*, VI.28.4, VI.28.6, VI.28.18–45; VI.30.11.
77. *Lettres Persanes*, CXIII; *De L'Esprit Des Lois*, VI.28.1; Cohler, 33; Schaub, 135; Rahe, "Forms of Government," 84.
78. *De L'Esprit Des Lois*, III.19.21; VI.28.39; VI.28.42; Cohler, 30, 62.
79. *De L'Esprit Des Lois*, VI.28.39; VI.28.4.
80. *De L'Esprit Des Lois*, VI.28.28; VI.28.37; VI.28.42; VI.30.19.
81. *De L'Esprit Des Lois*, III.18.24; VI.26.6; VI.31.3; VI.31.9; Cohler, 65; Pangle, *Theological Basis*, 74.
82. *De L'Esprit Des Lois*, VI.28.15–45.
83. *De L'Esprit Des Lois*, II.11.8; Cohler, 65; Loy, 103; Schaub, 149; Pangle, *Theological Basis*, 58; Carrithers, "Democratic and Aristocratic Republics," 140–44; Mosher, "Monarchy's Paradox," 173, 181.
84. *Lettres Persanes*, XXI, XXXVII, XCII, CXL, CXLVIII, CL; Pangle, *Theological Basis*, 58–59, 61.
85. Radasanu, 290–92, 294, 298.
86. Radasanu, 302, 306.
87. *De L'Esprit Des Lois*, III.19.27; Radasanu, 301.
88. *De L'Esprit Des Lois*, III.19.27; Loy, 163; Rahe, *Logic of Liberty*, 84, 96–7.
89. *De L'Esprit Des Lois*, IV.21.6.
90. *De L'Esprit Des Lois*, IV.21.7.
91. *De L'Esprit Des Lois*, IV.21.7.
92. *De L'Esprit Des Lois*, IV.20.4–5; Schaub, 137.
93. *De L'Esprit Des Lois*, IV.21.11.
94. *De L'Esprit Des Lois*, IV.20.2; IV.21.4–6; IV.21.21; Pangle, *Theological Basis*, 101–102.
95. *De L'Esprit Des Lois*, III.19.27; Carrithers, "Democratic and Aristocratic Republics," 128.
96. *De L'Esprit Des Lois*, IV.20.2; Joseph Cropsey, *Polity and Economy* (South Bend: St. Augustine's Press, 2001), 37n79; Cohler, 22; Pangle, *Theological Basis*, 139; Courtney, "English Liberty," in *Montesquieu's Science of Politics*, ed. Carrithers, Mosher, and Rahe, 276.
97. *De L'Esprit Des Lois*, IV.20.2.
98. *De L'Esprit Des Lois*, IV.20.4; IV.20.6.
99. *De L'Esprit Des Lois*, IV.21.21.
100. *De L'Esprit Des Lois*, I.1.3.
101. *De L'Esprit Des Lois*, I.1.3; II.9.9–10; II.10.1–4.
102. *De L'Esprit De Lois*, I.1.3; II.10.1–3.
103. *De L'Esprit Des Lois*, I.1.3; II.10.1–3.
104. *De L'Esprit Des Lois*, I.1.3; Larrere, "Montesquieu on Commerce and Economy," 337–38.

105. *De L 'Esprit Des Lois*, IV.21.11.
106. *De L 'Esprit Des Lois*, IV.21.11.
107. *Considérations*, ch. IV; *De L 'Esprit Des Lois*, IV.21.11.
108. *Considérations*, ch. I; De *L 'Esprit Des Lois*, II.10.14; II.11.5.
109. *De L 'Esprit Des Lois*, VI.30.3–8.
110. *De L 'Esprit Des Lois*, IV.21.21.
111. *Lettres Persanes*, CXXI; De *L 'Esprit Des Lois*, IV.21.21.
112. *Lettres Persanes*, LXXXI; *De L 'Esprit Des Lois*, IV.21.11–16.
113. Conroy, 56; Loy, 56.
114. *De L 'Esprit Des Lois*, VI.31.34; Virgil, *Aeneid*, III.523.
115. *De L 'Esprit Des Lois*, VI.30.10; Carrithers, "Democratic and Aristocratic Republics," 141.
116. *De L 'Esprit Des Lois*, V.26.23; VI.28.15,17–18,23; VI.29.1, 13,16; VI.30.12.

Chapter 8

Equality and Excellence in Rousseau's *Emile*, Book III

PAMELA K. JENSEN

Introduction

Jean Jacques Rousseau's masterwork, *Emile, or On Education*, is a "philosophical novel."[1] It follows its protagonist Emile from birth to marriage. Rousseau presents Emile as the personification of "man in general"; he represents the species writ small.[2] What sets Emile apart from others is not an exceptional mind or extraordinary natural gifts, but his education according to nature. In this respect he is unique. Adopting the persona of Emile's tutor or, preferably, "governor,"[3] Rousseau aims in Book III of *Emile* to give his pupil a love of the sciences and the methods to acquire them. Although he expresses here some of the same hesitation about lifting the veil nature employs to conceal its secrets as he does in the *Discourse on the Sciences and Arts (First Discourse)*, the governor-Rousseau nevertheless effects Emile's enlightenment (*FD*, 13, 21; *E*, 312). Judging by the illustration Rousseau designed to front this chapter of *Emile*, portraying Hermes, mythic inventor of writing, engraving the elements of the sciences on stone columns to protect them from a flood, Book III is also about the transmission and preservation of knowledge. We have then one reason why writing and books are prominent here. Book III also develops the order or hierarchy of the arts and sciences,

143

a task we may consider to be rather the legislator's responsibility than that of the inventor of the art or science.[4]

Ostensibly repudiating Hermes's project along with writing altogether, Rousseau (author of many books) insists: "Well-prepared minds are the surest monuments on which to engrave human knowledge" (*E*, 331). In this respect Rousseau imitates the Socratic repudiation of writing, as presented in Plato's *Phaedrus*, becoming, so to speak, his own Plato.[5] With *Emile* Rousseau has written a book about engraving knowledge on a human mind, in which his imaginary experiment can be repeated countless times.

Ultimately, we should read Book III in the context of the whole *Emile*. At the end of the chapter, looking back with satisfaction at his creation, Rousseau writes: "Emile has little knowledge, but what he has is truly his own. [He] has a mind that is universal not by its learning but by its faculty to acquire learning. With this method one advances little, but one never takes a useless step, and one is not forced to go backward" (*E*, 358). Alluding to the moral component of Emile's education in the sciences, Rousseau says "the games of philosophy" lead naturally in Books IV and V to learning "the true functions of man" (*E*, 323). "We have made an active and thinking being. It remains for us, in order to complete the man, only to make a loving and feeling being—that is to say, to perfect reason by sentiment" (*E*, 353). Nevertheless, it seems important to remember that the sentimental education of Emile rests on its solid intellectual base. Rousseau calls Book III the most "useful" part of *Emile*; it is also the chapter we are likely to find most familiar. Experimental and skills-based educational practices as well as critical thinking are emphasized in contemporary educational theory.[6]

By attending especially to the relationship between Emile and his governor (and between both of them and the author Rousseau, who stands behind them) we may better see the relationship between equality and excellence in Book III. In our day, as part of Rousseau's legacy, effort is made in education at the very least to balance equality or inclusion and excellence, and, in some quarters, to adopt "equity" as a goal, even to the point of depreciating aspirations to excellence. Without compelling him in any way, indeed without speaking of excellence, the governor-Rousseau intensifies Emile's desire to learn by intensifying his curiosity.

Moreover, it is difficult for us to imagine the desire for excellence without competition or comparison to others. By contrast, Emile's own quest for knowledge is meant to be entirely self-motivated. He is to seek what is useful to himself rather than what might make him shine in others' eyes. Further, Emile must submit to no authority nor do anything he doesn't want to do. But there is a catch: "Doubtless he ought to do only what he wants; but he ought to want only what you want him to do" (*E*, 258). It is up to the governor, in other words, to "give birth" to Emile's desires (*E*, 326). And, as much as possible, the governor's rule, while all-encompassing, must be invisible. As Rousseau clarifies, "Let him always believe he is the master, and let it always be you who are. There is no subjection so perfect as that which keeps the appearance of freedom" (*E*, 258).

The educational principles adopted in Book III correspond in nature to the all-too-short interval between late childhood and the onset of puberty (in the book, roughly ages twelve to fifteen). While pointing ominously and emphatically to the turbulent times lying ahead, for which governors must prepare far in advance, Emile's passions are as yet "calm," and he has, like the "savage" Rousseau describes, more faculties and strength than he needs. Looking ahead to Emile's future, the governor says that "the robust child will make provision for the weak man," channeling his surplus of strength into new activities that will always serve him in good stead. "This is the time of labors, of instruction, of study." Rousseau continues: "[I]t is not I who arbitrarily make this choice. It is nature itself that points to it" (*E*, 310).

The goal is not to make Emile in this brief window of time learned, but to preserve him from prejudices and to teach him how to judge the true utility of things.[7] From the perspective of nature—and most importantly— one learns in this way as well how to judge the order of society. For this, Emile will have to be introduced to the state of nature. As Rousseau puts the matter in the *Discourse on the Origins of Inequality (Second Discourse)*, "[I]t is no light undertaking to separate what is original from what is artificial in the present Nature of man, and to know correctly a state which no longer exists, which perhaps never existed, which probably never will exist *and about which it is nevertheless necessary to have precise Notions in order to judge our present state correctly*" (*SD*, 13; emphasis added).

Emile and "the magician-Socrates"

Amour-propre is completely antithetical to Rousseau's educational goals for his imaginary pupil. According to Rousseau, the passion of amour-propre is a form of self-love that arises when we begin to compare ourselves to others. "[T]his sentiment, preferring ourselves to others, also demands others to prefer us to themselves, which is impossible" (*E*, 364). In every-day life we nod to amour-propre when we detect status-seeking in others and especially when we complain about it. The race for status seems to place each in competition with all others. In this circumstance, some might fall prey to envy, while the successful equate happiness with being envied. In either case we become dependent upon the opinions of others to measure the degree of our own happiness and no longer take our bearings by ourselves. Our desire to learn is controlled (and distorted) by the desire for recognition. To nip amour-propre in the bud, the governor-Rousseau arranges for Emile, giddy with a little philosophy, to be publicly humiliated by "the magician-Socrates."[8]

Rousseau begins his story with a defense of himself intended for impatient readers regarding his lengthy, roundabout way of proceeding. He insists on the necessity of details in general and on the importance of each element of this episode in particular. The lesson in question begins with what looks like the opposite of utility—the standard for study employed in Book III. In what seems to be an impromptu bit of entertainment, Emile and the governor idly play around with magnetic attraction, noting how iron can be magnetized. "How long this quality entertains us without our being able to see anything more in it!" (*E*, 318). To enjoy the game Emile doesn't need to put forth much effort, but the governor-Rousseau has also insisted that boredom must at all costs be prevented. Magnetism must be shown to Emile to have a use.

With no apparent aim in mind, Emile and the governor drop in on a fair, where they see the magician attract a wax duck, which is floating in a shallow tub of water, with a piece of bread. The spectators are meant to think they see something wondrous, but Emile and his governor don't believe in magic and are merely curious. After discussing the puzzle at home, they are prompted to imitate the magician. They make their own wax duck, put a magnetized needle in it, and successfully attract it by using a magnetized key.

The intoxicated Emile is so eager to show off that as soon as he learns the first truth about magnets, he and his governor rush back to the fair the same day. Apparently sharing Emile's barely controllable enthusiasm, the governor deliberately leads Emile to think he is wiser about magnetism than he is, setting him up for a big fall.[9]

At the fair, Emile challenges the magician, boldly asserting that "this trick is not difficult and that he himself will do as much" (*E*, 318). Pulling from his pocket his own magnet hidden in some bread, he performs as well as the magician. The crowd applauds wildly and Emile gets "dizzy." The governor whisks Emile away covered with glory. The magician invites him

Equality and Excellence in Rousseau's *Emile*, Book III | 147

to come back the next day, promising to gather an even larger audience to applaud his skill. Every move Emile makes the following day, however, repels rather than attracts the duck. No matter how hard he tries, nothing works, and instead of applauding, the crowd jeers and mocks him. Even when Emile uses the magician's own piece of bread, the duck resists him. The *coup de grace* comes when the magician apparently demonstrates that he can command the duck's movements with his voice alone. Deflation complete, Emile and the governor quickly escape to their rooms, utterly ashamed and humiliated and probably with the intention of never trying to do anything further with the duck or magnets. But that is just the beginning of the story.

With Emile's humiliation Rousseau apparently means to show how to suppress the desire to learn or know out of vanity or amour-propre, that is to say, for the sake of praise or honor alone. Yet it is also possible to suppress or even destroy a nascent curiosity altogether by associating it with shame or dishonor—to punish Emile for *trying* to learn and, in the process to incense him against the person who demeans him. This requires "the magician-Socrates" not only to debunk Emile's claim to wisdom, for which Socrates is famous, but also to nurture his desire to learn. Emile must become attuned to his own ignorance, but not at the cost of losing his interest in the sciences.

As if on his own, "the magician-Socrates" appears the next morning on their doorstep. He complains, but "modestly." He candidly admits that his life is devoted to something quite petty, but it is the only way he can earn a living. "Magic" is his trade. As a proficient in this lowly art, with skills well-honed during a lifetime of practice, he has even more tricks up his sleeve to stop silly would-be rivals who have merely dabbled in it. Then, changing tone somewhat, the magician entreats Emile and the governor not to take away his only means of subsistence merely for the honor of exposing him as a charlatan or trickster (*E*, 320; cf. 342). This particular complaint is meant to alert Emile, who is an aristocrat by birth, to the lowly people who must work to live. Later in Book III Emile himself learns the trade of carpentry, not so much in order to earn a living but so that he will not despise trades and will respect the dignity of work, that is, so that he and his governor may "raise ourselves to the station of carpenter" (*E*, 351). Apart from the moral lesson, this aspect of the episode also provides a convenient excuse for those who write books: it is or can be a means of earning a living.

No more than Socrates does "the magician-Socrates" teach his lessons for pay. "I leave you obliged to me in spite of yourselves. It is my only vengeance. Learn that there is generosity in every station. I get paid for my tricks and not my lessons" (*E*, 320). Thus, he says, "I come out of the goodness of my heart to teach you the secret that perplexed you so" (*E*, 320). The magician-Socrates imparts to Emile and the governor an esoteric truth, taking them behind the scenes. Producing a large lodestone to show his new students, he explains that a child hidden under the table simply moved the magnet in response to the magician's orders. The magician merely deceived the eye of the untutored audience.

Emile's experience of philosophic generosity has an importance far beyond the little drama being enacted here. It may also explain why the magician is explicitly identified with Socrates just at this point (*E*, 321). This part of the story points to the governor-Rousseau's regard for Emile's education, but also responds to the need to insulate philosophy from criticism. The episode in effect creates a conspiracy among the knowers. Emile is initiated into a small but important secret society, establishing a basis for friendship between philosophers and non-philosophers. Having agreed to keep "Socrates's" secrets, an enlightened Emile and the governor once again appear at the fair. Underlining the importance of this episode to Rousseau the philosopher, Rousseau as governor sternly writes, "If [Emile] dared so much as to open his mouth, he would deserve to be annihilated" (*E*, 321).

The final part of Rousseau's little drama is the prearranged scolding of the governor by "the magician-Socrates"; an admonition to attend to his responsibilities to Emile. He must warn his charge against making avoidable mistakes that will come back to haunt the governor when the child is grown. Knowing that his relationship with Emile must change, and that in the future he will have to exert more explicit control over his pupil, the apparently chastened governor-Rousseau promises in front of Emile to heed the warning; in truth, the governor accepts it as a secret treasure given well in advance of the likely rainy day (*E*, 320).

In a critical review of *Emile*, a well-known man of letters dismisses out of hand the episode recounted here; it is entirely implausible, a mere fantasy. In the second edition of *Emile*, an amused Rousseau replies to him that of course he prearranged every feature of the entire story, from beginning to end; nothing so important could be left to chance.[10] "[I]ndeed, I did not say so. But on the other hand, how many times have I declared that I did not write for people who have to be told everything?" (*E*, 748; ed. n6). Like the magician's invisible assistant, Rousseau the writer is the invisible motor of the whole episode; he tells his critic that the magician was of course "instructed about the role he had to play"; he does not say that the magician himself is, in fact, a figment of Rousseau's imagination.

Emile and *Robinson Crusoe*

Following the episode with "the magician-Socrates," we are told that Emile's amour-propre will remain dormant "for a long time." In addition to this ostensible theme, the successful resolution of the matter without in any way dampening or impeding Emile's curiosity allows the scientific education to proceed apace. Indeed, the governor and Emile simply pick up where they left off. They make the magic trick truly useful, delving more deeply into the study of magnetism and finally producing or at least conceptualizing a compass. From there they proceed to physics (*E*, 321–22). Referring to the order of their objects of study, Rousseau says he doesn't follow the chain of the sciences philosophers use, but instead the chain linking one science to another that most people use. That is to say, while studying magnetism, the text enacts the magnetic attraction of one study to another, such that each thing calls forth the next, with the aim of fixing the order of the sciences and ensuing experiments in Emile's memory (*E*, 317, 323).

A little later, Rousseau describes two failed experiments he did with "a child" that convince without persuading.[11] "It is easy to prove to a child that what one wants to teach / him is useful; but to prove it is nothing if one does not know / how to persuade him. In vain does tranquil reason make us / approve or criticize; it is only passion which makes us act—and how can one get passionate about interests one does / not yet have?" (*E*, 331).

The governor's turn to the novel *Robinson Crusoe* reveals, however, not only that in order to *persuade,* poetry and an appeal to the imagination are necessary, but also that a kind of amour-propre must be smuggled back into Emile's education in another guise. To avoid any rivalry or competition between Emile and his governor, Rousseau establishes a rivalry between Emile and Robinson Crusoe. The novel provides the necessary "stimulant" to awaken and sustain Emile's curiosity, making him willing to put forth the considerable effort needed to acquire sound intellectual and manual skills (*E*, 331). At the same time, Emile can expend his amour-propre harmlessly on an imaginary being.

After abruptly announcing "I hate books," which "only teach one to talk about what one does not know," shortly Rousseau just as abruptly reverses himself. "Since we absolutely must have books, there exists one which, to my taste, provides the most felicitous treatise on natural education . . . *Robinson Crusoe*" (*E*, 332). Robinson Crusoe finds himself alone and "lacking the instruments of all the arts." In his situation we can see all our natural needs, and, in addition, "the means of providing for these needs emerge in order" (*E*, 331). As a castaway from civilization, marooned on a desert island, Robinson, so to speak, returns to the state of nature. "[I]t is by the lively and naïve depiction of this state that the first exercise must be given to [Emile's] imagination" (*E*, 331).

In its heavily redacted version as Rousseau describes it, *Robinson Crusoe* looks like a child's version of *Emile*; as a work meant for "few Readers" *Emile* is perhaps less "felicitous" than a child-friendly edition of *Robinson Crusoe*.[12]

While admitting that this state is unlikely to be Emile's (*E*, 332), its importance cannot be overestimated. It establishes the fundamental principle of the natural education, that is, the natural standard and its implications for judging the order of society. "But it is on the basis of this very state that he ought to appraise all the others." Rousseau continues: "The surest means of raising oneself above prejudices and ordering one's judgments about the true relations of things is to put oneself in the place of an isolated man and to judge everything as this man himself *ought* to judge of it with respect to his own utility" (*E*, 332; emphasis added). We might say that, by comparison to the *Discourse on the Origins of Inequality (Second Discourse)*, Emile must begin to see rather how the species ought to have developed than how it actually developed (*SD*, 19–20).

Rousseau says that as soon as the child begins to reason, the governor must be on guard against amour-propre. "Moreover, let there never be any comparisons with other children, no rivals, no competitors, not even in running" (*E*, 331). It is imperative that nothing Emile learns be motivated by "jealousy or vanity" (*E*, 331). To avoid such comparisons while nevertheless providing a needed "stimulant" to animate Emile's efforts, he is encouraged by his governor to become his own competitor: "However, every year I shall note the progress he has made; I shall compare it to that which he will make the following year. Thus I arouse him without making him jealous of anyone. He will want to outdo himself. He ought to. I see no problem in his being his own competitor" (*E*, 331). However sound the notion of becoming his own competitor is, it will not entirely solve the problem. A child with as few needs as Emile has might just as easily incline to rest on his laurels, looking backward, as voluntarily to put in all the effort required to continue improving his skills and abilities. As the governor-Rousseau himself explains, "I imperceptibly give my pupil, with the habit of exercising his body and of manual labor, the taste for reflection and meditation. This counterbalances in him the idleness which would result from his indifference to men's judgments and from the calm of his passions. He must work like a peasant and think like a philosopher so as not to be as lazy as a savage" (*E*, 352–53).

Competition with others would seem to work just as well, if not better, as a "stimulant," incentivizing, by the prospect of winning, the dedication required to advance. Nor do we usually regard such competition, which can generate, along with hope of victory, camaraderie, and mutual respect, to be ill-advised. But Rousseau is adamant. His turn to books is an admission that an alternative "stimulant" is necessary to motivate and sustain Emile's curiosity. Emile needs someone else to compare himself to, and the most obvious choice is also the most risky one—not "other children," but the governor. To prevent the dangerous competition between Emile and his governor, which threatens to issue in a power dynamic or battle of wills between them that might derail everything, Emile's attention must be diverted.

Even the question greeting Emile at every turn as the watchword of this part of his education—"What is that good for?"—is meant to leave the governor "less exposed" than otherwise (*E*, 326). Nothing must encourage the pupil to spy out the governor's weaknesses or to take pleasure in seeing him tongue-tied. The governor can always profess ignorance in response to Emile's question about the utility of something and change the subject. If he does talk, the governor must be careful to answer his pupil's questions only with reasons he can understand and must speak only of things that are useful for his age. "In thinking about what can be useful to him at another age, speak to him only about things whose utility he sees right now" (*E*, 331). This, Rousseau writes is "perhaps the most difficult trap for a governor to avoid" (*E*, 325). Rousseau warns other young governors: "If at the child's question you seek only to get out of it and give him a single reason he is not in a condition to understand, he will see that you reason according to your ideas and not his and will believe that what you tell him is good for your age and not for his. He will no longer rely on you, and all is lost" (*E*, 325–26). Extraordinary care must be taken to prevent even the barest suspicion on Emile's part that the governor's interests diverge, however slightly, from his own. To this end, Rousseau says that the governor will gain more credit with the pupil by admitting to failings he does not have than by insisting on his superiority in wisdom. The student may ask many questions, but the governor is always free to say "I don't know" when he cannot provide an answer that will keep Emile's attention on things and not on the governor, that is to say, the governor's will. The reason Rousseau gives—to the effect that otherwise children will pummel their governors endlessly with silly questions, for instance, "Why is the sky blue?"—is only a bit of the story. The governor must always be alert to the motive of the child's questions; if he is merely "subjecting you to his interrogation," the conversation must cease (*E*, 317). At bottom, a fear lurks that Emile will become too sensitive to the governor's rule or authority over him. Emile's feeling of perfect freedom could be shattered. *Robinson Crusoe* lets the governor off the hook.

As governor, Rousseau does not plant Emile on a real desert island or leave him to fend for himself. Emile is to imagine himself as Robinson Crusoe, not actually to live like him. Less than reading it, Emile uses the novel as a prompt-book or script for an all-engrossing but supervised game of make-believe; the novel is his entire "entertainment and instruction" for this period (*E*, 332). "I want him to learn in detail, not from books but from things all that must be known in such a situation; I want him to think he is Robinson himself, to see himself dressed in skins, wearing a large cap, carrying a large saber[13] and all the rest of the character's grotesque equipment, with the exception of the parasol, which he will not need" (*E*, 332).

Emile is transfixed, even obsessed, by his imaginary life. Much of the "action" occurs, though, as in a seminar, in conversations with the governor. "The child, in a hurry to set up a storehouse for his island, will be more ardent for learning than is the master for teaching. He will want to know all that is useful and he will want to know only that. You will not need to guide him; you will have only to restrain him" (*E*, 333).

Nor does Emile accept his rival's choices uncritically as if they are authoritative. "I want him . . . to examine his Hero's conduct; to investigate whether he omitted anything, whether there was nothing to do better; to note Robinson's failings attentively; and to profit from them so as not to fall into them himself in such a situation" (*E*, 332). We can certainly expect Emile to quarrel with some of Robinson's priorities, for example, his eagerness to secure the tobacco and rum taken from the shipwreck. In the main, though, Emile has found his "'castle in Spain,'" the treasure island of his daydreams—the regime he has founded and where he passionately wants someday to go. "For do not doubt that he is planning to go and set up a similar establishment" (*E*, 332).[14]

As if a father had been listening to the governor-Rousseau's conversation, an objection is made on Rousseau's own grounds, with the father in effect asking, "What is that good for?" That is to say, what is the utility of this "imaginary order," this imaginary republic? (*E*, 334) He calls the time Emile spends with the novel useless, if not harmful, and in a manner that calls Machiavelli to mind: "And many have imagined republics and principalities that have never been seen or known to exist in truth; for it is so far from how one lives to how one should live that he who lets go of what is done for what should be done learns his ruin rather than his preservation."[15] The almost irate parent basically complains that Rousseau's own book is a kind of "castle in Spain" that ill prepares a young person for the true way of the world. Since he will not be living with wise men but with "madmen," he needs to learn how to get them to do what serves his interests. "The real knowledge of things may be good, but that of men and their judgments is even more valuable, for in human society the greatest instrument of man is man, and the wisest is he who best makes use of this instrument" (*E*, 334). The complaint further asserts that there is no point in giving children an idea of an order that is entirely opposed to the established one according to which they must govern themselves; why waste time with cities in speech or model cities?

Rousseau in turn complains about the specious maxims and "false prudence" of fathers and makes a case for his approach. Such parents, he avers, merely make their children slaves of prejudice; the playthings of those whom they seek to control. Rousseau doesn't endorse Machiavelli's advice, but neither does he exactly denounce it. He merely denies that the worldly-wise types can achieve their aims. Precisely because Emile does not resemble others, he is best suited to lead. There is a proper route to knowing and managing people without imitating their weaknesses. But Emile must first be given a standard or yardstick to *evaluate* worldly sentiments. To note the jarring contrast between the proper order of things and current conditions is the ultimate purpose of the comparison. "It is thus that he will know how to compare the opinion to the truth and to raise himself above the vulgar; for one does not know prejudices when one adopts them, and one does not lead the people when one resembles them" (*E*, 335). Rousseau uses a phrase that clearly points to the Socratic enterprise, that is, the dialectical ascent from opinion to knowledge. Rousseau suggests that in the end Emile will be endowed with a rare practical wisdom or prudence (*E*, 649). But neither Emile nor the reader is as yet ready for the study of politics. Politics only appears in Book V, toward the end of the whole *Emile*.[16] Thus, Rousseau adroitly changes the subject. "[Emile] is still almost only a physical being. Let us continue to treat him as such" (*E*, 335).

The governor says that he never permits Emile to go far into the sciences (*E*, 358). If Emile resembled those teachers under whom (via the governor) he learns, those "preceptors of the human race," spoken of in the *First Discourse*, namely, [Bacon], Descartes, and Newton, it would not be possible to hold him back (*FD*, 21). Not even the best education can produce genius. But if he is not in training for a theoretical life, a life of philosophy, Emile's superiority in the practical realm will become evident. Throughout Book III, Rousseau reminds readers several times that his aim is not to make Emile learned, but to make him judicious (*E*, 341).[17] In the end, the distinction between philosophers and non-philosophers is maintained. It is in the friendship between philosophers and non-philosophers that we may see what is for Rousseau the most important reconciliation of equality and the highest excellence.

Emile's education in Book III is undergirded by what we might call a "noble lie." With benevolent intent, the governor-Rousseau imbues Emile with the myth that, apart from natural necessity, he is perfectly free. When Emile is older, the governor is more forthcoming. In revealing his constant labors on his pupil's behalf, the governor presents himself to the young man Emile as his most steadfast confidant and friend. These very bonds of affection between them form the new chains on which the governor relies to complete his pupil's education (*E*, 402, 484–87).

Rousseau and "the magician-Socrates"

We can discern a kind of kinship between "the magician-Socrates" and Rousseau. One of the magician's admonitions to the governor and Emile is that one should not be in a hurry to show off one's wisdom. "If I did not show you my master strokes right off, it is because one ought not to be in a hurry to show off giddily what one knows" (*E*, 320). The comment is reminiscent of Rousseau's own hesitation reflected in the *First Discourse* not to lay out his "system" or fundamental principles immediately. As the magician-Socrates puts it: "I am always careful to keep my best tricks for the proper occasion" (*E*, 320). By so acting, the magician who is identified with Socrates may have regard for his own self-preservation, as might Rousseau. In one of his published replies to critics of the *First Discourse*, Rousseau says, "Some precautions were thus at first necessary for me, and it is in order to be able to make everything understood that I did not wish to say everything. It was only gradually and always for few Readers that I developed my ideas" (*FD*, 184).[18]

In keeping with Rousseau's practice of shielding philosophy from criticism, being fully aware of the consequences of forgetting one's own self-preservation, the episode with "the magician-Socrates" serves as an excellent example of how to protect philosophy from the anger of those who might feel aggrieved by an encounter with a clever speaker, perhaps accusing him of being a sophist and making the weaker argument the stronger, or even of corrupting the youth.[19] Emile's first reaction to being bested by the "magician-Socrates" is an outburst of anger—momentarily blaming his own mortification on the magician, whom he accuses of cheating and of deceiving him (*E*, 319). In the episode itself not only is Emile's anger mollified, as discussed above, Emile and the governor in fact make an alliance with "the magician-Socrates."

To clarify his prudent care for philosophy and for his own freedom, we can consider here as well Rousseau's invocation in the *First Discourse* of the dead Fabricius (*FD*, 11); employing a rhetorical device called a "prosopopeia." Rousseau draws his account of Fabricius from Plutarch's "life" of Pyrrhus.[20] Notably, he excises from Plutarch's story the vehement attack Fabricius makes on Greek and in particular on Epicurean, that is, highly irreligious, philosophy.[21] In the midst of war Fabricius was sent on a diplomatic mission to the Samnites, where he met with their King Pyrrhus. Cineas, another guest, "by accident" opened the controversial discussion of philosophy with Fabricius and Pyrrhus, who had been trying to intimidate the rustic Roman. Although he is unmoved by ostentatious shows of Samnite wealth or even by the sudden appearance of an elephant, Fabricius forcefully interrupts Cineas to proclaim: "O Hercules! [M]ay Pyrrhus and the Samnites entertain themselves with this sort of opinions as long as they are at war with us" (*FD*, 11; *Life of Pyrrhus*, 481).

Rousseau claims to have written his "prosopopoeia" just after visiting his friend and fellow philosopher Diderot, who was imprisoned for some of his published writing. Rousseau also says that the first thing he wrote for the *First Discourse* was the prosopopoeia.[22] We might expect Rousseau in the *First Discourse*, then, to employ Fabricius's horrified speech to bolster his own barrage of criticisms of luxury and devotion to high civilization, to say nothing of modern philosophy. And yet Rousseau refrains. In doing so he mimics the caution of "the magician-Socrates" and shows his fidelity to his own "trade."

By contrast, when we consider the perilous consequences to Rousseau of publishing the *Emile*, we are reminded that the art of writing, to which Rousseau lays claim, is often no match for established religious and political authorities.[23] Thankfully, the pleasures of reading *Emile* remain ours for the having.[24]

Notes

I wish to thank John Ray, Ann Charney Colmo, and Jalene Fox for their help. All references to Rousseau's works are to *Collected Writings of Rousseau*, ed. Roger D. Masters and Christopher Kelly, 13 vols. (Hanover, NH: University Press of New England, 1991–2011). References in the text use the following abbreviations: *E* for *Emile, or On Education*; *FD* for *Discourse on the Sciences and Arts (First Discourse)*; *SD* for *Discourse on the Origins of Inequality (Second Discourse)*; *C* for *The Confessions*; *S* for *On the Social Contract*; PN for: "Preface to *Narcissus.*" See also Joseph Cropsey, "The Human Vision of Rousseau: Reflections on *Emile*," in *Political Philosophy and the Issues of Politics* (Chicago and London: The University of Chicago Press, 1977), 315–29.

1. Rousseau uses the term to describe Xenophon's Cyropaedia, FD,8.

2. Rousseau uses the phrase "man in general" in *SD*, 19. See also *E*, 167. Ann Charney Colmo suggested the formulation "the species writ small."

3. See *E*, 175–76.

4. Plato, *Phaedrus*, 274d-e.

5. Plato, *Phaedrus*, 274e–275d; *FD*, 10.

6. For the foundation of contemporary theory see, for example, John Dewey, *Democracy and Education: An Introduction to the Philosophy of Education* (New York: Simon and Schuster, 1916).

7. Rousseau makes a comment at the end of the chapter suggesting that his initial claim about what Emile learns is provisional. "He seeks to know things not by their nature but only by the relations which are connected with his interest. He estimates what is foreign to him only in relation to himself. But this estimation is exact and sure" (*E*, 359).

8. I use the designation "the magician-Socrates" instead of "sleight-of-hand artist" *(le lendemain)* (*E*, 318–20) and also instead of "the trickster-Socrates," who is identified as such (and linked explicitly with Socrates) only once (*E*, 321). First, on my reading, the connection with Socrates is made throughout the episode. Second, for me, Allan Bloom's expression "the magician-Socrates" better connotes the "trade" of the character. See Jean-Jacques Rousseau, *Emile, or On Education*, trans. Allan Bloom (New York: Basic Books, 1979), 173.

9. Emile and the governor know beforehand what a magnet is and that it can attract at a distance, but how do they divine that there is a magnet hidden inside both the duck and the magician's piece of bread? Does the governor-Rousseau have a trick of his own to make this fact clear to Emile?

10. In Book V, when recounting a meeting with an English governor that suggested to him a significant feature to include in *Emile*, Rousseau expresses real surprise that the incident in question happened by chance and not by the governor's deliberate design (*E*, 663–64).

11. The difference between convincing or proving (*de convaincre*) and persuading (*de persuader*) is very important in Rousseau's works. Most famous is his phrase "to persuade without convincing," that is, not to rely on rational argument, but rather on an appeal to feelings, owing perhaps to an inability of an audience to understand (*S*, VII, 156). Regarding the *First Discourse*, Rousseau replies to his critics that he didn't care about persuading his adversaries, and sought only to convince them. That is, he didn't appeal to their feelings or seek their esteem because he didn't care about winning their esteem for himself (PN, in *FD*, 186 and ed. n3, 223).

12. Perhaps Rousseau just doesn't want to boast about *Emile*. For a deeper analysis of *Robinson Crusoe*, see Thomas S. Shrock, "Considering Crusoe: Part I," *Interpretation: A Journal of Political Philosophy* 1 (September 1970): 76–106 and Part II in *Interpretation* 2 (Winter 1970): 169–232. I thank Timothy W. Burns for the citation.

13. Rousseau illustrates the *Second Discourse* with an engraving of an indigenous man who "goes back to his *equals*," leaving behind everything the Dutch missionaries who raised him had given him; he keeps only a necklace and a cutlass (or saber) (*SD*, Frontispiece and Rousseau's note, 93; emphasis added).

14. As governor Rousseau begins to accustom Emile to the differences between the sexes, a prominent theme in Books IV and V.

15. We can compare Emile's fantasy with Gonzalo's praise of the island in Shakespeare's *The Tempest* (II.i.150–70).

16. Machiavelli, *The Prince*, trans. Harvey C. Mansfield (Chicago and London: The University of Chicago Press, 1998), 61.

17. Rousseau first offers for Emile's consideration "the true principles of political right" in a summary of *On the Social Contract* (*E*, 649–60). "It is necessary to know what ought to be in order to judge soundly about what is" (*E*, 649). Second, Emile and the governor travel abroad and observe actual European politics through the lens of Fenelon's novel *Telemachus*, the book accompanying them (*E*, 660 and ed. n70, 760). As governor, Rousseau asks the reader to "imagine our travels" or to make them himself. That is to say, we are not privy to the discussions he and Emile have about contemporary politics and morals.

18. See Denise Schaeffer, *Rousseau on Education, Freedom, and Judgment* (University Park: The Pennsylvania State University Press, 2014).

19. See "Preface to a Second Letter to Bordes," in *FD*, 182–85. Rousseau also writes here, "Having so many interests to contest, so many prejudices to conquer, and so many harsh things to state, in the very interest of my Readers, I believed I ought to be careful of their pusillanimity in some way and let them perceive only gradually what I had to say to them" (*FD*, 184).

20. Plato, *The Apology*, 23 c-d to 24 b.

21. Plutarch, "Life of Pyrrhus," *The Lives of the Noble Grecians and Romans*, trans. John Dryden (New York: Modern Library, n.d.), 467–93.

22. Just before Fabricius "speaks," Rousseau himself disparages "Epicurus, Zeno, [and] Arcesilaus" (*FD*, p. 10). The two different responses stem perhaps from the same motivation. On the one hand, Rousseau dissociates himself from the atheistic modern philosophers, who resemble the ancient attackers of religious faith—the *villains* of the *First Discourse*; on the other hand, Rousseau refuses to give Fabricius, one of the *heroes* of the *First Discourse* an antiphilosophy remark.

23. *C*, Book VIII, 284–85.

24. The *Emile* was condemned by the *Parlement* of Paris and burned in Geneva (1762). With a warrant out for his arrest, Rousseau was forced to leave France, and his habitation was precarious and unsettled for a number of years (FD, x).

Chapter 9

Hegel's Evaluation of Liberalism
Equality of Rights without Human Excellence

Andrea E. Ray

The relation of Hegel's political philosophy to liberalism has been a persistent question for readers of the *Elements of the Philosophy of Right*. Interpretations of Hegel's own position have cast him as everything from a proto-totalitarian to a communitarian to a near liberal.[1] As a consequence, there has been a similarly wide range of interpretations of Hegel's evaluation of liberalism, as for each assumed standpoint there has been an assumed angle of critique on liberalism as well. For the purposes of our own examination of the relation of equality to excellence in Hegel's political philosophy, we will take as our starting point an observation by Allen Wood, who notes that "Hegel's political ideas leave the liberals' state pretty much intact. Hegel's ethical theory on the other hand, shreds the liberal rationale for it."[2] On the face of it, this seems quite curious. If Hegel disagrees so strongly with the rationale for the liberal state, why would he want to largely maintain that state, and, furthermore, which are the aspects of the liberal state that appeal to Hegel?

In the *Philosophy of Right*, Hegel describes liberal market-states as societies that simultaneously recognize individuals as equals insofar as they are all rights-bearers and deeply alienate those individuals from society by way of that recognition. While later theorists such as Marx take this alienation as an indication of a need to radically rethink our claim to property rights, for Hegel, rights, and particularly property rights, structure much of how we come to understand our relation to other individuals and thus cannot be done away with so readily. Instead, Hegel approaches the problem of liberal alienation by examining how we are deficient under liberalism, how we fail to flourish[3] within such a society. In doing so, Hegel suggests that the problem with liberalism is not so much that recognizing individuals as rights-bearers is wrong, as that such recognition is not enough. By exploring what Hegel wishes to retain from liberal market-states and his reasons for doing so, as well as his critique of the liberal understanding of the individual, we discover that Hegel considers this recognition of equals in the liberal state to be deficient insofar as it hinders human excellence. For a society to be conducive to human excellence, therefore, Hegel argues that we must look beyond the form of life described by seventeenth-century liberalism to *Sittlichkeit*—an ethical order that permits a broader array of recognition by conceiving of the individual as deeply interwoven with the group without simply reducing the individual to a mere part of the group.

The Rights-Bearer

From very early on in the *Philosophy of Right*, Hegel establishes the fundamentality of the right to property within his account of abstract right, or the formal sphere within which human beings may understand both themselves and one another as *persons,* as individuals with "the capacity for right" (§36).[4] This is because the right to property grounds both our conception of ourselves as persons and our capacity to relate to others as persons. First, it grounds our conception of ourselves as persons because it is by externalizing our will that we distinguish ourselves from mere things. As a person, the individual "has the right to place his will in any thing. The thing thereby becomes *mine* and acquires my will as its substantial end" (§44). By taking possession of an object, using it as one pleases, and even alienating that object from oneself, one objectifies one's will. The thing ceases to be simply a thing and, as property, becomes a representation of the will of the person with a right to that thing, and thus an indication of the capacity of that person to externalize his will. This means that, through property, we gain more than merely the tools or resources through which to externalize our wills; we gain the recognition of ourselves as the kinds of beings capable of doing so.

Because of this, Hegel argues that "from the point of view of freedom, property, as the first *existence* of freedom, is an essential end for itself" (§45A). To understand this claim, it is important to understand what Hegel here means by freedom.[5] The *Philosophy of Right* declares that "right is concerned with freedom, the worthiest and most sacred possession of man" (§215A), but it is often not immediately clear to readers what freedom is within the *Philosophy of Right*. The work discusses a number of different kinds of freedom, ranging from what Hegel calls "*negative* freedom or the freedom of the void" (§5R)—the rejection of all determination that Hegel regards as characteristic of both the "pure contemplation" of Hindu meditation and the "fury of destruction" of the initial stages of the French Revolution, to more prosaic and familiar kinds of freedom such as the freedom to resist one's inclinations or desires and the personal freedom from state interference that is a characteristic concern of liberalism.

However, the *Philosophy of Right* is primarily concerned with a different understanding of freedom, an understanding of freedom as a kind of relation of the self to action, and thus a kind of self-relation. As Robert Pippin writes, Hegel is interested in determining "the conditions that must be fulfilled such that my various deeds could be, and could be experienced by me as being, my deeds and projects, as happening at all in some way that reflects and expresses my agency."[6] This is because, for Hegel, "Freedom is to will something determinate, yet to be with oneself [*bei sich*] in this determinacy and to return once more to the universal" (§7A). Importantly, in the *Philosophy of Right*, the "will is a particular way of thinking." It is "thinking translating itself into existence, thinking as the drive to give itself existence" (§4A). This means that, contrary to many views of freedom, for Hegel, one is not free insofar as one could act in a number of ways, but insofar as one does act in a particular kind of way. Specifically, an individual is free insofar as he acts in such a way that his actions are both the translation of his thinking into existence and taken by him to be so. He is "with himself" in his actions insofar as he recognizes them as reflecting and expressing his will. Over the course of the *Philosophy of Right*, Hegel expands and enriches this view of freedom to eventually argue that freedom requires a particular kind of social relation as well as this self-relation, but even from this more simplistic account of Hegelian freedom, it is easy to see why property serves as the "first *existence* of freedom." In claiming something as one's own, one must externalize one's will, that is, one must translate one's will, and thus one's thought, into existence and understand oneself as doing so.

We can start to see the beginnings of Hegel's argument that a particular kind of social relation is demanded by his account of freedom when we realize that in addition to grounding our recognition of ourselves as persons, the right to property also grounds our capacity to relate to one another as persons. It does so because it is through this right that we are able to make contracts with one another, and it is through contracts that we recognize each other as fellow rights-bearers. For Hegel, "it is only as owners of property that the two [persons] have existence for each other" (§40). In transferring property, each party to the contract must recognize the other as someone with the right to property, and thus as an individual with the capacity for right. If this were not the case, the transferring would be meaningless. One party would perceive himself as simply taking immediate possession of a thing, and the other would in turn perceive himself as losing immediate possession. Even conceptualizing such an exchange as theft would be beyond either of the two individuals, as theft only makes sense in the case of one person who, lacking the right to the object, takes the object from another person with a right to the object. If neither individual recognizes the other as a person, neither can recognize such a taking as a violation of right.

Liberalism and Its Problems

For Hegel, this way of understanding personality first appears in Roman law, but in many ways it attains its full expression in liberalism. Readers of Locke are likely to recognize significant parallels between Hegel's account of the priority of the right to property and Locke's own. For Locke, a thing "is *by* the *Labour* that removes it out of that common state Nature left it in, *made* his *Property* who takes that pains about it."[7] Hegel disagrees with Locke that labor exclusively grounds the right to property, since for Hegel even marking a thing as mine, a "mode of taking possession which is not actual in itself but merely represents my will," suffices to transform a thing into property (§58). However, he certainly agrees that labor is one way in which one can externalize one's will and thereby lay claim to an object. Locke further holds that as property, the object is "a part of him, that another can no longer have any right to it."[8] This implies that for Locke, property not only serves as a means by which an individual distinguishes himself from mere things, but also as a means by which he establishes himself as distinguishable from mere things for other individuals. His property is his, not only to him, but to others as well because in claiming something as his property, others no longer have a right to it. Hence, to phrase Locke's account in Hegelian terms, by externalizing my will in an object through my labor, the object is no longer simply a thing, but my property. This shift from thing to property entails both my recognition of myself as having a right to property, and thus as capable of bearing rights, and a recognition by others of me as capable of bearing rights.

Furthermore, in Locke's account of property, the right to property is universal, as "every Man has a Property in his own person."[9] Therefore, property also allows each individual to recognize others as having a right to property, and thus as capable of bearing rights. Hegel's account of property eventually specifically excludes one's own person,[10] because property must be alienable for Hegel, but it shares this tendency toward universality. Hegel is particularly concerned with excluding one's own person from the realm of property in part because he sees Roman slavery as tied to a basic misunderstanding of the human being as potential property. He argues that "in Roman law . . . no definition of a *human being* would be possible, for the slave could not be subsumed under it; indeed, the status of the slave does violence to the concept" (§2R). Insofar as a human being is not a thing but a person, it must be the sort of being that has rights rather than the sort of being over which persons have rights. Thus, while Hegel differs with Locke on the specifics of whether one might correctly understand one's own person as property, his disagreement with Locke's position stems from an underlying agreement concerning the importance of establishing the universality of the right to property. The right to property is crucial to a satisfactory form of interpersonal recognition and thus to a satisfactory political order because it is through this right that we may even recognize ourselves and one another as persons at all. Hence, in order to follow the commandment of right, in order for one to "be a person and respect others as persons" (§36), Hegel holds that there must be a right to property, and that this right is only fully expressed once it is understood as a right held equally.

Since liberalism recognizes individuals as bearers of natural, and thus universal, rights, it seems to fulfill much of what Hegel regards as necessary for political life. Under liberalism, the commandment of right largely holds. The individual is able to conceive of himself as a person rather than as a thing, to likewise understand others as persons, and to live in a society in which other persons understand him as a person. Consequently, the individual is able to safely externalize his will and pursue his desires as he sees fit so long as doing so does not impede another's personhood. Together, these ways of understanding one another form a constellation of goods that follows from the specifically equal character of rights-bearing found in the liberal state. While other, earlier forms of political organization such as that found in Roman law certainly recognized some individuals as capable of bearing rights, by only recognizing some individuals as persons rather than recognizing all equally as persons, even those select few could merely enjoy some of these goods individually. The constellation as a whole requires that not only one take oneself to be a person, but that broadly speaking, others, whom one likewise takes to be persons, take one to be a person. Hence, the equality of rights-bearing found under liberalism allows a full expression of this combination of goods in ways that are unavailable in other, earlier conceptions of rights-bearing.

Yet, problems remain in liberalism according to Hegel, problems that are directly implied by these same benefits that liberalism provides the individual. While the form of recognition afforded by the equality of rights found in liberalism is necessary for political life, it is simultaneously an insufficient form of recognition. Within civil society, Hegel's term for liberal market economies, at the same time that the individual enjoys recognition as an equal, he suffers an alienation from his society through that same recognition. The modern liberal state "is represented as a unity of different persons, as a unity which is merely a community [of interests]" (§182A). As such, in civil society, "each individual is his own end, and all else means nothing to him" (§182A).[11] This means that in the state as envisioned by liberalism, the fact that each individual may pursue his desires provided he does not infringe another's rights is simultaneously a kind of freedom, a relaxation of limits on him, and a limitation itself. It is a limitation because insofar as he is recognized by his society as a person, that recognition is purely negative—to others, he is simply someone against whom they cannot offend in various ways. As such, while his status as a person is guaranteed by the equality of right found in civil society, it is simultaneously guaranteed that what it means for him to hold the status of a person is devoid of any positive meaning, and particularly any positive meaning tied specifically to him as an individual. In gaining the freedom and security to do as he pleases through the equality of rights found in civil society, he simultaneously guarantees that *he* will mean nothing to any of his fellow persons around him. Hence, within the state described by liberalism, the individual indeed enjoys equal recognition as a person, but also *merely* as a person.

For Hegel, this has a twofold importance for the question of human excellence, or perhaps more precisely an importance for the question of human excellence that a liberal would mistake to be twofold. To understand why, it is important to recall that in many ways, Hegel has an understanding of the human good according to which human excellence is basically flourishing as a human being. First, considering human excellence with respect to the individual, insofar as the recognition afforded by liberalism is a limitation on the individual, both with respect to his understanding of himself and his relation to his state, it curtails his self-actualization as an individual. This is most pronounced when we consider the fact that, by Hegel's view, under liberal theory, a member of the liberal state cannot be a citizen of his state in a meaningful way. He is merely one individual among many "private persons who have their interest as their end" (§187). From Hegel's perspective therefore, the liberal understanding of the state guarantees that being a citizen of a state entails that the individual be a bad citizen, and thus that there are expressions of human excellence that liberalism denies the individual because of the liberal state under which he lives.

Furthermore, Hegel suggests that liberal market-states not only render the individuals within them indifferent to one another, but that left unchecked they tend to produce a class of degraded human beings, some of whom are not only alienated from their society and its members, but plainly hostile to their society. Hegel writes:

> When the activity of civil society is unrestricted, it is occupied internally with *expanding its population and industry*.—On the one hand, as the association of human beings through their needs is *universalized*, and with it the ways in which means of satisfying these needs are devised and made available, the *accumulation of wealth* increases; for the greatest profit is derived from this twofold universality. But on the other hand, the *specialization* and *limitation* of particular work also increase, as do likewise the *dependence* and *want* of the class which is tied to such work; this in turn leads to an inability to feel and enjoy the wider freedoms, and particularly the spiritual advantages, of civil society.
>
> When a large mass of people sinks below the level of a certain standard of living—which automatically regulates itself at the level necessary for a member of the society in question—that feeling of right, integrity [*Rechtlichkeit*], and honour which comes from supporting oneself by one's own activity and work is lost. This leads to the creation of a *rabble*, which in turn makes it

much easier for disproportionate wealth to be concentrated in a few hands. (§243–44)

The economic interdependence of the liberal market-state thus presents two points of concern for Hegel when considered in light of the question of human excellence. First, like Adam Smith, Hegel believes that in modern economies there are kinds of work that degrade the worker. Excessive specialization has the effect of not only increasing the economic dependence of the worker, but also of numbing him to his society. This is particularly striking as, while Hegel enumerates a variety of "spiritual advantages" in his discussion of civil society, perhaps the most important one is simply being recognized as a person. Notably, Hegel does not here imply that the worker is no longer recognized as a person, but that he is unable to "feel and enjoy" such recognition. It seems likely that this is because one recognizes oneself as a person insofar as one sees oneself as able to externalize one's will. If the worker is rendered so dependent that he is no longer able to pursue his own desires meaningfully, he, in a sense, ceases to recognize himself as a person. This degradation of the individual is brought to further extremes in Hegel's second point of concern—that unrestricted civil society lends itself to the breakdown of right, integrity, and honor among large numbers of its poor and "the creation of a rabble." Hegel makes an important distinction between the class of workers unable to feel and enjoy the freedoms of civil society and the rabble. The rabble is not only alienated from society, but is specifically "against society" (§244A). As such, it is the result of an "inward rebellion" that takes society and government as its foe. Hence, as a member of the rabble, the individual within unrestricted civil society is alienated to the point he is not merely unable to feel and enjoy the freedoms of his society, but is actively hostile to the state within which he lives.

Second, considering human excellence with respect to the state, it is easy to see that parallel problems emerge for liberalism. Since the liberal understanding of the state guarantees that the state's citizens be bad citizens, it likewise guarantees that the state be a state of bad citizens. As Hegel writes, "If the state is confused with civil society and its determination is equated with the security and protection of property and personal freedom, the interests of the individuals as such becomes the ultimate end for which they are united" (§258R). Since the liberal state, by its own self-understanding, is nothing more than a collection of members each pursuing their own desires without regard for one another, it can at best be a state in which deficient individuals largely leave one another alone. At worst, in producing the rabble, it produces a class of individuals opposed to the state. The unity of those individuals under any given state is thus rendered shallow and even illusory. It is merely the result of "the selfish end in its actualization . . . establish[ing] a system of all-round interdependence" (§183). This is to say that together, such individuals might have the appearance of a citizenry but little more. Hence, while liberalism allows for the equality of rights necessary for the mutual recognition of our status as persons, it simultaneously hobbles both the individual and the state, at best limiting the individual to the status of a mere person and thereby restricting him from attaining certain forms of human excellence, and limiting the state to a mere collective of interdependent bad citizens.

Ethical Life

Hegel's solution to the deficiencies found in liberalism comes through what he terms *Sittlichkeit,* or "Ethical Life." Importantly, an equal claim to the ability to bear rights, and thus an equal claim to personality, is maintained under Hegel's rethinking of the liberal state. Civil society does not simply vanish under Hegel's state. Hegelian sublation entails negation, but also preservation. Hence, while the liberal rationale for the state, and with it the liberal understanding of the relation of civil society to the state, must be overcome, civil society remains an important part of Hegel's understanding of political life even as the individual's relation to the state and to his fellow citizens becomes radically altered.

In contrast to the liberal understanding of the state, which conflates civil society with the state, in modern ethical life, Hegel argues, "The relationship of the state to the individual [*Individuum*] is of quite a different kind. Since the state is objective spirit, it is only through being a member of the state that individual [*Individuum*] himself has objectivity, truth, and ethical life. *Union* as such is itself the true content and end, and the destiny [*Bestimmung*] of individuals [*Individuen*]is to lead a universal life; their further particular satisfaction, activity, and mode of conduct have this substantial and universally valid basis as their point of departure and result" (§258). Statements such as this have often prompted readings of Hegel as a totalitarian or thoroughgoing communitarian, but a note of caution is required here. Hegel continues, "Rationality consists in general in the unity and *interpenetration* of universality and individuality," (§258; emphasis mine) not simply the subsumption of individuality within universality. As Wood notes, the *Philosophy of Right* "is dictated not by collective ends but by a certain conception of the modern human individual . . . the rational state is an end in itself only because the highest stage of *individual* self-actualization consists in participating in the state and recognizing it as such an end."[12] Similarly, Paul Franco argues "while it is perfectly true . . . that Hegel rejects the individualistic standpoint of liberalism, this does not mean that he leaps into a diametrically opposed collectivism."[13] Hence, to understand this passage and the kind of relation of the state to the individual Hegel is describing, it is crucial that we grasp the interpenetrative quality of this relation.

As discussed earlier, freedom in the *Philosophy of Right* is a kind of relation of the self to action. When considered with regard to the treatment of property in abstract right and even the economic interdependence of civil society, the consequences of this view of freedom on our relation to others and the state remain relatively bare and abstract. The individual is free insofar as his ability to externalize his will through his property remains unrestricted except when incompatible with the right of other individuals to do so as well. This has some implications for the individual's relation to others and the state—that he not interfere with others unduly, that the state not interfere with him unduly, and so forth—but the conditions imposed on the social relation remain fairly sparse. Whereas in liberalism this sparseness is taken *to be* freedom, Hegel argues that in *Sittlichkeit* we come to recognize that, properly understood, this sparseness instead hinders the freedom of the individual and must be overcome by a reinterpretation of the individual's relation to the state such that the individual finds his freedom *as an individual* in his relation to others.

If this strikes us as strange and unfamiliar, the introduction to the *Philosophy of Right* suggests it should not, because even in social orders that fall short of the freedom of *Sittlichkeit,* we already implicitly hold such a view of freedom. Hegel writes: "We already possess this freedom in the form of feeling, for example in friendship and love. Here, we are not one one-sidedly within ourselves, but willingly limit ourselves with reference to an other, even while knowing ourselves in this limitation of ourselves" (§7A).

We will take friendship as an illustrative example. As a friend, the individual does not experience the need to take his friends into account as a restriction on his freedom, but as a reflection of his being a friend to them. He willingly considers them in his actions, and recognizes himself reflected in his actions by doing so—that is by *being a friend* to them. He is thus "with himself in an other," in Hegel's terminology. Were he to instead consider taking these others into account a simple restriction on his freedom, and to either disregard them entirely or only unwillingly limit his actions in light of his relation to them, he would not be a friend to them and would neither recognize himself as such nor be recognized as such provided his attitude toward them was known. Hence, it is only by understanding his freedom as a friend in the way Hegel describes that the individual is able to be a friend and to recognize himself as a friend. As a form of human excellence, therefore, friendship implicitly presupposes a Hegelian understanding of freedom. Without one, the individual can be a friend in name only, and thus must be a bad friend.

Through his exploration of *Sittlichkeit,* Hegel reinterprets the social relation as a relation of the kind found in friendship or love. Rather than only being with oneself in another individual, or even in one's family, one is now able to be with oneself in the state. Importantly, just as one does not lose one's particularity in being a friend, neither does one lose one's particularity in being a citizen of the state. This is crucial because, in contrast to the ancient relation of individual to state, in which "the subjective end was entirely identical with the will of the state; in modern times, however, we expect to have our own views, our own volition, and our own conscience" (§261A). Hence, in order to satisfy these modern expectations, the state in *Sittlichkeit* neither demands that the individual set aside his particular interests, nor that he suppress them, but instead serves to "harmoniz[e]" them with the universal, "so that both they and the universal are preserved" (§261R). The state thus recognizes the individual as an individual, as a particular being with particular interests. This is distinct from the indifference of the state in liberalism. In liberalism, the state recognizes the individual as a person—as a rights-bearer entitled to certain state protections, but all personality itself is devoid of any particularity that marks an individual as the individual he is. In contrast, Hegel believes such a relation to the individual can be achieved by the state largely through social institutions—most prominently, corporations. Such institutions allow the individual to realize his freedom *as an individual* through an activity directed toward a universal end. They are thus "pillars on which public freedom rests, for it is within them that particular freedom is realized" (§265). The result of such a reinterpretation of the liberal state is that the individual is able to self-actualize, both in relation to the state and in relation to other individuals, and thereby flourish as a human being.

Perhaps the most striking form of human excellence to become available to the individual in modern ethical life is patriotism—and with it being a citizen. In contrast to the alienation from society and degradation of the individual that Hegel finds characteristic of the liberal understanding of the individual-state relation, in *Sittlichkeit* the individual gains a "political *disposition*" of trust toward his society. Far from the antipathy of the rabble, the individual's relation to the state is characterized by a habitual "consciousness that [his] substantial and particular interest is preserved and contained in the interest and end of an other (in this case, the state), and in the latter's relation to [him] as an individual" (§268). He thus finds himself to be free in the state, and willingly regards the state's ends as his own, not because they subsume his particular interests, but because they harmonize with his. By fulfilling his duties to the state, he not only gains the state's protection of him and his property, but also "consciousness and self-awareness of being a member of a whole" (§261R) and thus self-actualizes as a citizen. Hence, unlike in liberalism, in *Sittlichkeit* the individual is able to genuinely be a citizen while remaining a modern individual, to view the state's end as his own and to pursue his own particular interests and ends. He is able to do so because ethical life preserves the equality of rights-bearing and freedom to pursue particular desires found in the liberal state while negating the atomistic, contractual individualism underlying the liberal understanding of the relation of man to state.

Hence, through the interpenetration of universality and individuality, ethical life overcomes the restraints on human excellence imposed by liberalism while maintaining the equality of rights and individual liberty characteristic of the liberal state. While in liberalism individuals gain equal recognition as persons, that recognition entails a hindering of their excellence by limiting them to mere recognition as persons. As such, they find themselves alienated from their society and one another. In contrast, within ethical life the individual is recognized by the state as a particular being with particular interests and recognizes himself in the state's ends. Not only is he able to pursue his own particular ends, but he is also able to feel himself a member of a whole and to relate to others as fellow members. This reinterpretation of his relation to others itself enables him to actualize his being in ways barred to him under liberalism. In ethical life by enjoying a broader, richer form of recognition than in liberalism, he attains kinds of excellence as a human being that were previously unavailable to him.

Notes

1. Anti-liberal readings of Hegel are commonly taken to begin with Rudolf Haym's *Hegel und Seine Zeit* (Berlin: Rudolf Gaertner, 1875). See Karl Popper's *The Open Society and its Enemies* (Princeton: Princeton University Press, 1963) for a totalitarian interpretation. A more liberal reading can be found in Shlomo Avineri's, *Hegel's Theory of the Modern State* (Cambridge: Cambridge University Press, 1972). Charles Taylor's *Hegel* (Cambridge: Cambridge University Press, 1975) is a classic communitarian reading. See Allen W. Wood, *Hegel's Ethical Thought* (Cambridge: Cambridge University Press, 1990), Steven B. Smith, *Hegel's Critique of Liberalism: Rights in Context* (Chicago: The University of Chicago Press, 1989), and Paul Franco, *Hegel's Philosophy of Freedom* (New Haven: Yale University Press, 1999) for responses to the liberal versus communitarian interpretive debate.

2. Allen W. Wood, *Hegel's Ethical Thought* (Cambridge: Cambridge University Press, 1990), 258.

3. As Wood notes, "In Hegel's ethical theory, the final good is not happiness but freedom," 77. See also Wood, "Happiness," 53–74. Flourishing here should not be taken to mean happiness, but self-actualization.

4. G. W. F. Hegel, *Elements of the Philosophy of Right*, ed. Allen W. Wood, trans. H. B. Nisbet (Cambridge: Cambridge University Press, 1991). *Philosophy of Right* references are given by paragraph number.

5. See Wood, 36–52; Robert Pippin, *Hegel's Practical Philosophy: Rational Agency as Ethical Life* (Cambridge: Cambridge University Press, 2008), 36–43 and 121–79.

6. Pippin, 36.

7. John Locke, *Two Treatises of Government*, ed. Peter Laslett (Cambridge: Cambridge University Press, 1988), 290.

8. Locke, 287.

9. Locke, 287.

10. Early passages in the *Philosophy of Right* suggest that Hegel does think of one's own person as property. For example, §57 asserts that the human being "takes possession of himself and becomes his own property as distinct from that of others." Yet even in these early remarks Hegel argues that slavery and similar forms of exploitation "depend on regarding the human being simply as a *natural being*" (§57A). I take Hegel's later remarks on slavery and serfdom at §66R to be an exploration of the contradiction inherent in regarding the human being as such and a more accurate account of his final view. For a contrasting interpretation, see Wood, 99–101, who holds that "Hegel would have done better simply to hold consistently to his 'self-ownership' theory."

11. Notably, Hegel acknowledges that because of the economic interdependencies demanded by civil society, the individual "cannot accomplish the full extent of his ends without reference to others." Yet, this merely means that for the individual,

"these others are therefore means to the end of the particular [person]" rather than genuinely other individuals as such (§182A).

12. Wood, 21.

13. Paul Franco, "Hegel and Liberalism," *The Review of Politics* 59, no. 4 (Autumn 1997): 855.

Chapter 10

Democracy, Nobility, and Freedom
The Political and Moral Aesthetics of Tocqueville

John C. Koritansky

Can nobility of soul be at home in a democracy? If the question is not flatly unintelligible today, it must be admitted that it does seem archaic. Nobility is not a word that we typically associate with democracy. It's not part of our conversation, and even to bring it up risks giving annoyance. It is surely the case that, despite a claim to "openness," democracy is antithetical to a distinct class such as would be styled and self-styled "the nobles," to whom belong the prerogatives of cultural dominion and political rule. Despite this certainty, though, are we not aware that there might be at least some individuals, perhaps not fully socialized to the democratic ethos, who long to possess and to express what might be called a nobility of soul, even though the term has no clear articulation? Perhaps one feels a certain restlessness, an impulse to self-assertion, whatever that might mean, which neither venal self-gratification nor service to others can really satisfy.

The interpretation of the restlessness of our spirits as a longing for an amorphous nobility, and a consequent hostility toward the psychological oppression of democratic equality, makes us receptive to the works of Friedrich Nietzsche, if he is not himself responsible for that receptivity. Probably no one of our era, perhaps no one ever, wrote so movingly about nobility. One might describe his book *Beyond Good and Evil* as a lead toward his philosophy of the future by way of inducing the experience of a pathos of nobility. However that might be, though, it is the case that any contemporary concern for nobility derives largely, whether directly or indirectly, from Nietzsche. His concern for nobility and his uncompromised hostility to equality is *the* challenge to the democratic way of life in our day. This must be confronted.

Yet even in anticipating such a confrontation, we are aware that we are resuscitating something that is more than a century old. That is, it belonged to the dawn of the twentieth century, whereas we live in its aftermath. Between Nietzsche's day and ours the whole modern world was threatened with destruction. The outcome was that democracy, liberal capitalist democracy, was left standing in victory. So we are compelled to be more cautious and circumspect in our concern for nobility, if we do still feel it. Today we are compelled to consider whether there may be some edition of nobility that is not incompatible with democracy, lest we retrace the path to perdition.

So it is, then, that for reasons that are especially pressing today, we turn back to Alexis de Tocqueville and his masterpiece, *Democracy in America*. We turn back because Tocqueville does not confine his discussion to formalities: institutional arrangements and legalities such as preoccupy even prescriptive writings on democracy among our contemporaries. He does write of these things but his central concern is for the soul. He treats of democracy itself as having a sort of collective animus and he then treats of the effects of democratic equality on the individual human being. His concern is always for the health and strength of the soul. If there is a version of nobility compatible with democracy, we expect Tocqueville will help us recognize and nurture it. That is a big "if," though. Tocqueville is relevant for us today because of a concern for strength of soul that is awakened by Nietzsche together with our cautious resistance to follow Nietzsche to his conclusions.

Every careful reader of *Democracy in America* knows that Tocqueville intends to present a "new political science" that is prescriptive. Although the unique circumstances of America preclude her institutions and arrangements being followed in any detail, America does show very broadly that it is possible for democracy to resist the generic pathology of democratic despotism, under which a central authority would administer all the affairs of its subjects by treating each equal to each of the others in one homogenous mass. Tocqueville intends instead to preserve freedom democracy, in which the active participation in citizens' own self-government on a provincial level substitutes for the heavy hand of central administration. However, preserving this distinction is not simply a matter of legislating the right sort of political and institutional arrangements. It is, rather, primarily a matter of the citizens having the right attitude and spirit, jealously to guard their own collective self-reliance against the seductions and pressures from Big Brother. All democratic citizens love equality; it is their dominating passion. However, there is a difference in how they understand equality and in the way that they assert their love for it. Only if they understand and assert their love of equality in the right way will freedom be preserved. Indeed, the right sort of love of equality is practically indistinguishable from the love of freedom. Thus, the fundamental opposition is psychological: "There is in fact a manly and legitimate passion for equality that incites men to want all to be strong and esteemed . . . but one also encounters a depraved taste for equality . . . that reduces men to preferring equality in servitude to inequality in freedom" (*DA*, 52).[1]

From this beginning it is easy to understand the structure of at least the first volume of Tocqueville's great work. The five chapters that follow the statement of the two forms of the love of equality describe, in considerable detail, the complex governmental structures all of which preserve provincial freedom. They also show how these complex American structures depend on physical circumstances that make them useless as models for other democracies. European statesmen ("legislators") will have to exercise their own intelligence, Tocqueville having shown them what is at stake. The gist of the argument is that in America the principal animus for administrative centralization lies in the state governments. The provinces would be helpless in resisting the oppression from their state governments except for the fact that the states lack the full prerogatives of sovereignty. That belongs to the national government. That government, though, is something far away and although it does bear the ultimate responsibility for the protection of America from foreign dominion, the actual demands of foreign policy for America, in 1825, are few and weak. There are other factors too, all tending in the same direction: the openness of the continent, the brevity of the nation's history, the peculiarities of its founding, Tocqueville is at pains to indicate how all of it works to preserve the remarkable vigor and vitality, the activeness, of Americans' love of equality.

The institutions in America work, but as the saying goes, "It works for us," for "us" Americans. It would not be so among other peoples. Therefore, in the second half of his first volume Tocqueville writes of extralegal matters. We learn here of the omnipotence of the democratic majority, so powerful that it dominates the precincts of thought without even needing thought police. On this point Tocqueville is especially insistent, the majority's omnipotent power cannot be limited or "checked" by anyone or anything that would be seen as standing in opposition. It can, however, be "tempered," an important distinction. That is to say, the majority can exercise a sort of self-restraint. The modes of the self-restraint of the democratic majority are what Tocqueville calls "mores," and these are the "Principal Causes Tending to Maintain a Democratic Republic in the United States," as reads the title of the chapter that formally concludes the argument of Part 2 Volume I. (The final chapter of Volume I is strictly speaking an addendum, being more about things specifically American as versus things democratic but incidentally American.) Not surprisingly, the discussion of mores contains as its longest part Tocqueville's treatment of religion in America. This extremely rich and subtle section would require very careful analysis. Suffice it to be said in the present context that in America religion provides the finial crown of the mores whereby the democratic majority is tempered so as not to run roughshod over the all-important provincial liberties.

Have we then arrived at Tocqueville's implicit answer to our question of nobility in democracy? That is, shall we say that Tocqueville shows us a democratic sort of nobility that he expresses as the "manly love of equality?" Such a notion of nobility would of course not entail a noble caste; indeed it would preclude that. Still, the manly love of equality does have something important in common with nobility more traditionally understood. The common element is the spirit of defiant resistance, intractable pride. In America this is what gives the principle of popular sovereignty its salutary form. We imagine Tocqueville's Americans resisting the despotical oppression of central administration thinking and feeling, "We can do for ourselves, thank you, 'cause who's better than us?" Tocqueville's entire political science would be lost on us if we were not moved to admire that spirit and to seek ways for its nurture. We may call this nobility if we so choose, provided that we bear in mind that we are talking about nobility without *a* nobility.

Is this satisfactory, though? That is, if the word *nobility* is appropriated in the way suggested above, so as to make of it a democratic phenomenon, does this not involve an abstraction from certain connotations that, if brought to the surface, suggest a serious challenge to democracy even at its best? We are reminded that the manly love of equality entails a prideful spirit. The serious question, though, is whether the desire to be "strong and esteemed" can exist without its being somehow *comparative* in a way that anyone who loves of equality would consider invidious. In short, does not all pride entail a feeling of superiority, being elevated over what is low and common? If that is so, then must we not think that the "manly love of equality" is only precariously alive in democracy because it preserves something that can really belong only to a noble class and be openly expressed only among them? We are laboring to bring into confrontation Tocqueville's ultimate judgment, that democracy is the condition whereby "the natural greatness of man" is revealed (*DA*, 5), versus Nietzsche's, that democracy is the reign of "the last man," the product of the triumph of a morality of slaves: petty, venal, and vapid, men who feel no satisfaction except the satisfaction of their revenge—against anything noble. Nietzsche versus Tocqueville: Who is right?

Tocqueville published the second volume of *Democracy in America* in 1840, five years after the first volume. In his first volume Tocqueville had written thematically of the tyranny of the democratic majority such that many of his readers, then and now, would likely be caused to think that his aim was to find a way to check democracy's tyrannical impulses through various governmental and social institutional arrangements. This reading, though, actually involves a certain distortion of Tocqueville's thought for which his second volume offers a correction. A sign that such was Tocqueville's intention is that the very term *tyranny of the majority* does not occur at all in Volume II.[2] Tocqueville actually holds that majoritarian tyranny is generic to democracy. It cannot be effectively checked, not by anything of an alien or contrary spirit. But while the democratic majority cannot be checked, it can be "tempered" and ennobled so as to resist "despotism." This might seem an overly subtle distinction initially but it is fundamentally important for understanding the movement of his argument.[3] What he is pointing toward is for us to see what sort of despotism democracy has to fear, to fear but *not* to accept. To clarify and insist on this point Tocqueville needed to elaborate the effects of democracy on the individual democratic subject or citizen. He needed to show more directly than he had in his first volume what happens to an individual's mind and heart in a society where all are equal and more or less alike.[4] Would the democratic individual be spiritually crushed or might one be rather sustained, even enhanced? Since this is the issue of Volume II, we might turn to it in hope that some further light will be shed of the question of nobility in democracy.

Volume II of *Democracy in America* is a rich treasure trove of observations all of which bear on our question. We can make a selection, though, of two chapters from Part 3, the part that shows the "influence of democracy on mores properly so-called" (*DA*, 533). This part draws upon and then succeeds the two previous parts that show how democracy affects "intellectual movement" and "sentiments." What Tocqueville means by "mores" is the defining features of one's character. The two chapters at issue are numbers 14 and 18, on "manners" among democratic subjects and on "honor." Their selection is recommended insofar as these chapters assert Tocqueville's strongest concession to a hostility to democracy on behalf of nobility. He shows that he understands what is probably the hardest thing to be abandoned if we must be reconciled to the triumph of democracy; and he even indicates a certain sympathetic sadness for the loss.

This sympathy must be considered carefully. So far as manners are concerned, Tocqueville confesses that he is himself annoyed by the lack of refinement, the boorishness of manners among Americans. Democracy is the reason. "Genuine dignity of manners consists in always showing oneself in one's place, neither higher nor lower; that is within the reach of the peasant as of the prince. In democracies, all places appear doubtful; hence it happens that manners, which are often haughty, are rarely dignified. In addition, they are never either well regulated, or well informed" (*DA*, 579). This fact cannot but pain such a person as Tocqueville himself, whose every paragraph, if one may say so, exhibits the most exquisite refinement of taste and sensitivity. For while "there is nothing, at first sight, which seems less important than the external form of human actions . . . there is nothing to which men attach more value" (*DA*, 578). So if despite such inclination Tocqueville is ultimately to judge democracy favorably, that requires that he exercise some self-containment and judge democracy from a certain remove. One might put it that Tocqueville's posture on this point is itself a model of refinement and good manners and he invites his readers to share intimately that same posture. "For to experience the kind of refined pleasure procured by distinction and choice in manners, habit and education must prepare the heart, and one easily loses the taste along with the use of them . . . . One must not attach too much importance to this loss; but it is permissible to regret it" (*DA*, 581).

While his chapter on manners bids us to grant to the subject matter only so much seriousness as the subject deserves, that is, to keep it light, his chapter on "honor" is deeply, heavily serious. Perhaps we should not attach too much importance to the loss of refinement of manners, but the loss of honor would seem another matter. Why, though, does democracy impose this cost? There is a difference between the moral laws that derive from permanent and general needs of mankind and more particular rules that are connected with interests of a specific nation or class. The former define what human beings understand to be "doing good" or "doing evil."

The latter state what men feel to be honorable; they explain how a specific group communicates praise or blame. Note, this is not to say merely that differently situated peoples have divergent notions of right and wrong but rather that such groups, aware of their distinctness and proud of it, will feel some behaviors to be honorable for themselves that they do not hold to apply to others. Those others are simply "without honor." Tocqueville's example is the refusing of a duel. This might be forbidden by a particular, aristocratic, code of honor or it might be commanded by another. This example also shows that there is a measure of caprice in a code of honor and yet it is never entirely capricious. What is honored can vary from group to group but only within certain limits; and those limits derive from the actual circumstances of the group. Thus, feudal aristocracy honored military courage most of all. This example will prove to be more than *an* example in what follows.

The feudal code of honor was not only very demanding but also extremely complex. Patriotism counted for very little; what mattered, what honor bound one to exhibit, was fidelity to one's lord; and one would not tolerate being dishonored by the infidelity of one's vassal. Tocqueville explains that he draws out his description of feudal honor at some length because it shows "more and better marked features than any other [example]" (*DA*, 593). It is not the only example, though. He mentions the Romans and, with the help of Plutarch's "Life of Coriolanus," says that among the Romans prowess and valor were honored above all other virtues—indeed, to be felt to be virtue itself. This would be to be expected of a people "formed for the conquest of the world" (*DA*, 593).

Is there, then, an example of a code of honor among a democratic people? Yes, there can be, if or insofar as they too might have some distinguishing circumstances that pertain to them as a people. America illustrates the point. For while there is no specific class that honors itself exclusively, Americans are a distinct people on the world's stage. Reprising a theme that he had already advanced toward the conclusion of Volume I (*DA*, 384–90, 387), Tocqueville here cites how Americans are propelled by circumstances toward commerce and industry and have therefore developed a code of honor that is consistent and compatible with those requirements. The ambitious love of money, severe condemnation of sloth, a profound respect for the sober duties and the sanctity of marriage, these are all features of American honor and they combine with a high tolerance for daring bordering on recklessness in commercial enterprise. We are not surprised, then, to learn that on one point the American sense of honor is in common with that of both feudal aristocrats and Romans. They all honor courage. To be sure the Americans do not think to exhibit courage on the battlefield—not ordinarily. That, though, is because Americans experience commerce and industry almost as an analog of the battlefield, what with its risks and sacrifices and its prospects for glorious victories. "The Americans put a sort of heroism into their manner of doing commerce" (*DA*, 387).

The question that remains, though, is whether this American version of honor is not an exception to the more general effect of democratic conditions. One may note that his description of the Americans' "heroism" in commercial enterprise in Volume I is contained in the final chapter, number 10 of Part 2, a chapter of which Tocqueville says that it contains things that "touch on my subject [but] do not enter into it; they are American without being democratic" (*DA*, 303). In the chapter on honor in Volume II we see why this must be so. The strength and complexity of a code of honor is reflective of the degree of distinctness of the group to which it belongs. It is a matter of the psychic energy required to maintain one's belonging to the distinct group. Thus, "the more exceptional the position of a society is, the greater number are its special needs, and the more the notions of its honor, which correspond to its needs, increase. Prescriptions of honor will therefore always be less numerous in a people that is not partitioned into castes than in any other. If nations in which it is even difficult to find classes come to be established, honor will be limited to a few precepts, and these precepts will be less and less distant from the moral laws adopted by common humanity" (*DA*, 596). Americans do exhibit honor but it is a weaker, looser thing than among feudal aristocrats and to the extent that it exists at all it is because of the circumstances of America that deserve to be called primitive. The democratic future will be different.

Having stated the basic reason why honor is most complex and rigorously demanding among aristocracies, Tocqueville goes on to mention several additional factors all tending in the same direction. He appears to want to leave no stone unturned regarding this very important phenomenon. (The chapter under consideration is the second-longest of the entire volume.) For one thing, in feudal aristocracy there was very little social mobility. One occupied a status according to a hierarchical pattern that remained fixed over generations. How one ought to behave was something received and then handed down as one's patrimony (*DA*, 596–97). Then too, the features of the code of honor were known and felt by a relatively small number of persons. Among such, "Honor is therefore easily mixed and confused in their minds with all that distinguishes them. It appears to them as the distinctive feature of their physiognomy" (*DA*, 597). To defend one's honor is to defend one's very self. Finally, Tocqueville observes that in a society where each person occupies a place he cannot leave, "where he lives in the midst of other men around him attached in the same manner . . . no one can hope or fear not to be seen; he encounters no man placed so low that he has no theater, who will escape blame or praise by his obscurity" (*DA*, 598).

Tocqueville calls attention to the meticulous pains he has taken in the chapter under present consideration and he expects that this will cause his reader to have "understood that there is a tight and necessary relation between inequality of conditions and what we have called honor" (*DA*, 598). Nevertheless, he is not fully confident that we will have grasped the lesson in all of its far-reaching consequences. So he states these; and here we must quote him directly so as to consider the words with requisite care.

> If it were finally permissible to suppose that all races should intermingle and all the peoples of the world should come to the point of having the same interests and the same needs, and of no longer distinguishing themselves from one another by any characteristic feature, one would cease entirely to attribute conventional value to human actions; all would view them in the same light; the general needs of humanity that conscience reveals to each man would be the common measure. Then one would no longer encounter in this world any but simple notions of good and evil, to which ideas of praise or blame would be attached by a natural and necessary bond.
>
> Thus, finally to include all my thought in a single formula, it is the dissimilarities and inequalities of men that have created honor; it is weakened insofar as these differences are effaced, and it should disappear with them. (*DA*, 599)

Tocqueville's chapter on honor cannot be other than deeply troubling; it especially troubles the very sentiments and hopes that he has himself encouraged throughout the rest of his work. For if honor is effaced from the democratic world, what of the "manly and legitimate" form of the love of equality that seeks to elevate all to the rank of the "*great*"? Must we think that Tocqueville could be reconciled to such a softening of the soul as would characterize the subjects of the new sort of despotism *that we have most to fear*, that despotism that "monopolizes movement and existence to such a point that everything around it must languish when it languishes, that everything must sleep when it sleeps, that everything must perish if it dies?" (*DA*, 88). That simply cannot be his final thought. On the contrary, in his penultimate chapter he insists that while democracy does pose the danger of the new, egalitarian form of despotism, we should not think the task of resisting it to be insurmountable (*DA*, 672). Ultimately, the ground for Tocqueville's hope is the spiritedness, the "intractability" that the love of equality entails. "I praise it principally for that. I admire it as I see it deposit that obscure notion and instinctive penchant for political independence at the bottom of the mind and heart of each man, thus preparing the remedy for the evil to which it gives birth. *It is on this side that I cling to it*" (*DA*, 640; my emphasis).

It appears that Tocqueville's chapter on honor does not sit well with the inspiriting message of the work as a whole. Perhaps we can gain a clearer perspective, though, if we reconsider the chapter in the context of how he concludes the third part of Volume II, the part about mores. Let us recall: of all the several, sometimes capriciously artificial virtues that existed among feudal aristocrats, the one that characterized all of them and the most fundamentally important was courage. This is part of a more general point; the more distinctive the circumstances that set one group apart from others, the more distinctive the mores of that group, the more prominent will courage be among those mores. The Romans were courageous too, in the service of their republic or their empire, but that was not so defining a feature of a citizen's character as it was of a feudal aristocrat. Still less prominent is courage among the Americans, although not absent to be sure. Wherever a code of honor exists, as Tocqueville employs the word, courage will always be a part of what is honored.

Is the converse true, though? That is, will it always be the case that honor will exist among the courageous? Framing the issue this way helps us see the connection between the chapter on honor and the several chapters succeeding it that actually and fittingly concludes the mores section. These chapters treat of war in democracy and, of what stands in direct relationship to our present subject, of military courage.

War, Tocqueville writes, is very dangerous in and to democracy— not only defeat in war but war itself. "War does not always give democratic peoples over to military government; but it cannot fail to increase immensely the prerogatives of civil government in these peoples; it almost inevitably centralizes the direction of all men and the employment of all things in its hands. If it does not lead to despotism suddenly by violence, it leads to it mildly through habits" (*DA*, 621). Nevertheless, war is not completely avoidable; and Tocqueville is not an unqualified peace theorist. "War, however, is an accident to which all peoples are subject, democratic as well as others" (*DA*, 617). Moreover, war is not simply or always bad. "I do not wish to speak ill of war; war almost always enlarges the thought of a people and elevates its heart. There are cases where only it can arrest the excessive development of certain penchants that equality naturally gives rise to, and where, for certain deep-seated maladies to which democratic societies are subject, it must be considered almost necessary" (*DA*, 620–21). If the civilian population of a democratic country might need to have its public spirit roused from time to time out of its bourgeois complacency, this humor is countervailed by an opposing one among the soldiers, especially the professional noncommissioned officers. These men want war, often to the point of recklessness. "The noncommissioned officer therefore wants war, he wants it always and at any price, and if he is refused war, he desires revolutions that suspend the authority of rules in the midst of which he hopes, thanks to the confusion and to political passions, to chase his officer out and take his place; and it is not impossible that he will give rise to them, because he exerts a great influence over the soldiers through their common origin and habits, although differs much from them by passions and desires" (*DA*, 625). It is easy to draw the recommendatory conclusion from these considerations. A democratic legislator should try to civilize soldiery and at the same time inspirit citizenship by adroitly mixing the contending humors. Tocqueville causes us to think of a democratic army made up of citizen soldiers (*DA*, 622).

Can such an army, a democratic army, fight, though? The importance of this question is not to be underestimated. For despite the confluence of causes that have brought about the triumph of democracy as Tocqueville describes them in his "Introduction," and which we today would describe as the direction of history, aristocracy still might hold back or cut back democratic growths from time to time by imposing military defeats. Nor is the question irrelevant to more contemporary circumstances. Is the question not still asked in some quarters whether democracy—our democracy—is fit to fight? So far as Tocqueville's reflections go, his discussion of this issue centers on the question whether democratic armies will exhibit the requisite discipline that will avail against armies drawn from more hierarchical and authoritarian societies. His answer is that they will not; but this disadvantage is, generally, more than offset by the advantage of a greater spirit among democracies soldiers. To see this we need to scratch beneath the surface of democratic citizens' pacific desires and habits and see the "hidden relation between military mores and democratic mores that war uncovers" (*DA*, 629).

> Most of them adore chance and fear death much less than trouble. In this spirit they lead commerce and industry; and this same spirit, transported by them onto the battlefield, brings them willingly to expose their lives so as to be assured, in a moment, the prizes of victory. . . . Thus, whereas interests and tastes turn the citizens of a democracy away from war, the habits of their souls prepare them to fight it well; they easily become good soldiers as soon as one has been able to tear them from their business and their well-being. (*DA*, 629)

This observation, regarding the connection between spiritedness and the often hidden features of democratic citizens' hearts is drawn out in the chapter that follows, chapter 25, Part III. It is the penultimate chapter among those devoted to the subject of war—therefore the penultimate chapter of the whole third part of Volume II, on "mores." Here, Tocqueville makes his point that in democratic armies there is often a relatively casual familiarity among soldiers of differing rank. This means that in democratic armies one will not observe the sort of scrupulous regard for discipline that is characteristic of aristocratic armies. Or so it might seem, especially if we are comparing the discipline between aristocratic versus democratic armies when they are at rest. However, when the fight is on, Tocqueville asserts that there is a sort of discipline that comes to the fore in a democratic army and is likely to prove decisive just when its competition cracks. "In democratic peoples military discipline ought not to try to negate the free flight of souls; it can only aspire to direct it; the obedience it creates is less exact, but more impetuous and more intelligent. Its root is in the very will of the one who obeys; it is supported not solely by his instinct, but by his reason; so it often tightens itself as danger renders it necessary. The discipline of an aristocratic army is often relaxed in war because this discipline is founded on habits, and war disturbs these habits. The discipline of a democratic army is on the contrary steadied before the enemy, because then each soldier sees very clearly that he must be silent and obey in order to be able to win" (*DA*, 630).

Already in these carefully constructed sentences we see that Tocqueville is building toward a rhetorical flourish. That is, he is inviting us to share something more than the keen observation of a neutral spectator. On the contrary, his words towards the end of chapter 25 are as stirring as any that ever flow from his pen. Suddenly, and dramatically, Tocqueville enlarges the field of our imagination. He recalls Plutarch, who in his *Lives* gives Tocqueville the general impression that in ancient armies soldiers spoke very freely to their commanders such that "[o]ne would say that they were as much companions as chiefs" (*DA*, 630). And then in a concluding paragraph that consists of but one sentence, Tocqueville strikes his final chord: "I do not know if Greek and Roman soldiers ever perfected the little details of military discipline to the same point as the Russians; but that did not prevent Alexander from conquering Asia, and Rome, the world" (*DA*, 630). Here more than anywhere else one is made to feel that "manly and legitimate passion for equality that incites men to want all to be strong and esteemed . . . [and which] tends to elevate the small to the rank of the great" (*DA*, 52).

What does Tocqueville permit us to say about whether nobility of soul can be at home in democracy? The answer is that pride in one's nobility for which one expects and demands to be honored will not be found. What was always at the root of honor and nobility though, a sort of raw intractable courage, does belong to democracy. And to reiterate, it is, finally, for this reason that Tocqueville clings to it.

Notes

1. Alexis de Tocqueville, *Democracy in America,* ed. and trans. Harvey C. Mansfield and Delba Winthrop (Chicago: University of Chicago Press, 2000).

2. I thank Thomas Pangle for this observation, shared with me in conversation. It is noteworthy that in his sober and friendly review, "An Appraisal of Volume I of *Democracy in America,*" John Stuart Mill treats "tyranny of the majority" as the danger in democracy and understates, almost to the point of oblivion, the problem of "despotism." Mill's hope, that mature democracy might harbor a "leisured class" whose very existence would mitigate democracy's tyrannical proclivity, is not supported by Tocqueville. Tocqueville's prescription is different because his diagnosis is different. Democracy's friends today, who ought not allow themselves to be blind to its defects, should consider carefully the divergence between these two exemplars of modern prudence. Mill's Review is printed in Alexis de Tocqueville, *Democracy in America,* Volume I (New York: Schocken Books, 1967), *v–xlix.*

3. One should consider carefully how Tocqueville distinguishes "tyranny" from "despotism" (*DA*, 235–49).

4. The second volume of *Democracy in America* was less well received than the first, especially in France. Whereas the French might be interested to learn what governmental and social arrangements the more primitive Americans had invented in the service of equality, the observations of the second volume would have been less flattering.

Chapter 11

Does Kierkegaard Have a Concept of Excellence?

Christopher A. Colmo

Does Kierkegaard have a concept of excellence? What is the relation of excellence to human equality in his view? These two questions suggest two different ways of understanding human nature. Should we think of humanity as determined by or measured against the most excellent human beings? Does human nature aspire to a perfection that defines it? Alternatively, is our humanity defined by something we all share equally, some common attribute? In the United States today we are likely to think of humanity in this second way, as an equality of rights that we all share. A political sign posted on the lawn by one of my neighbors includes the declaration that in this house we believe that "no human being is illegal," which implies that the rights we share equally belong to us not as citizens but as human beings. The transpolitical character of our humanity holds also if we define our humanity in terms of human excellence, but in this mode of definition there is a tension between perfection or excellence and our individual but still human nature. Kierkegaard wrestles with the problems of uniting the universal and the particular.[1]

A digression will help to position Kierkegaard in his historical context. Kierkegaard was as conscious as his contemporaries, Marx and Nietzsche, that the Enlightenment project had roots in the critique of Christianity. Indeed we might wonder whether Kierkegaard's *Attack upon "Christendom"* was not intended to finish what Hobbes started when he published "Of the

Kingdom of Darkness." If we accept the premise that Kierkegaard was aware of the modern critique of Christianity, we must accept also the possibility that Kierkegaard intended to announce the failure of the Enlightenment project, at least in its most extreme form, which aimed at the abolition of Christianity. Christianity had not been, indeed will not be, abolished. The reader might rebut this assertion by pointing to Kierkegaard's *Practice in Christianity* as describing bourgeois Europe as a place where no one is a Christian precisely because everyone is a Christian. Christianity has succeeded in defining European humanity in terms of an individual self claiming eternal validity in spite of the Enlightenment attempt to destroy the structure of belief that supported that eternal consciousness. Modern man believes more than ever in the self of which he is conscious, but he no longer has faith in the God that loves and sustains that self. The twilight of the Christian God in conjunction with the affirmation of the eternal self gives birth to European nihilism as Kierkegaard diagnoses it in *The Sickness Unto Death*.

Let us return to the bearer of rights who asserted his absolute equality with every other bearer of rights. Viewed in a merely finite perspective, this self-assertion quickly appears as mere vanity. While the self asserts its right to life, nature assures us only of our right to death. As Prince Hal reminds Falstaff, "Thou owest God a death" (1 *Henry IV*, 5.2.126). This is hardly a satisfactory response to human beings who have learned to look upon the self as an end in itself. Kierkegaard devotes his rhetorical power and dialectical wizardry to encouraging the finite self to choose the conditions that would support the self's own consciousness of being infinite and eternal.

Kierkegaard does not speak in terms of equality, excellence, and the relation between them. He prefers to work with the categories of the aesthetic, the ethical, and the religious. The aesthetic is the immediate, finite, historical self that lives and works in the world of more and less. The ethical is the universal. It is a good question why Kierkegaard does not call the ethical the categorical imperative. Why does he not simply endorse Kant?[2] One difference is that for Kierkegaard the rational universal is not imperative at all; it is a choice one must make. An example might be beneficial at this point. In *Fear and Trembling*, the merman comes to experience guilt over his conduct toward the young maiden. But how can he be guilty? Abducting maidens is simply what mermen do. That a beast of prey might experience guilt for being what he is is simply inconceivable. Aesthetically, the merman is a creature of conquest. The merman's world is one of stronger and weaker, faster and slower, but without right or wrong. The merman must choose to live in a world of good and evil. Only through this choice does he enter into sin and guilt. The merman does not discover himself under a categorical imperative. He must choose to be an ethical being.

Why does Kierkegaard need a third category, the religious? The religious sphere is that of the God as Teacher and Savior. Man does not discover the truth within himself. If the truth is within me, then no choice is necessary. I need merely to remember or rediscover that which I have been from all eternity. If choice is necessary, then the God as Teacher and Savior is also necessary in order to supply the eternal consciousness which as a self I have chosen.

Kierkegaard's dialectical acrobatics are surely beyond the reach of the ordinary person (for in the aesthetic realm, dialectic is a matter of more or less talent), but it is precisely the common man and woman that Kierkegaard most wants to reach. It is the common man who has come to realize that he is not common at all. Each of us is special, each is of infinite worth. But how so? We are transient creatures; all that we accomplish is vanity. An older language might have answered this question by saying that we are all children of God with an immortal soul. The Enlightenment set out to expose this God as a mere creature of our childish imagination. But the God of our imagination is dead, as is the God supplied by reason alone. Amazingly, the immortal soul, the eternal consciousness of self is not dead. Man's longing for the eternal is greater than ever, but without God the longing must turn to despair; indeed, it becomes a will to despair. If the gods of reason and imagination have failed us, our eternal consciousness can be sustained only by a God who is a discovery of neither reason or imagination. That God is the Absolutely Other. Whatever the imagination might suggest, that is not it. Reason cannot grasp it, for it is other than reason absolutely. It is the God as Teacher and Savior.[3]

These, then, are Kierkegaard's three categories: the finite aesthetic realm, the world of greater and lesser; the category of the ethical universal; and the religious, the God as Teacher and Savior.

In Kierkegaard's disenchanted modern world, the world of the twilight of the gods, why not simply retreat into the aesthetic? The aesthetic is not without its charms. Indeed, one needs to say that the beauties of this world all belong to the aesthetic realm. In the realm of more and less, higher and lower, talent, ability, and energy reign supreme. True, it is a world in which many, even the vast majority, are oppressed; nature is wasteful. But it is also the world of Shakespeare and Goethe, Socrates and Plato. Kierkegaard was particularly fond of Mozart, whom he placed in the aesthetic "realm of the gods."[4] The skilled dialectician also belongs to this world. The aesthetic category is the category of the genius, not the apostle.[5] *Philosophical Fragments* presents the highest human relationship as one in which the teacher serves as an occasion for the learner to discover the truth within himself. The highest relation of one human being to another is a finite, aesthetic relationship whose greatest practitioner was Socrates. To answer the question of our title, why not turn to the aesthetic? Kierkegaard's concept of excellence lies in the aesthetic realm where great talent and great strength become what they are. This flowering is not a choice any more than a plant chooses to grow. It is, however, an end in itself. The beautiful has its *telos* within itself (*Either/Or* II, 277).

Why not stop here? Why is the inequality of the aesthetic not enough? Why is it not even natural? For Kierkegaard, this is simply a historical question with a historical answer. In nineteenth-century Europe, the aesthetic achievement, however great, is measured against the longing of a self that wills itself as an eternal consciousness. Under the scrutiny of this infinite longing every aesthetic accomplishment is exposed as ephemeral and vain (*Either/Or* II, 198–99, 207). Where even the greatest achievement, work, and task are as nothing, the suffering of the oppressed is intolerable. Those who suffer are selves of infinite worth, and they are conscious of themselves as such. The equality of rights is grounded in the recognition of an equality of worth. Kierkegaard, the observer, sees that this equality of worth is ultimately grounded in the consciousness of our eternal self. But an eternal consciousness is not more than a false consciousness for a finite, aesthetic existence, an existence abandoned by God. Modern man was created in the image of God, a God in whom he no longer believes. Marx and Feuerbach taught us that this God was the mere projection of our own highest human aspirations. We must reclaim our own divinity. We must build the true and only heaven in the world of our finite experience. Kierkegaard sees that this is indeed the aspiration of modern man. Heidegger goes even farther down this road: conscience is man's call to himself.[6]

The eternal consciousness of the finite self—what Kierkegaard calls a historical point of departure for an eternal consciousness—is then simply a historical fact.[7] Oddly enough, it is possible to understand our eternal consciousness only if a certain kind of historicism is true. Christianity or Christianity plus philosophy has created in man the infinite longing of an eternal consciousness.[8] To repeat, under the scrutiny of this infinite longing every aesthetic accomplishment is exposed as ephemeral. "The aesthetical as such is despair" (*Either/Or* II, 259). *Vanity of vanities, all is vanity* (cf. *Either/*

Or II, 80–81). Judge Wilhelm addresses the two letters of the second half of *Either/Or* to a young man of seemingly boundless intellectual talent who tries to find completion in a merely aesthetic existence, but his accomplishment is always incommensurable with the *telos* he seeks. Judge Wilhelm's advice to this young man is really quite shocking: he tells him to despair (*Either/Or* II, 212). But of what is he to despair? He is to despair, not of his eternal consciousness, but of everything finite, of the whole realm of more and less, higher and lower. It is this despair that allows him to grasp the ethical universal, to choose to do his duty. This is the step that Kant leaves out. Kant tells us to obey the categorical imperative and in this way lead a life of rational consistency. But why? "As a particular individual I am not the universal, and to require that of me is absurd" (*Either/Or* II, 268). Why should the aesthetic man not lead a life of infinite variety if he is so able? Judge Wilhelm's answer is that the aesthetic individual is never satisfied because he already sees his existence in the light of his eternal consciousness, and from this point of view everything fails. One is in constant pursuit of happiness, but one never achieves happiness. The liberation from the Sisyphean pursuit of happiness is to choose despair, the ultimate and final despair of all things finite as ends in themselves. This is the step Kant skipped, the step that opens the way to the affirmation of the ethical universal. Some readers may be reminded of Nietzsche's effort to discover a new optimism by thinking pessimism through to its ultimate conclusion.

It is probably more important than it seems to note here the distinction that Judge Wilhelm draws between doubt and despair (*Either/Or* II, 215). Doubt is a natural response to the duality of things, to the fact that what is more in one sense is less in another. In the *Republic* (523b-c), Socrates calls such things summoners: they summon the mind to thought. For Descartes, our dreams become summoners when they force upon us the question of how we know we are awake. Judge Wilhelm distinguishes between doubt and despair in stipulating that doubt is not an act of the will; despair is a choice, an act of the will (*Either/Or* II, 217). His despair of all things finite is his choice of himself and of his eternal consciousness. In choosing himself in this sense, he also chooses God (*Either/Or* II, 218). The postulates of Kant's *Critique of Practical Reason* are all contained in the choice of the self that despairs of the finite and holds fast to its eternal consciousness: freedom from the finite world of pleasure and pain, the immortality of the soul, and belief in God.

That Judge Wilhelm does, indeed, hold fast to his eternal consciousness he states most emphatically. "I will not give up my sense of duty or the beauty that this brings to my life. I will let no one take these things from me."[9] But in holding fast to his eternal consciousness, Judge Wilhelm brings into sharp relief the suffering of this world. Where even the greatest achievements are as nothing compared to eternity, the suffering of the oppressed is intolerable. If we despair, as we must, of the Enlightenment project for bringing universal happiness in the realm of the aesthetic, is nihilism unavoidable? Those who suffer are selves of infinite worth, and they are conscious of themselves as such. How can the universal, the duty we fulfill, bring beauty to the suffering we all endure?

Judge Wilhelm gives various examples of how the universal might beautify life. His most extended discussion is of marriage; indeed, his two long letters to his aesthetic friend seem intended to persuade him to marry. A more manageable and equally serviceable example, however, may be found in the forty pages Judge Wilhelm devotes to viewing one's necessary labor as a task fulfilling one's duty (*Either/Or* II, 282–321).

Work is just that; as one of my colleagues, an economics teacher, once remarked, "They would not pay you for it if it were fun." From a purely aesthetic point of view, the labor I do from necessity is truly Sisyphean. The paycheck I earn this week is gone by next week. Life is, indeed, a joyless quest for joy. Of course, we all hope to get ahead, to save something, to find rest from our labors, to retire. One has no need of Kierkegaard's dialectical skill to see that retirement as the goal of life is a bleak picture. A teacher might be reminded of the student who wants to get her required courses "out of the way." The assumption is that the course in itself has no value. We might easily feel the same about a lifetime of work. Judge Wilhelm does not tell us to take courage, to suppress these feelings of meaninglessness. We are told instead to drain the cup. Despair and despair freely! The pain that racks your body from the jackhammer you grip, the ingratitude of the client whose tedious affairs you have resolved, the unteachable student over whom you labored with infinite patience, these, the Judge tells us, are as meaningless as they seem. Radical despair of each of these finite labors opens the way to seeing that labor as our individual task, our duty. In this sense, all lives are equal. If we look upon our fate, however lowly, as being our task, then it gains the significance of the universal, not in an abstract way, but through each of us fulfilling our own particular task. The task, which had become clear to us in its own utter futility, is now restored as a thing of infinite worth because it is our participation in the universal. Despair of the finite takes away everything, but by holding fast to our eternal consciousness, we get it all back again. Kierkegaard sometimes calls this "repetition" (*Either/Or* II, 144).

Is this story similar to the story of Job? Job loses all that he loves as a temptation to despair of God. He despairs of his earthly goods only in the sense that he has lost them, not in the sense that he has ceased to love them or see their beauty. As a reward for his faith in God, Job gets back, in some form, all the things that he loves. The loss of his earthly goods tempts him to turn away from God. At no point does he see the emptiness of the things he loves or cease to love them. Kierkegaard's story is quite different. Here, we begin by despairing over the finite in order to defiantly hold fast to our eternal consciousness. Our dilemma is one Job never faced. Judge Wilhelm exhorts his friend to despair of all things finite in order to have them restored as a manifestation of his duty and his relation to the Absolute. One is tempted to say that what is saved here is not the glory of God but the beauty of the earth. And all this through an act of the will.

Has Kierkegaard here simply fallen back on the Lutheran tradition in which we are all called by God to fulfill our task? In the Lutheran tradition, we owe our labor in our calling to the greater glory of God. It is a temptation on our part to labor for some finite, earthly good.[10] Kierkegaard's story reverses this drama. Viewing our task as our duty now ennobles our finite activity. Perhaps what Kierkegaard proposes can be found in Ivan Denisovich. Suffering the injustice of slave labor as a bricklayer in a prison camp, Ivan's sense of his own human dignity allows him to take pride in his craftsmanship.[11] Perhaps Solzhenitsyn ascribes this possibility to God's grace. Kierkegaard seems to ascribe it to human will:

We noted at the outset that equality in America today is thought of mostly as equality of rights. Kierkegaard finds equality rather in the universality of duty. Kierkegaard does not discuss the relation of rights to duties, and it is hard to know what he might say in this regard. Without passing over the issue entirely, we can note one similarity between rights and duties. We all have equal rights regardless of our unequal talents. In Kierkegaard's presentation, the universality of duty restores the dignity of our particular aesthetic task, but in such a way that all tasks are equal. From the aesthetic point of view, Mozart is far above Salieri, but judged in the light of our eternal consciousness, everything human fails, Mozart just as much as Salieri. And if we see both genius and mediocrity as doing their duty, then they are both restored equally to dignity. Each finds the beautiful within itself.

There is a strong element of egalitarianism in Kierkegaard, but it is hard to know the status of this egalitarianism. Is it a response to his own historical situation? Does Kierkegaard think there is anything deeper than history to which one might appeal? There is, of course, a problem with the ethical as we have presented it above. Judge Wilhelm assumes or insists that the universal can be reconciled with the particular. In his treatment of Abraham and Isaac, Kierkegaard raises the possibility that that might not be true. If things are as Abraham thinks they are, then he has an absolute duty toward God which stands in glaring contradiction to his ethical duty as a father. Here, the particular is higher than the universal. As Kierkegaard admits, if this is not the case, then Abraham is simply a murderer. Kierkegaard sometimes expresses the thought that the highest principles can be proved only negatively.[12] Perhaps the thought that is necessary to acquit Abraham is a thought we cannot think. Certainly, it is the pseudonymous author of *Fear and Trembling* who boasts that if he ever meets a thought he cannot think, he will have the courage to recognize it. Is the author's boast also an exhortation to the reader?

The other hero who stands out prominently in Kierkegaard's writings is Socrates. In *Sickness unto Death* we are even told that what the present age most needs is a Socrates. Would Socrates help us to see that we should not despair of the finite? Is Judge Wilhelm's injunction to despair of the finite once and for all in order to get it all back again with the blessing of duty a risky proposition? What could make it a risk worth taking? Christianity set an impossibly high standard for the goodness of life on earth. In the light of this standard, the finite world of more and less seems hardly worth the candle. Unlike Marx or Nietzsche, who each in his own way urges us ruthlessly to attempt to build heaven on earth, Kierkegaard urges us to see the inevitable vanity of all earthly action, to despair of the world, but in such a way as to get it all back again by virtue of our own infinite self-worth. In a spirit of resignation to his own historical situation, Kierkegaard seems to have tried to teach the men and women of the post-Christian world to "bloom where you are planted."[13]

I have neglected in this essay to say anything directly about Kierkegaard's emphasis on indirect communication. Kierkegaard sometimes published in his own name, but almost all of the works cited in this essay were published over various pseudonyms, such as Judge Wilhelm.[14] I have taken great liberty in stating Kierkegaard's opinions, since technically speaking these are only the opinions of the fictional authors who are the characters in his drama. This neglect is perhaps less important than it seems once one recognizes, as Kierkegaard did, that all communication is indirect communication (*Postscript*, 274). Voice and pen never communicate directly, since the listener or the reader must always try to rethink the thought he or she has heard or read. One must always ask, even of a prophecy, "What does it mean?" As long as this question is possible, philosophy is possible. In the case of Abraham, God had promised to make of him a great nation. The question is then unavoidable, What does it mean when God tells Abraham to sacrifice Isaac? As Judge Wilhelm might point out, this question is not an act of the will but rather a necessary part of trying to obey God's command. The problem in the Binding of Isaac is not only what God commands, but how he might command it.

The Socratic relation is for Kierkegaard the highest relation between one human being and another. Socrates cannot give another human being the truth. He can only act as an occasion for another to discover the truth. If Kierkegaard has a concept of excellence, to us it seems more Socratic than prophetic.

In an essay on equality and excellence in Kierkegaard, it would be an evasion to stop here without mentioning the vexed topic of his relation to the emancipation of women. Certainly, Judge Wilhelm gives vent to the most violent objections to the emancipation of women. Feminist interpretations of Kierkegaard have found the root of this antipathy in a fear of women's emancipation as a threat to patriarchal dominance.[15] Kierkegaard would seem to agree. Judge Wilhelm is a married man whose glowing description of his relation with his own wife is part of his rhetorical strategy in recommending marriage to an aesthetic bachelor with whom Wilhelm and his wife are both friends. We do not learn until nearly the end of the book that Wilhelm is somewhat jealous of his unmarried friend, a fact that he reveals only by denying it (*Either/Or II*, 330). Wilhelm also seems threatened by the comic romance of Scribe, whose plays suggest to Wilhelm that a married woman is being advised to spice up her otherwise boring marriage by occasional judicious affairs. Kierkegaard's portrayal of Judge Wilhelm certainly supports the feminist interpretation of patriarchy as based on fear of both women's rights and women's freedom. Whether Kierkegaard could paint such a picture of an insecure and jealous husband while at the same time identifying with him seems to me debatable. We are probably on safer ground if we limit ourselves to saying that emancipation was central to an Enlightenment project the success of which Kierkegaard had come to despair, and that his own project for enabling men and women to inherit the earth depended more on their recognition of their equal duties than of their equal right.

Notes

1. Søren Kierkegaard, *Either/Or* II, translated by Walter Lowrie (Garden City, NY: Doubleday Anchor, 1959), 268.

2. Joseph Cropsey raised this question in the margin of my Master's paper. I owe much to his engagement with Kierkegaard during the course he taught on that author at University of Chicago in 1971.

3. Kierkegaard's *Philosophical Fragments* draws out the consequences of the hypothesis of the God as Teacher and Savior. See Søren Kierkegaard, *Philosophical Fragments* and *Johannes Climacus*. Trans. Howard V. Hong and Edna H. Hong (Princeton: Princeton University Press, 1985).

4. Søren Kierkegaard, *Either/Or* I. Trans. David F. Swenson and Lillian Marvin Swenson (Garden City, NY: Doubleday Anchor, 1959), 47 and *Either/Or* II, 297.

5. See Søren Kierkegaard, *The Present Age* and *Of the Difference between a Genius and an Apostle*. Trans. Alexander Dru (New York: Harper and Row, 1962).

6. Martin Heidegger, *Being and Time*. Trans. John Macquarrie and Edward Robinson (New York: Harper and Row, 1962), 320, sec. 57.

7. This is my interpretive gloss on the question Kierkegaard poses on the title page of *Philosophical Fragments*.

8. This is Kierkegaard's version of what Leo Strauss, in his early writings, called the "unnatural" cave, a sort of cave beneath the cave. Leo Strauss, *Philosophy and Law: Contributions to the Understanding of Maimonides and His Predecessors*. Trans. Eve Adler (Albany: State University of New York Press, 1995), 135–36. Strauss tried to work his way back to the cave as Xenophon and Plato saw it, i.e., as it was before Plato called it a cave. Kierkegaard saw this as possible only for very few, i.e., as politically impossible.

9. I have invented this speech. See *Either/Or* II 243, 280.

10. Max Weber, *The Protestant Ethic and the Spirit of Capitalism*. Trans. Talcott Parsons (New York: Scribner, 1958), ch. 3, 79–92; see also 216, "ad gloriam Dei."

11. Alexander Solzhenitsyn, *One Day in the Life of Ivan Denisovich*. Trans. Ralph Parker (New York: Signet, 1963), 93–106.

12. Søren Kierkegaard, *Concluding Unscientific Postscript to Philosophical Fragments* I. Trans. Howard V. Hong and Edna H. Hong (Princeton: Princeton University Press, 1992), 220.

13. By way of contrast, Leo Strauss once wrote that "our fate is not our task." Quoted in Liisi Keedus, *The Crisis of German Historicism: The Early Political Thought of Hannah Arendt and Leo Strauss* (Cambridge: Cambridge University Press, 2015), 77, cf. 114. What I have presented as Kierkegaard's resignation to his historical situation would appear to Strauss to be a species of historicism that should be rejected.

14. The only exceptions are *Attack Upon Christendom* and *Of the Difference between a Genius and an Apostle*, the content of which Kierkegaard published over his own name.

15. For example, Céline Léon, "(A) Woman's Place Within the Ethical," in *Feminist Interpretations of Søren Kierkegaard*, ed. Céline Léon and Sylvia Walsh (University Park: Pennsylvania State University Press, 1997), 103–30.

Chapter 12

Nietzsche

The Indignity of Equality

Timothy Sean Quinn

Few thinkers have written so movingly about nobility, or with such undisguised hostility toward equality, as has Nietzsche. Nietzsche's teaching would therefore seem to pose the greatest challenge, if not the most terrible threat, to liberal democracy. Indeed, as the political and cultural crises of the early twentieth century made abundantly clear, perversions of Nietzsche's thought armed an unprecedented assault on liberal democracy on behalf of an empire of masters and slaves. In spite of this catastrophe, Nietzsche still appeals to those individuals who aspire to a nobility of soul and a potent individuality unsatisfiable within the constraints of liberal democratic notions of human equality. It is in Nietzsche, then, that questions about the possibility of ennobling democracy reach their most intense pitch.

Even though these are political questions, Nietzsche is not a political philosopher in the same manner as, for example, Marx or Hobbes. He offers no theory of government, nor any discrete plan for political renewal. In fact, he cautions against political action, urging passivity in the face of the "monstrous logic of horror" sweeping across Europe in the wake of the "death of God" and the collapse of Christian morality.[1] Neither does Nietzsche align himself with the political movements of his age, but labels himself "the last antipolitical German."[2] On the other hand, Nietzsche reflects deeply throughout his writings, but especially in *Beyond Good and Evil*, on human dignity, and therefore on the cultural and political conditions that allow it to see the light of day. These conditions, in turn, require a critique of those values shaping contemporary political practice, in an effort to "put the knife to the roots" of forces that efface human dignity. Central to these forces is a belief in equality.

We find an intimation of Nietzsche's later, more full-throated attack on equality in his essay of 1871, "The Greek State."[3] There, Nietzsche argues that the goal of the Greek state was to produce an "Olympian existence and constantly renewed creation and preparation of the genius" (*TGS*, 173). On behalf of this task, "the misery of men living a life of toil" is necessary: "slavery," therefore, "belongs to the essence of a culture" (*TGS*, 166).[4] By contrast, "we moderns" extoll both "the dignity of man and the dignity of work;" social equality and instrumentality of human beings go hand in hand. The servility of modern culture, "nourished by Communists and socialists as well as their paler descendants, the white rage of 'liberals' of every age," blinds it to the necessity for slavery, as well as to the servile values of the age. Consequently, the genuine sources for human dignity remain obscure. They can be recovered only to the extent that a society recuperates a distinction between the "few" and the "many": "every man . . . is only dignified to the extent that he is a tool of genius" (*TGS*, 172–73). In this early essay, in short, Nietzsche advocates what Georg Brandes would later identify as an "aristocratic radicalism," recognizable later in the well-known distinction between aristocratic and slave moralities.[5]

In the second *Untimely Meditation*, Nietzsche deepens his analysis of the modern suppression of human greatness in light of an excess of what he labels "the historical sense."[6] Our age, Nietzsche writes, is the result of an "antiquarian" devotion to the accumulation of facts without value: "There is a lack of that discrimination of value and that sense of proportion which would distinguish between the things of the past in a way that would do true justice to them . . . everything old and past that enters one's field of vision at all is in the end blandly taken to be equally worthy of reverence" (*ADH*, §3). Antiquarian history is therewith a horizon of equality; with equality comes degeneration: "When the senses of a people harden in this fashion . . . when the historical sense no longer conserves life but mummifies it, then the tree gradually dies unnaturally from the top downwards to the roots." This antiquarian inclination appears in our age, Nietzsche asserts, in the guise of modern natural science, specifically, "in the demand that history be a science" (*ADH*, §4). This demand, Nietzsche argues, proliferates "facts" at such velocity that it becomes impossible to assimilate them. Instead, "we moderns," filled with "indigestible knowledge stones," have become "walking encyclopedias" unable to muster the resolve to be dynamic actors in the world. Unable to fashion strong horizons within which to thrive, modern souls drift aimlessly through life without strong convictions, "weakened personalities" who remain spectators on the world scene. As Nietzsche trenchantly observes: "The war is not yet over and already it has been transformed a thousandfold into paper" (*ADH*, §5).

Central to Nietzsche's critique of modernity in this essay is his conviction that modern political life and modern natural science march hand in hand: social equality is the political correlate of scientific objectivity. The decline into mediocrity characteristic of modern society is consequently the effect of our belief that "'science is beginning to dominate life'" (*ADH*, §7). As in "The Greek State," a crucial symptom of this domination is the reduction of human beings to utility: "The present age," Nietzsche writes, "is supposed to be an age . . . of labor of the greatest possible common utility . . . the words 'factory,' 'labor market,' 'supply,' 'making profitable' . . . come unbidden to the lips when one wishes to describe the most recent generation of men of learning. Sterling mediocrity grows even more mediocre, science ever more profitable in the economic sense" (*ADH*, §7). These modern pathologies, however, have premodern roots, evident in the modern inclination to understand itself as the culmination of history, an inclination that bears the indelible mark of Christian eschatology. Thus, Nietzsche observes, "history is still disguised theology: just as the reverence with which the unlearned laity treat the learned class is inherited from the reverence with which it treated the clergy. What one formerly gave to the church one now gives . . . to learning: but that one gives at all is an effect of the church's former influence" (*ADH*, §8).

Modernity so conceived resembles a secularized Christianity, to which Nietzsche opposes "the Greeks." The Greeks, Nietzsche tells us, confronted a danger "similar to that which faces us," a chaos of overwhelming influences. The Greeks learned "to organize the chaos," achieving "victory over all other cultures" through "the superior strength of their *moral* nature," resulting in "a new and improved *phusis* (*ADH*, §10).[7] To return to the Greeks and therewith to liberate again the possibilities of human greatness over and against the mediocrity of the present age requires a critical annihilation of antiquarian culture, that is, of the Biblical and therewith the modern.[8] This task, in turn, requires Nietzsche to disinter modernity's roots. He undertakes this task in earnest in *The Gay Science*.

Nietzsche's theme in *The Gay Science* is, by and large, a restoration of human dignity after its undermining by the spread of egalitarian passions. We may take our bearings from a passage in Book V that spells out his relationship to the "petty politics" of his age:

> We "conserve" nothing; neither do we want to return to any past; we are by no means "liberal"; we are not working for "progress"; we don't need to plug our ears to the marketplace's sirens of the future: what they sing—"equal rights," "free society," "no more masters and no servants"—has no allure for us. We hold it absolutely undesirable that a realm of justice and concord should be established on earth (because it would certainly be the realm of the most profound levelling down to mediocrity and *chinoiserie*); we are delighted by all who love, as we do, danger, war, and adventure . . . we contemplate the necessity for new orders as well as for a new slavery—for every strengthening and enhancement of the human type also involves a new kind of enslavement. (*GS*, §377)[9]

Although Nietzsche distances himself from both conservative and liberal camps, he writes with particular venom about the "profound levelling" effect of liberal politics. In *The Gay Science*, Nietzsche notes that the mildness of modern souls—"common natures"—makes all "noble, magnanimous feelings" seem unbelievable because inexpedient; the irrationality of passion is what the common "despises" in the noble (*GS*, §3). In particular, the hegemony of the useful blunts nobility of strong passions that to the vulgar can seem to be nothing but madness owing to their inexpediency (*GS*, §55). By comparison, the regnant modern culture is an "industrial culture," comprised of "workers and employees" rather than warriors and artists (*GS*, §40). The modern condition is therefore an unwitting state of slavery: "a creature who is not at its own disposal and who lacks leisure is by no means something despicable to us . . . perhaps each of us possesses too much of such slavishness in accordance with the conditions of our social order and activity, which are utterly different from those of the ancients" (*GS*, §18).

The mediocrity fostered by liberalism is especially evident in its "religion of compassion." "Compassion," Nietzsche explains, "is the most agreeable feeling for those who have little pride and no prospect of great conquests" (*GS*, §13). It has rendered human beings "mild," "righteous," "inoffensive," "humane." These qualities Nietzsche takes to be signs of corruption characteristic of a society in decay, along with pacifism, desire for comfort and ease, and horror at cruelty (*GS*, §23). Seeking to tame "*all the dangers* which life once held," the religion of compassion (as Nietzsche states in *Daybreak*) demands that "everyone should assist" in the "common security"—"a tyranny of timidity" that for modern souls has become "their supreme moral law."[10] It is the root of the modern "herd morality."

Nietzsche's antidote to liberal mildness turns upon intensifying a "pathos of distance" evocative of Greek sensibilities surrounding nobility of soul: "The specific hue which nobility had in the ancient world is absent in ours because the ancient slave is absent from our sensibility." The failure of modern souls to ennoble themselves is therefore a direct consequence of being accustomed to "the *doctrine* of human equality, if not also equality itself" (*GS*, §18; emphasis in original). Equality imperils nobility. The distinction Nietzsche suggests here is noteworthy. While he avers, here and elsewhere, that Christianity is the source of the *doctrine* of equality, the *fact* of equality is the residue remaining after Christianity's gradual withdrawal from public life in Europe: one of the "shadows of God" still cast after the "death of God" and the waning of Christian conviction.[11] As Nietzsche explicitly states in *Daybreak*: "the more one liberated oneself from the [Christian] dogmas, the more one sought as it were a *justification* of this liberation in a cult of philanthropy" (*D*, §132; emphasis in original). By contrast, to vanquish these shadows and restore a "pathos of nobility and distance" demands new hierarchical orders rooted in "a new slavery." For Nietzsche, this task calls for a deconstruction of moral valuations in order to expose the roots of these valuations. These roots lie in the "pathos of distance" itself; disinterring these roots exposes the forces that attempted to erase the pathos of distance, in other words, the sources of the regnant moral values of pity and equality. Nietzsche's account therefore turns on a distinction between two principal types of moral valuation, the aristocratic or noble and the "slave morality." According to Nietzsche, the concepts "noble" and "aristocratic in the social sense" are the sources from which a notion of "good" originally developed, where "good" meant "'spiritually noble . . . highminded . . . privileged." By contrast, everything common or plebeian becomes "bad." Nietzsche cites as evidence the German word *schlecht,* which not only means "bad" but also "simple," "plain," "common." Originally, then, "bad" simply designated "the common man with no derogatory implication" (*GM*, §4). More significant for Nietzsche is the acknowledgment of the fundamentally egoistic character of these original moral valuations; it is only with the collapse of "aristocratic value judgments" that the antithesis between egoistic and unegoistic actions arises. This collapse begins in the priestly-ascetical morality embraced by Judaism, which rejects the equation of goodness with nobility, beauty, and power, and identifies the good with suffering, poverty, and powerlessness (*GM*, §7). Underpinning this act of revaluation is the psychology of *ressentiment*. While "all noble morality" grows out of self-affirmation, "slave morality" begins "when *ressentiment* itself turns creative and gives birth to values: the *ressentiment* of those who, denied the proper response to action, compensate for it only with imaginary revenge" (*GM*, §10). This revenge involves a psychological-linguistic act boiling up from the self-loathing of the slave. Rather than the egoistic self-affirmation of the noble, the slave morality, finding its servitude intolerable, directs its self-loathing away from itself toward the noble character it now blames for its own servile abasement.[12] The noble henceforth is "evil"; in that case, the servile, the weak, the impotent becomes, by contrast, "good." For Nietzsche, the "slave revolt" in morality begins with this epochal "revaluation of values."[13]

The "levelling" Nietzsche associates with liberal democracy and socialism is the direct descendent of the slave morality. It is therefore, vestigially, Judeo-Christian in origin. As he observes in *Beyond Good and Evil*: "*Morality in Europe these days is the morality of herd animals*. . . . And in fact, with the aid of a religion that indulged and flattered the loftiest herd desires, things have reached the point where this morality is increasingly apparent in even political and social institutions: the *democratic* movement is the heir to Christianity" (*BGE*, §202; emphasis in original). While the "death of God" that Nietzsche famously proclaims in *The Gay Science* represents the collapse of Christian belief and of "our entire European morality" that "was built on this faith, leaned on it, had grown into it" (*GS*, §343), Nietzsche is clear that "shadows of God" remain that still must be vanquished. These shadows are various: Nietzsche is particularly critical of modern natural science, and the modern state, both of which share a basis in the leveling of humanity's highest aspirations: science has become an instrument for gratifying the lowest, most utilitarian passions, and the modern state is rooted in notions of equality, "herd morality." Interestingly, both of these phenomena bear the distinctive traces of a religious faith in their fundamental convictions.

Most significantly, then, it is modern values, broadly construed, which translate the values of the Judeo-Christian slave morality into secular terms. In his discussions of these values, which permeate the entire ambit of his thought, Nietzsche's goal is twofold: to expose the Judeo-Christian roots of modern moral valuations, and therewith of those political institutions they sustain; and to indicate the mendacity of these values, which are in fact just as egoistic as the noble and aristocratic they claim to disdain. A few examples will suffice.

In aphorisms from Book I of *The Gay Science*, Nietzsche pillories the praise of selflessness or "neighbor-love," of compassion and pity, and of pacifism that he sees at the basis of modern notions of equality. He notes, to begin: "Compassion is the most agreeable feeling for those who have little pride and no prospect of great conquests; for them, easy prey . . . is something enchanting. Compassion is praised as the virtue of prostitutes" (*GS*, §13). On the one hand, compassion appears to be an expression of the equality of human beings; it "feels with" the suffering of others and wishes to share their suffering. On the other hand, compassion is at the same time a means for reversing the order of superior and inferior individuals: compassion implicitly debases the object of compassion with whom it supposedly sympathizes.[14] It is a weapon for "mediocre souls." Immediately, in the next aphorism, Nietzsche identifies "love of neighbor," a virtue arising directly from Christianity, as "a craving for new property" rather than a paradigm of selflessness, indistinguishable from sexual desire. Love of neighbor, therefore, while intending to be "the opposite of egoism . . . may in fact be the most candid expression of egoism" (*GS*, §14). The attempt to establish an equality of souls through the suppression of egoism is in short but a mask for asserting a bold egoism. The passions that serve to promote equality, in that case, are not what they seem; equality, a pervasive modern value, is but a disguise for power.

In short, "the popular superstition of Christian Europe" is the assumption that "what is characteristic of morality is selflessness, self-denial, self-sacrifice, or sympathy and compassion" (*GS*, §345). These qualities however have "no value in heaven or on earth"; they are instead symptomatic of the nihilism that has steadily eroded European politics. It would seem then that nobility of soul is impossible within modernity. Yet Nietzsche attempts throughout his writings to evoke a feeling for nobility. *Beyond Good and Evil* is, perhaps, his most noble attempt at reviving the noble.

"What is Noble?" is the title of the final part of *Beyond Good and Evil*. As Leo Strauss observes, the word *vornehm* is not the exact equivalent of "noble," the word typically chosen to translate it: *vornehm* "is inseparable from extraction, origin, birth."[15] Earlier, in aphorism 188, Nietzsche had characterized nature as noble; the first aphorism in this chapter addresses "the enhancement of the type 'man,' the constant 'self-overcoming of man'" on behalf of the rise of a "noble caste" (*BGE*, 257). The connection between these two senses of *vornehm*—as noble and as natural—is "will to power":

noble natures are born to rule.[16] Thus, Nietzsche invokes Alcibiades and Caesar, examples of noble natures he contrasts with "herd men," whom Nietzsche deems brutes (*BGE*, 200). But Nietzsche also notes that from noble natures will arise "new philosophers." Nobility therefore points in two different but related directions: toward statesmen, and toward philosophers. The role of the former is to secure the political conditions necessary for "new philosophers" to see the light of day: in a passage that recalls his early essay, "The Greek State," Nietzsche writes that the "fundamental belief" of an aristocratic society "must always be that society *cannot* exist for the sake of society, but only as the substructure and framework for raising an exceptional type of human being up to its higher duty and to a higher state of being" (*BGE*, §258; emphasis in original). This sort of society, Nietzsche adds, "will have to be the embodiment of will to power . . . because it is alive, and because life *is* precisely will to power" (*BGE*, §259; emphasis in original).

The emergence of a society that embraces will to power is impeded by the persistence of what Nietzsche deems "herd morality"; a consideration of the vicissitudes and weaknesses of the prevailing herd morality constitutes Nietzsche's theme in the three chapters preceding the final chapter, "What Is Noble?" For Nietzsche, all morality is herd morality since morality (or, as he sometimes calls it, "the political") is for the sake of the survival of communities (*BGE*, §201). The present European version of herd morality, "the democratic movement," suppresses any urge toward human greatness. In keeping with the argument of his *Genealogy*, Nietzsche writes, "everything that raises the individual over the herd and frightens the neighbor will henceforth be called *evil*; the proper, modest, unobtrusive, equalizing attitude and the *mediocrity* of desires acquire moral names and honors" (emphasis in original). Nonetheless, Nietzsche observes at the same time an inchoate longing within liberal democratic and socialist societies for the very greatness of soul they suppress, as was evident in the Europe's response to Napoleon: "What a relief it is for these European herd animals, what a deliverance from an increasingly intolerable pressure, when, in spite of everything, someone appears who can issue unconditional commands; the impact of Napoleon's appearance is the last major piece of evidence for this" (*BGE*, §199). Those in whom this longing resonates most potently Nietzsche deems "free spirits"; Nietzsche writes *Beyond Good and Evil* precisely to appeal to and to direct their longings toward "a new *task*" of reordering society on behalf of the emergence of "new philosophers" (*BGE*, §203; emphasis in original). It must be the case, then, that these "free spirits" can be discovered within the prevailing democratic society. Nietzsche's Zarathustra looks for kindred spirits in a town named "The Motley Cow."[17] As Lawrence Lampert observes, what is motley about the town is its collection of diverse human beings, a collection only possible in a democratic age.[18] For this very reason, a democracy could serve as a breeding ground for "higher" human types. In a notebook entry from 1883 regarding the relationship between the "last man"—humanity as it currently exists—and the "overman"—humanity transformed—Nietzsche confirms this view: "The aim is *by no means* to conceive the latter as matters of the former. Rather, the two types are to exist beside each other—separated as much as possible; *like the gods of Epicurus, the one not meddling with the other*" (emphasis in original).[19] Democratic equality can eclipse but not wholly efface the possibility of human nobility; a basis for it remains in the egoism at the core of modern Christian-inspired values of selflessness and pity.

Free spirits, then, are a first step in the recuperation of nobility; they are the predecessors of the "new philosophers." But free spirits are of two sorts. The first are creatures of the prevailing Enlightenment morality, disenchanted with Christian values but nonetheless remaining in its throes. Early in *Beyond Good and Evil*, Nietzsche brands them "the levelers . . . scribbling slaves of the democratic taste and its 'modern ideas;'" lacking solitude and believing that philosophy ought to be edifying, they remain "ridiculously superficial" (*BGE*, §44).[20] At the end of the book, he reveals that their desire for freedom "and subtleties in the feeling of freedom necessarily belong to slave morals and morality"; it is not noble souls, but slaves who desire to be free. The second sort are "those of a different faith . . . who consider the democratic movement to be not merely an abased form of political organization, but rather an abased (more specifically a diminished) form of humanity" (*BGE*, §203). These free spirits look "towards new philosophers" who are at the same time commanders and leaders. At times, Nietzsche appears to blur the difference between the statesman and the philosopher; they converge in their shared effort to revalue all prevailing values. They depart, however, on their relation to civil society: genuine philosophy is not edifying, has no public teaching to offer. Unlike the bold self-assertion of the great statesman, the egoism of the philosopher drives him away from public life. Nietzsche's teaching about nobility preserves the doubleness of politics and philosophy by refraining from the attempt to justify philosophy in light of the political.

Nietzsche therefore precedes his statements about the nature of both nobility and philosophy with a reprise of the conditions needed for both to see the light of day. A noble soul embraces egoism while disdaining vanity (*BGE*, §265, §261); it feels an "instinct for rank" (*BGE*, §263); it is awakened by "long struggle" with "unfavorable conditions and through the ennobling effects of profound suffering (*BGE*, §262, §270). It rejects all duties except the one to exercise its own privileges and responsibilities (*BGE*, §272). Nietzsche does not yet reveal what these privileges and responsibilities are. Instead, he summarizes in a single aphorism the *problem* of nobility:

> What is noble? What does the word "noble" still mean to us today? How do noble people reveal who they are, how can they be recognized under this heavy, overcast sky of incipient mob rule that makes everything leaden and opaque?—There are no actions that probe who they are . . . and there are no "works" either. . . . It is not works, it is faith that is decisive here, faith that establishes rank order . . . some fundamental certainty that a noble soul has about itself, something that cannot be looked for, cannot be found, and perhaps cannot be lost either.—*The noble soul has reverence for itself.* (*BGE*, §28; emphasis in original)

Nobility is a problem not merely as a result of the way "the democratic taste" has fogged our vision of humanity's highest aspirations. It is a problem owing to its hiddenness, its distinction from the public life of action. The separation of the concept of the noble from works and deeds recalls Nietzsche's earlier assertion regarding the reverence the common has for the great, a reverence rooted in great deeds and great passions, that is, a reverence for what is public and shared. But what is public and capable of being shared is invariably vulgar. As Nietzsche states in aphorism 269, "the masses, the educated, the enthusiasts . . . admire 'great men' and prodigies who inspire people to bless and honor the fatherland, the earth, the dignity of humanity, and themselves, 'great men' who are pointed out to young people for their edification." What is truly great escapes the public eye. Here, Nietzsche effectively redefines the proper sphere of reverence: not what is public, but what is hidden, the reverence of the noble soul for itself.

Significantly, Nietzsche's revelation of the hiddenness of genuine nobility matches his insistence on the hiddenness of the philosopher. All philosophy is done in solitude; the philosopher "was always a hermit first" (*BGE*, §289). What is genuinely philosophic is therefore also concealed, "an abyss behind every ground," a cave beneath the cave. As Nietzsche points out much earlier in *Beyond Good and Evil*, it behooves the philosopher to disguise himself, to remain "hard to understand" in order to protect his thought from being debased by the many. Nietzsche repeats that admonition in the aphorism immediately following the one indicating the relationship between philosophical solitude and philosophical depth: "Every profound thinker is more afraid of being understood that of being misunderstood" (*BGE*, §290). The three aphorisms following this statement about the esoteric character of philosophy make plain why these distinctions and these measures are necessary: the first concerns the human race (*der Mensch*), the second concerns a philosopher (*ein Philosoph*), and the third, a true human being (*ein Mann*). In the first case, Nietzsche, writing in summary fashion, states that "the human being is a diverse, hypocritical, artificial, and opaque animal . . . the human being invented good conscience so that he could enjoy his soul as something simple . . . and the whole of morality is a brave and lengthy falsification that makes it possible to look at the soul with anything like pleasure" (*BGE*, §291). It is, however, the goal of the philosopher to plumb the heights and depths of the soul, "struck by his own thoughts as if from outside, from above and below." The philosopher therefore represents the highest instance of the human: "a person who constantly experiences, sees, hears, suspects, hopes, and dreams extraordinary things . . . a being who is frequently running away from himself, frequently afraid of himself,—but too curious not to always come back to himself" (*BGE*, §292). This description of the philosopher recalls Nietzsche's earlier characterization (from Part II of *Beyond Good and Evil*) of the "philosopher of the future" as an "attempter." The German word *Versucher*, "attempter," is deliberately ambiguous; it evokes the word *Versuchung*, "temptation."[21] To philosophize is to be tempted to attempt; philosophical knowledge, in short, begins and ends for Nietzsche in self-knowledge. But to feel the temptation toward self-knowledge requires strength of character: however terrifying the truths revealed to the philosopher about his soul, he remains "too curious not to always come back to himself." In returning to himself, the philosopher becomes *ein Mann*, a true man. The third aphorism in this group of three therefore considers the character necessary for the pursuit of philosophy: one must be loyal and unafraid to seek out and defend what is his own, "who has his anger and his sword . . . a man who is naturally a *master*." For such masters to arise, "the *unmanliness* of what is christened 'pity' . . . needs to be forcefully and thoroughly exorcised" (emphasis in original).[22] The exorcism will invariably be painful, since the "morbid over-sensitivity and susceptibility to pain" that now besets Europe portrays itself as "something higher" using "bits and pieces" of religion and philosophy. It has been Nietzsche's effort throughout *Beyond Good and Evil*—indeed, across the entire ambit of his thought—beginning with "The Greek State," to attempt an exorcism of the impoverished democratic vestiges of the Judeo-Christian morality that have held sway since the death of God.

Fittingly, then, *Beyond Good and Evil* concludes, after its consideration of human character, with the revelation of a new god to seduce the new philosophers. This new god, "that great hidden one," "the genius of the heart," is Dionysus (*BGE*, §295). Nietzsche makes two bold claims about Dionysus: first, that he is a philosopher, and second, that he, and indeed all gods, laugh (*BGE*, §294). The divine laughter is one shared by the new philosophers: the fact that "even gods philosophize" leads them to "a new and super-human laughter." The laughter of philosophizing gods and mortals is illustrative of their knowledge of rank, with the "*golden* laughter" (emphasis in original) of superhuman souls at the top and the coarse laughter of the vulgar at the bottom. Nietzsche's allusions to the "*gai saber*" of the Provençal poets (from which he gathers the title of the book that announces the death of God, *The Gay Science*) is meant to invoke both laughter and chivalry; it is the name he gives the antidote to the "cult of suffering" prevailing in Europe, in the age of "the last man." Human dignity, in short, can be restored only by rediscovering what is genuinely worthy of laughter.[23] But such laughter is only possible in light of the highest instance of humanity. That highest instance is the philosopher. If the reign of the "cult of suffering" and of "the democratic taste" is to come to an end, genuine philosophy must somehow see the light of day.

What is at stake in Nietzsche's political musings then is not a certain political order but the dignity of philosophy, for which a certain political order prepares.[24] Although Nietzsche praises Alcibiades and Napoleon, great statesmen are ultimately of lesser stature than the philosopher. Democracy, in its insistence that philosophy must be edifying, poses a unique set of threats to the dignity, as well as to the very possibility, of philosophy. Democratic equality inclines philosophy toward attempts at public edification. But once the philosopher aims at edification, he must appeal to prevailing moral convictions; since all morality is, for Nietzsche, political, all morality is "herd morality." When the philosopher seeks to align himself with the herd, he invariably ceases to be a philosopher, and becomes "a teacher of the purpose of existence" rather than "an attempter." The confusion of philosophy with public edification is a vestige of Christian neighbor love: it presumes equality of souls. As a result, it undermines the authentic, instrumental role of politics, that is, "as the substructure and framework for raising an exceptional type of being up to its higher duty and to a higher state of being" (*BGE*, 258). It therefore behooves the philosopher to disguise himself, to remain "hard to understand" in order to protect his thought from being debased by the many. As Nietzsche explains in Part II of *Beyond Good and Evil*, "Our highest insights must—and should!—sound like stupidities, or possibly crimes, when they come without permission to people whose ears have no affinity for them" (*BGE*, §30). Consequently, "Every profound spirit loves a mask . . . a mask is constantly growing around every profound spirit, thanks to the consistently false (that is to say *shallow*) interpretation of every word, every step, every sign of life he displays" (*BGE*, §40; emphasis in original). The preservation of the dignity of philosophy, in short, requires not only a distinction between "high" and "low," the noble and the vulgar, but also between exoteric and esoteric writing. Philosophy and the city, so to speak, remain at odds. In this way, as in others, Nietzsche points us back to the ancients, who (with the notable exception of Socrates, in Nietzsche's view) did not shirk from nobility of soul.

Dignity so conceived is not then a political virtue, but the virtue of the strong individual. There is no way, then, to ennoble democracy, except as a staging ground for a nascent aristocratic order. Abandoning the modern "democratic taste," Nietzsche therefore yearns for "the Greek conception of culture" as a condition for the restoration of the noble (*ADH*, §10). In this way, we are returned to his original notion in "The Greek State" of a social order that requires slavery. To reorder society in this fashion would represent a summary display of "will to power": "'Exploitation,'" Nietzsche writes, "does not belong to a corrupted or imperfect primitive society; it belongs to the *essence* of being alive as a fundamental organic function; it is a result of genuine will to power, which is just the will to life" (*BGE*, §259; emphasis in original). For there to be slaves or servile souls requires, of course, that there exist masters, noble souls. Nietzsche thus anticipates an "enhancement" in "the type 'man'" as the task of an aristocratic society alive to "the pathos of distance" (*BGE*, 257). It is precisely this pathos that (among other things) the philosopher discovers in his exploration of the heights and depths of his own soul. One might catch a wisp here of Plato's philosopher-king who is able to judge the metals that define his citizens, and therefore their proper caste, a judgment that can only be delivered from the point of view of the noble or "high."[25]

Nietzsche's return to the "Greek," however, is vexed by the demand to liberate "philosophers of the future," free from the values that have rendered this age the age of the "last man." Illustrative of this dilemma is Zarathustra's longing for the "overman," for the "self-overcoming of man," as harbinger of a return to Dionysian service. The freedom of the "free spirits" therefore leads to a new sort of bondage; philosophy is the highest expression of will to power, that is, of grinding necessity, of life. The dignity of philosophy does not consist, then, in the ideal of a soul noble and ennobling, but in the philosopher's clear-eyed embrace of the compulsion to create values at once new and ancient.

In the end, Nietzsche's teaching concerning the indignity of equality is ambiguous. Responding to the failure of desiccated Christian values to sustain hope in the highest human possibilities, Nietzsche looks to a future whose contours remain obscure, a "sea of infinite possibility." On the other hand, Nietzsche looks backward, to a return to the Greeks on behalf of liberation from those Christian and modern values that have rendered this a nihilistic, life-denying age. An aphorism from the final book of *Beyond Good and Evil* offers a perfect and succinct expression of this ambiguity: " 'Too bad! What? Isn't he going—backwards?'—Yes! But you understand him badly if you complain about it. He is going backwards like someone who wants to take a great leap" (*BGE*, 281). Longing for a new divinity, Nietzsche asserts the hegemony of the human; human dignity consists but in the endless effulgence of the will, exploring its own heights and depths, that is, in eternal return, *amor fati*.

Notes

1. Friedrich Nietzsche, *The Gay Science* (*GS*), trans. Josephine Nauckhoff and Adrian del Caro (Cambridge: Cambridge University Press, 2001), 199. All future references will be to *GS* and the aphorism number.

2. Nietzsche's self-characterization appears in the first German edition of *Ecce Homo*, but is dropped from subsequent editions. See *Kritische Studienausgabe* (*KSA*), ed. Giorgio Colli and Mazzinio Montinari (Munich: Deutscher Taschenbuch Verlag, 1967–1977) Band 14, 462; 472–73. Compare *Ecce Homo* (*EH*), in *The Anti-Christ, Ecce Homo, Twilight of the Idols: And Other Writings* (Cambridge: Cambridge University Press, 2005), "Why I am so wise," §3.

3. "The Greek State" (*TGS*) in *On the Genealogy of Morality* (*GM*), trans. Carol Diethe (Cambridge: Cambridge University Press, 1997), 164–73.

4. According to Walter Kaufmann, "There is no more basic statement of Nietzsche's philosophy in all his writings than this statement. Here is . . . the clue to his 'aristocratic' ethics and his opposition to socialism and democracy." See *Nietzsche: Philosopher, Psychologist, Antichrist* (Princeton: Princeton University Press, 1950): 149, 319.

5. See Georg Brandes's letter to Nietzsche, and Nietzsche's reply of 2 December 1887 (KGB III/6, *Brief* 500), in which Nietzsche approves of the expression "aristocratic radicalism." See also Renato Cristi, "Nietzsche, Theognis, and Aristocratic Radicalism," in *Nietzsche as Political Philosopher*, ed. Manuel Knoll and Barry Stocher (Berlin and Boston: De Gruyter, 2014): 173–94.

6. Nietzsche, "Advantage and Disadvantage of History for Life" (*ADH*), *Untimely Meditations*, trans. R. J. Hollingdale (Cambridge: Cambridge University Press, 1997).

7. Although it is tempting to associate Nietzsche's use of the word *phusis* with Heidegger's later use of the term, their sense of *phusis* differs: For Heidegger, it designates an original understanding of Being, while for Nietzsche, it designates physiology. A "new and improved *phusis*" thus refers to a new breed of human beings; it is an aspect of Nietzsche's "biologism." See Note 16.

8. In his notebooks from Winter 1869–70, Nietzsche puts the matter bluntly; in his outline for a proposed book, "Sokrates und Instinkt," which would eventually become *The Birth of Tragedy*, Nietzsche indicates that the theme of his third chapter, religion, ought to begin in this fashion: "Monism as Impoverishment. Victory of the Jewish world over the weakened will of Greek culture." See *KSA* Band 7, 80.

9. See also *GS* 24: "China . . . is a country where large-scale discontentment . . . became extinct centuries ago; and in Europe too the socialists and state idolaters, with their measures of making life better and safer, might easily establish Chinese conditions and a Chinese 'happiness.'"

10. *Daybreak: Thoughts on the Prejudices of Morality* (*D*), trans. R. J. Hollingdale (Cambridge: Cambridge University Press, 1997), §175; emphasis in original.

11. See also *Beyond Good and Evil* (*BGE*), trans. Judith Norman (Cambridge: Cambridge University Press, 2002), §202; and *D* §132.

12. As Deleuze puts it, the difference between noble and slave expressions of moral values is the difference between "active" and "reactive" modes of will to power. See Gilles Deleuze, *Nietzsche and Philosophy*, trans. Hugh Tomlinson (London and New York: Continuum, 1986): 111.

13. Interestingly, Tocqueville seems to have anticipated Nietzsche's distinction between noble and slave moralities when he observed that aristocracy and democracy reflect "two distinct kinds of humanity." See *Democracy in America* II. iv. 8.

14. See Michael Frazer, "The Compassion of Zarathustra: Nietzsche on Sympathy and Strength," *Review of Politics* 68, no. 1: 49–78. For the contemporary devotion to compassion, see Martha Nussbaum, "Compassion: The Most Basic Social Emotion," *Social Psychology and Policy* 13 (1996): 27–58. See also Nussbaum's essay, "Pity and Mercy: Nietzsche's Stoicism," in *Nietzsche, Genealogy, Morality: Essays on Nietzsche's 'On the Genealogy of Morality,'* ed. Richard Schlacht (Berkeley: University of California Press, 1994): 139–47.

15. Leo Strauss, "Nietzsche's *Beyond Good and Evil*," in *Studies in Platonic Political Philosophy*, ed. Thomas Pangle (Chicago: University of Chicago Press, 1983): 174–91.

16. In keeping with this dual sense of the noble, Nietzsche also offers two senses of the natural: as *Natur* and as *phusis*. While *Natur* and *naturlich* designate nature in what we may call an ordinary sense, Nietzsche reserves the term *phusis* for human physiology transformed and beautified, "new and improved" humanity.

17. *Thus Spoke Zarathustra* (*TSZ*), trans. Adrian Del Caro (Cambridge: Cambridge University Press, 2006), "On the tree on the mountain."

18. Lawrence Lampert, *Nietzsche's Teaching: An Interpretation of Thus Spoke Zarathustra* (New Haven and London: Yale University Press, 1986), 33.

19. *KSA* 10:7 [21]; emphasis in original.

20. In *Ecce Homo*, Nietzsche states with characteristic bluntness: "[N]othing is more foreign and unrelated to me than this whole European and American species of *libres penseurs*. Just with dyed-in-the-wool idiots and clowns of 'modern ideas,' I find myself even more in conflict with representatives of this Anglo-American species. . . . They also want to 'improve' humanity in their own way, in their own image" (*EH*, 114).

21. See Michel de Montaigne, "To the Reader," in *The Complete Essays of Montaigne*, ed. Donald Frame (Stanford: Stanford University Press, 1958). The French word *essai* from which Montaigne draws the title of his work means "attempt." Nietzsche himself was a serious reader of Montaigne.

22. As Nietzsche states in *EH*: "I consider the overcoming of pity a *noble* virtue" ("Why I Am So Wise, §4; emphasis in original.)

23. See Leo Strauss's essay, "Kurt Riezler," in *What Is Political Philosophy?* (Westport, CT: Greenwood Press, 1959), 259. See also Strauss's remark in his Preface to *Spinoza's Critique of Religion* (New York: Schocken Books, 1965), 3: "It is safer to try to understand the low in the light of the high than the high in the light of the low. In doing the latter one necessarily distorts the high, whereas in doing the former one does not deprive the low of the freedom to reveal itself fully as what it is." Nietzsche would find this insight agreeable.

24. Commenting on *Beyond Good and Evil* in *Ecce Homo*, Nietzsche states that his book "is in essence a *critique of modernity*, including modern science, modern art—even modern politics—, along with indication of an opposite type who is as un-modern as possible, a noble, affirmative type" (emphasis in original). See *EH*, 135.

25. In his lectures on Plato, delivered when he was still a young professor of classical philology at Basel, Nietzsche praises the aristocratic element in Plato's thought. See his "Einführung in das Studium der platonischen Dialoge," chapter II: "Platons Philosophie als Hauptzeugniß für den Menschen Plato," in *Werke: Kritische Gesamtausgabe*, vol. II. 4, ed. Giorgio Colli and Mazzino Montinari (Berlin and New York: De Gruyter, 1995), 148–88.

Chapter 13

The Good and the Excellent
John Rawls's Egalitarian Liberalism

Michael Zuckert

It may be difficult to remember more than fifty years later what an explosive impact John Rawls's *A Theory of Justice* had when it appeared in its bright green cover in 1971. It was the book many had been yearning for, a book that made normative sense of the post–New Deal political world. It provided a rationale for government provision of security and welfare-promoting measures without demanding socialism, complete equality of outcomes, or curtailment of liberty. If Rawls was not a man for all seasons, his theory was a doctrine for all desiderata. He was clearly one of the breed we might denominate an egalitarian liberal—indeed, in some ways the originator of the late-twentieth-century version of that breed. But though an egalitarian, he was also a liberal in the original sense of that term, a thinker committed to liberty. He thus seemed the perfect pilot to steer the ship of state between the Charybdis of illiberal, unfree regimes such as Nazi Germany or the Soviet Union and the Scylla of Darwinian survival of the fittest libertarianism.

A Theory of Justice also had an amazing ability to appeal to a very broad and diverse audience on the grounds of intellectual style. It had a very clear, easy to grasp dominant narrative: justice can be discovered via the procedure of an agreement arrived at in an easily grasped situation of choice, what Rawls called the original position. Justice, that so elusive concept, could be stated in two quite specific and readily grasped principles. Here was a doctrine within relatively easy reach of all. At the same time, it was philosophically sophisticated, responding to most of the concerns then dominant in the ethical and political philosophy of the day as practiced by the professionals. It had something for nearly every turn of mind. Among the problems to be overcome was the opposition between equality and excellence. Although an egalitarian, Rawls was no leveler. There is room, he avers, for excellence in his capacious theory.

But before I can proceed to explain how Rawls attempts to make room for liberty and excellence along with equality, I must pause to clarify one aspect of my procedure. As is well known, Rawls developed two different systems or theories of justice, theories that relate to each other in ambiguous and somewhat uncertain ways. Rawls's readers—indeed, sometimes Rawls himself—in some instances find the two theories to be almost identical and in other instances see them as separate and different. I am among those who see them as different in the decisive respect, but similar in most of their conclusions about justice. In the second version of his theory, developed in his *Political Liberalism*, Rawls unveils a distinction between two types of theory—ones he calls comprehensive doctrines and the other he calls political doctrines. The latter does not merely designate the subject matter of the theory but also the grounding and scope of it.

Of the two, comprehensive doctrines are most familiar, for they are the kind of "religious, philosophical, and moral doctrines" that citizens typically hold *(Political Liberalism*, xvi). "They are comprehensive in that they relate to a very wide range of moral and political phenomena" (*PL*, I. 22). "Religious and philosophical doctrines express views of the world and of our life with one another . . . as a whole" (*PL*, II. 2.4). Moreover, comprehensive doctrines appeal for their validity to what Rawls loosely calls "metaphysics," which seems to include such disparate things as "specific metaphysical or epistemological doctrines" and the kind of deep-going faith commitments one finds in religious believers (*PL*, I 1.4; cf. I 5.1). Comprehensive doctrines appeal to what we might call ultimate truths of philosophy or religion.

By contrast, a political theory, in Rawls's special sense of the term, differs from a comprehensive one in that its subject matter is limited to the political realm, to what Rawls calls "the basic structure of society," defined as a "society's main political, social and economic institutions" (*PL*, I 2.1; cf. *PL*, VI 4.1). Many important moral matters lie outside its coverage. It is also "free-standing" in that "it is neither presented as, nor as derived from . . . comprehensive doctrines" *(PL,* I 2.2). It is "presented independently of any wider religious or philosophic doctrine" *(PL,* VI 4.1). It thus offers no specific metaphysical or epistemological doctrine beyond what is implied by the political conception itself" *(PL,* I 1.4).

Although Rawls's later system might be taken to supersede the earlier *A Theory of Justice,* my attention will be exclusively on the earlier version. My topic—equality and excellence—demands that, for our topic is among the many themes that receive far less attention in the later Rawls.

There are many places in Rawls's justice theory where he leaves room for excellence. To name a few—he affirms as part of justice a norm of "fair equality of opportunity," which leaves room for the display and rewarding of merit, that is, potential excellence. He has a robust doctrine of liberty that leaves room for the individual pursuit of excellence. His egalitarian principle of distributive justice allows, indeed underwrites, unequal distribution of resources, which can be a platform for the pursuit and achievement of excellence. In this regard he counters notions of justice, such as those Tocqueville diagnosed as dangers in democracies, that require ever increasing actual equality in resources and social standing, that is to say, notions of justice directly counter to excelling in any way.

These are all aspects of Rawls's theory where significant openings toward excellence occur. But I think the most significant aspect of Rawls's thinking indicating his commitment to excellence lies within his treatment of the good. His "justice as fairness" as developed in his first system is a comprehensive rather than a political doctrine. It is also a deontological rather than a teleological theory. The two are distinguished in terms of the relation between two central concepts of morality—the right (including justice) and the good. Teleological theories are those that consider the right as that which maximizes the good. The good has definitive priority in such theories. Plato and Aristotle are thinkers who present theories of this type. Deontological theory "does not specify the good independently from the right or does not interpret the right as maximizing the good" *(TJ,* 30). One way to understand the difference between the two types of theories is in terms of priority: as Rawls puts it, "in justice as fairness the concept of right is prior to that of good" *(TJ,* 31). This formula means that justice is derived independently of the good and, one might say, it has priority over it in the sense of trumping it. That is to say, what people desire and seek as their good is subject to restraint by the principles of justice.

The priority of right or justice over good is one reason Rawls is not often seen as a thinker who valorizes excellence. Yet despite the ordering of priorities within justice as fairness, the good and excellence play a notable role in *A Theory of Justice*.

Let me first provide a brief sketch of the derivation of the principles of justice with an eye to the place of the good in it. The basic idea of the derivation is that justice is that set of rules that all members of society would agree to were they in a position of fairness vis-à-vis each other at the moment of striking their agreement. Fairness requires at least these two features of the choice situation: that it be defined in such a way that no individual's claims to justice be sacrificed to others or even to the whole, and that none be able to knowingly demand rules that will specially favor themselves. In order to meet these requirements Rawls posits a situation he calls the original position in which the deliberators are free to demand principles that do not sacrifice their personal good or interests, but in which they lack information that would allow them to seek self-favoring rules. No sacrifice and no self-favoring. The latter is achieved via a veil of ignorance according to which the deliberators know nothing specific about themselves as they are in the real world. They do not know their gender or their abilities, interests, conceptions of the good, or their place in society or even what type of society they are members of. As is often noted, this is something like the state of nature as posited in earlier liberal theory. But Rawls is quite clear that this is no real situation: it defines the constraints that limit and channel the deliberations in the original position and thus the principles of justice that can be agreed to.

The good, or the conception of the good, that the deliberators have is among the things of which they are ignorant, as I have said. But they do know that they have some conceptions of the good, or of the ends that they pursue in life. They know *that*, but not *what*. Possessing only formal knowledge of the that, it would seem they lack enough information to choose desirable principles of justice, for they do not know what they desire. To solve that problem Rawls posits a set of goods that he calls primary goods, which, roughly speaking, are all-purpose goods that, no matter what the deliberators' particular conceptions of the good are, they can be presumed to want or need. The primary goods are "things which it is supposed a rational man wants whatever else he wants" (*TJ*, 92). Rawls identifies "broad categories of these primary goods": "rights and liberties, opportunities and powers, income and wealth," and a "sense of one's worth."

One consequence of the abstractness and identicalness of the deliberators is that one "representative person" can act on behalf of all. What that person rationally chooses will be the principles of justice, for it is the same as all the others would "choose." They (or he, she, or it) choose, Rawls argues, his two principles of justice. The two principles embody a more general basic single principle: "All social values . . . are to be distributed equally unless an unequal distribution of any, or all of these values is to everyone's advantage" (*TJ*, 62). This single principle bifurcates into the two principles, according to which of the primary goods is under consideration. According to the first principle, basic rights and liberties are to be distributed equally and are to have a certain priority in that they are not to be traded off against other sorts of primary goods. "Since opportunities and powers," including offices and positions, cannot be held equally by all, they are governed by one branch of the second principle, the rule of fair equality of opportunity, a very robust notion of equal opportunity. Finally, "income and wealth" are to be distributed according to the other branch of the second principle: any inequality in the possession of such goods can be justified if and only if it benefits the least advantaged persons in the society.

The good and with it the excellent receive a largely negative treatment in the derivation of the principles. Rawls considers as a potential principle something he calls perfectionism. This is a teleological principle in that it proposes to "define the duties and obligations of individuals so as to maximize the achievement of human excellence in art, science, and culture." He identifies Nietzsche and Aristotle as among the canonic philosophers who have affirmed some version of this principle. The treatment of perfectionism is the most direct and overt treatment of excellence in the entire *A Theory of Justice*. That treatment is negative insofar as Rawls concludes that this principle would be rejected and thus does not qualify as a correct principle of right for society. In the form of perfectionism the concern for excellence is "a counterpoise to egalitarian ideas" and stands for a certain sort of incompatibility between equality and excellence, with Rawls favoring equality (*TJ*, 326). The parties in the original position know that they have a conception of the good to which they are attached. It expresses what they particularly value. They also know, Rawls stipulates, that that these conceptions of the good, including matters of religious faith, differ among individuals and that therefore there is no one uniform conception of the good that prevails throughout their society. Accordingly, "they do not have an agreed criterion of perfection" or excellence.

> To acknowledge any such standard would be, in effect, to accept a principle that might lead to a lesser religious or other liberty, if not to a loss of freedom altogether to advance many of one's

> own spiritual ends. . . . The parties have no way of knowing that their claims [to their conceptions of the good and all that entails] may not fall before the higher social goal of maximizing perfection . . . thus it seems that the only understanding that the persons in the original position can reach is that everyone should have the greatest equal liberty consistent with a similar liberty for others. They cannot risk their freedom by authorizing a standard of value to define what is to be maximized by a teleological principle of justice such as perfectionism. (*TJ*, 327–28)

Individuals' conceptions of the good may be constrained by the principles of justice but not by others' conceptions of the good.

Rawls is emphatic, then, in rejecting perfectionism. The maximization of excellence is not to be the primary goal of society. But his position can be and often has been misunderstood. He does not mean to claim that all human "activities and accomplishments are of equal excellence" (*TJ*, 329). "Very often it is beyond question that the work of one person is superior to that of another. . . . Clearly there are standards . . . for appraising creative efforts" (*TJ*, 328). So Rawls denies that maximization of excellence is the standard of justice, but he by no means rejects excellence altogether or consigns it to the realm of indefeasible subjectivity.

Not only does he affirm the reality and relevance of excellence but he also attempts to provide for it in another feature of his complex system of justice. The reader might have noticed that the two principles contain no provision for the distribution of one further primary good, "the sense of one's worth." As it happens, this is the one most intimately related to our theme of excellence; it is also the primary good that Rawls pronounces "perhaps the most important" of them all (*TJ*, 440). Just as the distribution rule for the primary good is not present in the two principles, so it does not play a role in the main deduction of the principles in the original position. The chief way in which this good is realized in society is in terms of a natural "duty of mutual respect" that all members incur (*TJ*, 337). The primary good of self-respect is most visible in this duty, which makes it different from the goods provided for in the two principles, where the chief manifestation of justice is in terms of rights. Thus, the agent has a right, for example, to speak freely or to have certain opportunities on fair terms or to have a certain share of material wealth. There are, of course, duties that accompany these rights, but the duty bearers vary according to the aspect of the right involved. So, for example, the duty to provide fair equality of opportunity might fall to an individual employer to recruit employees in certain ways or to the state to provide basic education to all in order to fit all members with the intellectual wherewithal to pursue opportunities fairly. The individual has a right as specified or implied in the relevant principle of justice and the duties vis-à-vis that right lie scattered. In the case of self-respect the focal point is, rather, the duty of mutual respect, which is the operationalization of the primary good of the sense of one's worth. The connection between the primary good of sense of self-worth and the duty of mutual respect, that is, of respect by others, is forged via the thought that our sense of self-respect is at least in part dependent on receiving the respect of others. At the very least, "their self-respect and their confidence in the value of their own system of ends cannot withstand the indifference much less contempt of others" (*TJ*, 338). That is to say, active disrespect by others undermines one's self-respect. But Rawls goes even farther: "finding our person and deeds appreciated and confirmed by others" is a necessary support, it seems, for our self-esteem, "the sense of our own worth." We are to esteem others so that they will esteem us, so that we will esteem ourselves, a long chain of esteem finally reaching the primary good at issue.

Rawls derives the duty of mutual respect in a line of reasoning rather like the one that generates the two principles:

> Now the reason why this duty would be acknowledged is that although the parties in the original position take no interest in each other's interests [i.e., your desire for esteem does not in itself prompt me to grant it] they know that in society they need to be assured by the esteem of their associates. (*TJ*, 338)

So they accept a mutual duty to respect; the mutuality is the crucial feature of the reasoning for the duty.

Self-respect, Rawls implies, is a good in itself in that it provides a "sense of the person's own value," which is in itself, it seems, universally valued (*TJ*, 440). It is also instrumentally valuable in that it "implies a confidence in one's ability, so far as it is within one's power, to fulfill one's intentions" (*TJ*, 440). This latter formulation seems infelicitous; as stated, it appears to be tautological. I believe a better way to capture Rawls's point is to say that self-respect contributes to one's ability to fulfill one's intentions through fortifying one's confidence and thereby prompting effort and action.

One does not always know in advance one's capabilities for any given task but a general sense of self-esteem makes one likelier to pursue one's goals despite not knowing if they are achievable.

The link to our concern with excellence should now be clear. Excellence in any given pursuit implies and usually requires achievement beyond the ordinary and thereby a willingness to take risks and submit to the discipline that makes extraordinary achievement possible. Rawls identifies in the human psyche a motive force that tends to move in the direction of excellence, though it by no means guarantees its achievement. This is his Aristotelian principle: "other things equal, human beings enjoy the exercise of their realized capacities (their innate or trained abilities), and this enjoyment increases the more the capacity is realized" (*TJ*, 426). This principle is not normative; it is simply a fact about human motivation (*TJ*, 427). Nor does he understand it to be a teleological fulfillment of human potential. He derives its attraction from simpler and less cosmic features of the human constitution. "Presumably complex activities are more enjoyable because they satisfy the desire for variety and novelty of experience, and leave room for feats of ingenuity and invention. They also evoke the pleasures of anticipation and surprise" (*TJ*, 427). As a "psychological law governing changes in the pattern of our desires," the Aristotelian principle is not to serve as a standard for ranking the various conceptions of the good to which Rawlsean individuals adhere. But it does affirm a sort of natural impulsion toward these more complex developments of human capacities and thus supply a natural support for excellence or for movement in that direction.

Let us now see how these various elements of Rawls's theory of excellence, if it can be called that, work together. "Mutual respect," a necessary bulwark of self-esteem, is shown, he says, in our willingness to see the situation of others from their point of view, that is to say, to see it sympathetically and in a positive light. It is to view their situation "from the perspective of their conception of the good," and thereby to see it as a good. It is to accept limits on our actions or at least "to give reasons for our actions whenever the interests of others are materially affected" (*TJ*, 337). "Also respect is shown in a willingness to do small favors and courtesies, not because they are of material value but because they are an appropriate expression of our awareness of another person's feelings and aspirations" (*TJ*, 338). This is not to say that one must approve of all the actions and conceptions of the good of all others. The principles of justice set standards to govern our approbation and disapprobation. The duty of mutual respect does not mandate approval of unjust deeds and goals (*TJ*, 425). Moreover, as we indicated earlier, there are standards implicit in social practices that serve to regulate our approbations. There are more and less competent pianists or sprinters. The duty of mutual respect does not require that these differences be ignored. It is a duty of mutual but not of equal respect. But that mutuality requires at the same time that we be sensitive to "another person's feelings and aspirations" (*TJ*, 338).

The duty of mutual respect protects and fosters the sense of self-worth of individuals, which, in the ways specified above, builds confidence and competence and thus, together with the Aristotelian principle, conduces to the pursuit of excellence. The duty of self-respect does a lot of the work in the provision of the goods of self-respect and excellence so far as that is a feature of Rawlsean society. But it does not do all of it. The entirety of the system of justice as fairness, not only the duty of mutual respect, contributes to the achievement of self-respect. "Justice as fairness," Rawls pronounces, "gives more support to self-esteem than other principles" of justice and this fact provides "a strong reason for [the parties in the original positon] to adopt it" (*TJ*, 440). This is surely an important claim, but Rawls presents surprisingly little direct discussion of it. I believe the missing discussion can be supplied on the basis of what he does say in this context and throughout the book.

Part of his broader case is implied in the following observation: "Nor plagued by failure and self-doubt can we continue in our endeavors" (*TJ*, 440). Failure in our life projects undermines our self-esteem and drains us of aspiration and vigor. While justice as fairness by no means guarantees success in our ventures it does ensure that all members of society possess at least a floor of resources that guarantees that one's subsistence is not endangered or that one must engage in esteem-busting activities in order to survive. The provision of equal liberties and substantial material resources under the difference principle means that all members have fair prospects for success in their life ventures, certainly more than the less-advantaged members of society would have under other versions of social justice.

More important, it seems, is a feature of Rawls's system that can perhaps be best expressed in the Hegelian language of recognition. The provision to each and every member of a share of the resources of the society and of liberty to largely shape his or her own life is recognition of each and all as beings with value and rightful claims on the society. Not only are all affirmed as beings with value, but their values, that is, what they value as contained in their conceptions of the good, are all and equally affirmed. *That* they have a conception of the good, equally and presumably universally possessed, is more germane than *what* particular conception of the good they possess. There may be unequal achievement in the pursuit of any particular good but the various goods do not stand in a hierarchy vis-à-vis each other. All persons are thus validated not merely as persons but in terms of the particular goods they value. The society does not value Christians over Muslims or scholars over counters of blades of grass (*TJ*, 432). In sum: equal recognition in conjunction with enhanced prospects for success and insurance against abject failure conduce to self-esteem, which in turn conduces to the striving for and the possession of substantial resources for achieving excellence.

But does Rawls achieve the reconciliation of equality and excellence he seeks? Does the Rawlsean philosophy provide a theoretical reconciliation of the two? Does it promise to achieve that reconciliation in practice? Perhaps the most significant feature of Rawls's treatment of excellence is his rejection of perfectionism. The basis for that rejection, it may be recalled, is the fact that persons in the original position know that but not what. Any agreement on a perfectionist doctrine threatens the (unknown) conception of the good that the parties may have. Therefore, Rawls concludes, the only answer they can arrive at is to reject perfectionism in favor of "the greatest equal liberty consistent with a similar liberty for others" (*TJ*, 327–28).

As many critics of Rawls have pointed out, there is no reason the parties in the original position should be debarred from deliberating about the good just because they are ignorant of their own conception. Indeed, it is that very ignorance that guarantees that any answer they reach can satisfy the requirement that the deliberators not select self-favoring principles of justice. Not knowing their own conception of the good, their deliberations can be free of any infection by the common human tendency to believe one's own way is best. Rawls rules out a deliberation on the good behind the veil of ignorance via his stipulation that the parties "are assumed to be committed to different conceptions of the good and they are entitled to press their claims on one another to further their separate aims" (*TJ*, 327–28). In effect, this means that conceptions of the good are declared off-bounds from the outset; the parties are defined to be unwilling to put at risk their conceptions of the good to be. But is that rational for the parties in the original position to do? He implies that they are unalterably committed to their different conceptions of the good, but is this valid? At times he also emphasizes their ability to change conceptions of the good as justification for practices such as freedom of speech. If change is possible and parties in the original position know that, might they not deliberate about the good in the peculiarly favorable conditions in which they find themselves with the hope of reaching an agreement on the true good that could serve as what Lincoln called "a standard maxim" for a good society, a standard of good to which all aspired? Rawls is too hasty, it seems, in rejecting the good.

But in ruling out perfectionism Rawls is endorsing a more or less standard version of liberal theory, as developed by Locke or Mill. The arguments advanced by these thinkers are more promising than Rawls's. According to Locke, the primary justice issue posed by politics is the problem of coercion: What, if anything, might justify the use of coercion by government against individuals? Locke notices that the use of coercion against others is generally forbidden, but even in the absence of government is permissible in defense of person and property. That rightful power is the basis of governmental coercive authority and does indeed rule out global perfectionism as not among the legitimate uses of coercion. However, favoring certain conceptions of the good over others might conduce to the maintenance of a just (rights-securing) society, so Locke does not draw so hard and fast a line against governmental pursuit of the good as Rawls does.

Even though Rawls's own argument for rejecting perfectionism is flawed, let us grant him the point as better defended within the antecedent liberal tradition. There are two other places in Rawls's scheme that are problematic. The first concerns the duty of mutual respect, a central feature in his attempt to secure self-esteem and with that a precondition for the pursuit of excellence. The most obvious problem with a duty to esteem all others is that esteem cannot be commanded. Indeed, the attempt to command esteem often leads those so commanded to dig in their heels and extend disesteem instead. Consider the backlash against political correctness in large segments of the society.

Although he does not dwell on it, Rawls seems aware of this problem and thus he outlines a fairly minimal duty of esteem. We are to act with sensitivity to the feelings of others and not disesteem them because of the content of their conceptions of the good. We might summarize by saying that the duty of mutual respect is equivalent to a norm of civility. This surely can be the subject of a duty but even in this attenuated form it seems difficult to command. Has any human society ever lived up even to Rawls's fairly minimal standard of civility? In his society do we imagine that those who benefit from the difference principle by earning more primary goods than those beneath them in the chain of social positions never would fail in this duty? Might not the difference principle itself accentuate the problem in establishing the public understanding that those in the upper reaches earned and in a sense deserve their greater advantages by virtue of their benefiting those beneath them, who are better off than they would otherwise be if not for them?

Moreover, as we have seen, the duty of mutual esteem allows, perhaps even encourages, unequal esteem to be given for unequal achievement. This is an important feature of the Rawlsean opening toward excellence, but Rawls seems to be ignoring a fact of human nature that cuts against his duty of mutual esteem. Even if not intended in this way is it not the case that unequal esteem is often (always?) interpreted as disesteem, at least to some degree? One can damn with faint praise, after all. This is all to say, the duty of mutual respect cannot do as much work as Rawls believes it can. But that is a problem built into all societies no matter what conception of justice prevails within them. As Hobbes said, an honor everybody has nobody has. And an honor some have implies some degree of dishonor to others.

A related point. Rawls affirms as a psychological law his Aristotelian principle providing that individuals naturally prefer and value more highly activities calling on or calling forth development of more complex faculties. He is careful to affirm that this is not to be a normative principle and within his theory does not provide a basis for rating more highly some goods or activities than others. Thus, he confirms that the good of counting blades of grass as one's life plan is no less valuable as a conception of the good than any other. However, if the Aristotelian principle is indeed a law of human nature is it not inevitable that those who pursue the more complex and more useful goods will disesteem those, like the blade of grass counter, whose pursuits do not call forth the more complex faculties?

Probably the best defense of the Rawlsian position on the good is in terms of the plurality of human goods and the difficulty of arranging them in some incontestable hierarchy. This, again, is an insight characteristic of the liberal tradition, which receives strong defense from theorists such as Isaiah Berlin and William Galston. But this notion of pluralism of goods is not what Rawls affirmed. For him, what is significant is the "that" but not the "what" of conceptions of the good. That is to say, the moral power, as he calls it, of forming a conception of the good, any conception not ruled out by the principles of justice, is the basis for the esteem due to everyone's conceptions of the good. But we seem to have a "considered moral judgment," to use another of his terms, that though there is a plurality of goods and that a simple rank ordering of them eludes us, not every conception of the good is equally estimable. The liberal tradition has generally been content to leave it at this formulation without inquiring too closely into the basis for making the distinctions that we do. Rawls's Aristotelian principle together with a standard of usefulness to society or to specific others seems a good first cut at articulating the basis for these discriminations. Once we concede the other side of esteem and its limits as a universal commodity we see that Rawls expects much more from his duty of mutual respect than it can possibly deliver. Accordingly, we can expect in a Rawlsean society less achievement of the good of a sense of self-worth and thus less support for excellence than he expects.

To conclude: Rawls aims to reconcile equality and excellence and so far as he does so he hews fairly closely to the way the liberal tradition has done so. On reflection, however, it does not appear that Rawls's version of egalitarian liberalism has improved on the liberal tradition as a reconciliation of these two standards. Neither he nor the liberal tradition has effectuated a perfect reconciliation of equality and excellence but thinking through Rawls's attempt to do so brings out some of the tensions inherent in human nature and society that make anything but an imperfect and fraught reconciliation impossible.

Selected Bibliography

Allen, Danielle. *Why Plato Wrote*. West Sussex: Blackwell, 2010.
Annas, Julia. *An Introduction to Plato's Republic*. Oxford: Oxford University Press, 1981.
Aristophanes, *Clouds*. Translated by Alan H. Sommerstein. Warminster, UK: Aris and Phillips, 1982.
Aristotle. *Aristotle's Nicomachean Ethics*. Translated by Robert C. Bartlett and Susan Collins. Chicago: The University of Chicago Press, 2011.
———. *Aristotle's Politics*. Edited by Carnes Lord. Chicago: University of Chicago Press, 2013.
———. *Nicomachean Ethics*. Translated by H. Rackham. Cambridge: Harvard University Press, 1999.
———. *The Eudemian Ethics of Aristotle*. Translated by Peter L. P. Simpson. New Brunswick, NJ: Transaction, 2013.
Avineri, Shlomo. *Hegel's Theory of the Modern State*. Cambridge: Cambridge University Press, 1972.
Bartuschat, Wolfgang. "The Ontological Basis of Spinoza's Theory of Politics." In *Spinoza's Political and Theological Thought*, edited by C. De Deugd, 30–36. Amsterdam: North-Holland, 1984.
Benardete, Seth, trans. *Plato's Philebus: The Tragedy and Comedy of Life*. Chicago: University of Chicago Press, 1993.
Berlin, Isaiah. *Against the Current*. Princeton: Princeton University Press, 2001.
Burger, Ronna. *Aristotle's Dialogue with Socrates: On the Nicomachean Ethics*. Chicago: University of Chicago Press, 2008.
Bobonich, Christopher, ed. *Plato's Laws: A Critical Guide*. Cambridge: Cambridge University Press, 2010.
Brann, Eva. *The Music of the Republic: Essays on Socrates' Conversations and Plato's Writings*. Philadelphia: Paul Dry Books, 2004.
Burckhardt, Jacob. *The Greeks and Greek Civilization*. Edited by Oswyn Murray. Translated by Sheila Stern. New York: St. Martin's Press, 1998.

Carrithers, David W., Michael A. Mosher, and Paul A. Rahe, eds. *Montesquieu's Science of Politics*. Lanham, MD: Rowman and Littlefield, 2001.

Cicero. *Letters to Quintus and Brutus, Letter Fragments, Letter to Octavian, Invectives, and Handbook of Electioneering*. Edited by D. R. Shackleton Bailey. Cambridge: Harvard University Press, 2002.

Clay, Diskin. *Platonic Questions: Dialogues with the Silent Philosopher*. University Park: Pennsylvania State University Press, 2000.

Cohler, Anne M. *Montesquieu's Comparative Politics and the Spirit of American Constitutionalism*. Lawrence: University of Kansas Press, 1988.

Colmo, Ann. "Magnanimity: The Upper Limits of Reason." *Northeastern Political Science Association*, no. 1 (2004): 1–34.

Conroy, Peter V. *Montesquieu Revisited*. New York: Twayne, 1992.

Cropsey, Joseph. "Justice and Friendship in the *Nicomachean Ethics*." In *Political Philosophy and the Issues of Politics*, 252–73. Chicago: University of Chicago Press, 1977.

———. "On Ancients and Moderns." *Interpretation: A Journal of Political Philosophy* 18, no. 1 (Fall 1990): 31–51.

———. "The Human Vision of Rousseau: Reflections on *Emile*." In *Political Philosophy and the Issues of Politics*, 315–29. Chicago and London: University of Chicago Press, 1977).

———. *Plato's World: Man's Place in the Cosmos*. Chicago: University of Chicago Press, 1995.

———. *Polity and Economy*. South Bend: St. Augustine's Press, 2001.

Curley, Edwin. "Donagan's Spinoza." *Ethics: An International Journal of Social, Political, and Legal Philosophy* 104, no. 1 (1993): 114–34.

———. "A Good Man Is Hard to Find." *Proceedings and Addresses of the American Philosophical Association* 65 no. 3 (1991–92): 29–45.

Davis, Michael. *The Politics of Philosophy: A Commentary on Aristotle's Politics*. Lanham, MD: Rowman and Littlefield, 1996.

Deleuze, Gilles. *Nietzsche and Philosophy*. Translated by Hugh Tomlinson. London and New York: Continuum, 1986.

Doherty, Lillian, and Bruce King, eds. *Thinking the Greeks: A Volume in Honor of James M. Redfield*. London and New York: Routledge, 2018.

Donagan, Alan. *Spinoza*. Chicago: University of Chicago Press, 1989.

Due, Bodil. *The Cyropaedia: Xenophon's Aims and Methods*. Aarhus, Denmark: Aarhus University Press, 1989.

Duncan, R. "Plato's *Symposium*: The Cloven Eros." *Southern Journal of Philosophy* 15 (1977): 277–90.

Fénelon, François de Salignac de la Mothe. *Fénelon: Moral and Political Writings*. Translated by Ryan Patrick Hanley. Oxford: Oxford University Press, 2020.

———. *Oeuvres*. Edited by Jacques Le Brun. Paris: Gallimard, 1983–1997.

———. *Œuvres complètes de Fénelon*. Edited by Jean-Edmé-Auguste Gosselin. Paris: J. Leroux et Jouby, 1848–1852.

Ferrari, G. R. F., ed. *The Cambridge Companion to Plato's Republic*. Cambridge: Cambridge University Press, 2007.
Franco, Paul. "Hegel and Liberalism." *The Review of Politics* 59, no. 4 (Autumn 1997): 831–60.
———. *Hegel's Philosophy of Freedom*. New Haven: Yale University Press, 1999.
Frankel, Steven. "Spinoza's Response to Maimonides: A Practical Strategy for Resolving the Tension between Reason and Revelation." *International Philosophical Quarterly* 45, no. 3 (2005): 309–25.
———. "Spinoza's Rejection of Maimonideanism." In *Spinoza and Medieval Jewish Philosophy*, edited by Steven Nadler, 79–95. New York: Cambridge University Press, 2015.
———. "Politics and Rhetoric: The Intended Audience of Spinoza's *Tractatus Theologico-Politicus*." *The Review of Metaphysics* 52, no. 4 (June 1999): 897–924.
———. "Determined to Be Free: Spinoza on the Meaning of Freedom." *The Review of Politics* 73, no. 1 (Winter 2011): 55–76.
Frazer, Michael. "The Compassion of Zarathustra: Nietzsche on Sympathy and Strength." *Review of Politics* 68, no. 1 (February 2006): 49–78.
Grace, Eve, and Christopher Kelly, eds. *The Rousseauian Mind* (London and New York: Routledge, 2019).
Gagarin, Michael. "Socrates' *Hubris* and Alcibiades' Failure." *Phoenix* 31 (1997): 22–37.
Gerson, Lloyd. "Plato's Rational Souls." *The Review of Metaphysics* 68 (2014): 37–59.
Gatens, Moira. *Feminist Interpretations of Benedict Spinoza*. University Park: Pennsylvania State University Press, 2009.
Gauthier, René Antoine, O.P., and Jean Yves Jolif, O.P. *L'Éthique à Nicomaque: Introduction, Traduction et Commentaire*. Louvain: Publications Universitaires de Louvain, 1959.
Gildin, Hilail. "Notes on Spinoza's Critique of Religion." In *The Philosophy of Baruch Spinoza*, edited by Richard Kennington, 155–71. Washington, DC: Catholic University of America Press, 1980.
———. "Spinoza and the Political Problem." In *Spinoza. A Collection of Critical Essays*, edited by Marjorie Grene, 377–87. Garden City NY: Anchor Books, 1973.
Gray, Vivienne J. *Xenophon's Mirror of Princes: Reading the Reflections*. Oxford: Oxford University Press, 2011.
Griswold, Charles, ed. *Platonic Writings; Platonic Readings*. University Park: Pennsylvania State University Press, 1988.
Hale, John R. *Lords of the Sea: The Epic Story of the Athenian Navy and the Birth of Democracy*. New York: Viking Penguin, 2009.
Halper, Edward C. "Spinoza on the Political Value of Freedom of Religion." *History of Philosophy Quarterly* 21, no. 2 (2004): 167–82.
Hanley, Ryan Patrick. "L'éducation du prince selon Fénelon: de l'amour-propre à la justice." *Revue française d'histoire des idées politiques* 53 (2021): 113–24.
———. *The Political Philosophy of Fénelon*. Oxford: Oxford University Press, 2020.

———. "Rousseau and Fénelon." In *The Rousseauian Mind*, edited by Eve Grace and Christopher Kelly, 87–97. London: Routledge, 2019.
Havlíček, A., and M. Cajthaml, eds. *Plato's Symposium, Proceedings of the Fifth Symposium Platonicum Pragense*. Prague: Oikoumene, 2007.
Haym, Rudolf. *Hegel und Seine Zeit*. Berlin: Rudolf Gaertner, 1875.
Hegel, G. W. F. *Elements of the Philosophy of Right*. Edited by Allen W. Wood. Translated by H. B. Nisbet. Cambridge: Cambridge University Press, 1991.
Heidegger, Martin. *Being and Time*. Translated by John Macquarrie and Edward Robinson. New York: Harper and Row, 1962.
Hillenaar, Henk. "Fénelon ancien et moderne." *Studies on Voltaire and the Eighteenth Century* 265 (1989): 1232–38.
Hindley, Clifford. "Xenophon on Male Love." In *Xenophon*, edited by Vivienne J. Gray, 72–110. Oxford: Oxford University Press, 2010.
Hobbes, Thomas. *Leviathan*. New York: Penguin: 1985.
Hooper, Anthony. "The Memory of Virtue: Achieving Immortality in Plato's *Symposium*." *The Classical Quarterly* 63 (2013): 543–57.
Hume, David. "Of the Balance of Power." In *Essays: Moral, Political and Literary*, edited by Eugene F. Miller. Indianapolis: Liberty Classics, 1985.
Hyland, Drew. *Finitude and Transcendence in the Platonic Dialogues*. Ithaca: State University of New York Press, 1995.
Irwin, Terence. *Plato's Ethics*. New York: Oxford University Press, 1995.
Joint Association of Classical Teachers' Greek Course Background Book (JACT). *The World of Athens: An Introduction to Classical Athenian Culture*. Cambridge: Cambridge University Press, 1984.
Kahn, C. H. "Plato's Theory of Desire." *Review of Metaphysics* 41 (1987): 77–103.
Kant, Immanuel. *Critique of Practical Reason*. Translated by Lewis White Beck. Indianapolis: Bobbs-Merrill, 1956.
Keedus, Liisi. *The Crisis of German Historicism: The Early Political Thought of Hannah Arendt and Leo Strauss*. Cambridge: Cambridge University Press, 2015.
Kelly, Christopher. *Rousseau as Author: Consecrating One's Life to Truth*. Chicago and London: University of Chicago Press, 2003.
Kierkegaard, Søren. *Attack upon "Christendom."* Translated by Walter Lowrie. Boston: Beacon Press, 1956.
———. *Concluding Unscientific Postscript to Philosophical Fragments I*. Translated by Howard V. Hong and Edna H. Hong. Princeton: Princeton University Press, 1992.
———. *Either/Or I*. Translated by David F. Swenson and Lillian Marvin Swenson. Garden City, NY: Doubleday Anchor, 1959.
———. *Either/Or II*. Translated by Walter Lowrie. Garden City, NY: Doubleday Anchor, 1959.
———. *Fear and Trembling and The Sickness Unto Death*. Translated by Walter Lowrie. Princeton: Princeton University Press, 1968.

———. *Philosophical Fragments and Johannes Climacus*. Translated by Howard V. Hong and Edna H. Hong. Princeton: Princeton University Press, 1985.

———. *Practice in Christianity*. Translated by Howard V. Hong and Edna H. Hong. Princeton: Princeton University Press, 1991.

———. *The Present Age and Of the Difference between a Genius and an Apostle*. Translated by Alexander Dru. New York: Harper and Row, 1962.

Knoll, Manuel, and Barry Stocher, eds. *Nietzsche as Political Philosopher*. Berlin and Boston: De Gruyter, 2014.

Lampert, Lawrence. *Nietzsche's Task: An Interpretation of "Beyond Good and Evil."* New Haven and London: Yale University Press, 2001.

———. *Nietzsche's Teaching: An Interpretation of "Thus Spoke Zarathustra."* New Haven and London: Yale University Press, 1986.

Lear, Richardson. *Happy Lives and the Highest Good: An Essay on Aristotle's Nicomachean Ethics*. Princeton: Princeton University Press, 2004.

Lesher, James, Debra Nails, and Frisbee Sheffield, eds. *Plato's Symposium: Issues in Interpretation and Reception*. Washington, DC: Center for Hellenic Studies, 2006.

Léon, Céline. "(A) Woman's Place within the Ethical." In *Feminist Interpretations of Søren Kierkegaard*, edited by Céline Léon and Sylvia Walsh, 103–30. University Park: Pennsylvania State University Press, 1997.

Locke, John. *Two Treatises of Government*. Edited by Peter Laslett. Cambridge: Cambridge University Press, 1988.

Lowenthal, David. "Introduction." In *Considerations on the Causes of the Greatness of the Romans and Their Decline*, by Montesquieu. Ithaca: Free Press, 1965.

Loy, J. Robert. *Montesquieu*. New York: Twayne, 1968.

Lynch, Christopher. *Machiavelli on War*. Chicago: University of Chicago Press, forthcoming.

Machiavelli, Niccolo. *Discourses on Livy*. Translated by Harvey C. Mansfield and Nathan Tarcov. Chicago: University of Chicago Press, 1996.

———. "Machiavelli to Vettori, 26 August 1513." In *Machiavelli and His Friends: Their Personal Correspondence*, edited and translated by James B. Atkinson and David Sices. DeKalb: Northern Illinois Press, 1996.

———. *The Prince*. Translated by Harvey Mansfield. Chicago: University of Chicago Press, 1996.

———. *The Prince*. Translated by Harvey C. Mansfield. Chicago: University of Chicago Press, 1998.

———. *The Discourses on Livy*. Translated by Harvey Mansfield and Nathan Tarcov. Chicago: University of Chicago Press, 1998.

Manent, Pierre. *An Intellectual History of Liberalism*. Princeton: Princeton University Press, 1994.

Mara, Gerald. *Socrates' Discursive Democracy: Logos and Ergon in Platonic Political Philosophy*. Albany: State University of New York Press, 1997.

Marks, Jonathan. *Perfection and Disharmony in the Thought of Rousseau*. New York: Cambridge University Press, 2005.

Melzer, Arthur. *The Natural Goodness of Man: On the System of Rousseau's Thought*. Chicago and London: University of Chicago Press, 1990.

Mignini, F. "Theology as the Work and Instrument of Fortune." In *Spinoza's Political and Theological Thought: International Symposium Under the Auspices of the Royal Netherlands Academy of Arts and Sciences, Commemorating the 350th Anniversary of the Birth of Spinoza, Amsterdam*, 24–27 November 1982, edited by C. De Deugd, 127–36. Amsterdam: North-Holland, 1984.

Mill, John Stuart. "An Appraisal of Volume I of *Democracy in America*." Reprinted in Alexis de Tocqueville, *Democracy in America*, v–xlix. New York: Schocken Books, 1967.

Miller Jr., Fred D. "Aristotle on Deviant Constitutions." In *Aristotelian Political Philosophy*, Vol. II, edited by K. I. Boudouris, 112–14. Athens: The International Center for Greek Philosophy and Culture, 1995.

Mitsis, Phillip, and Heather L. Reid, eds. *The Poetry in Philosophy: Essays in Honor of Christos C. Evangeliou*. Sioux City: Parnassos Press—Fonte Aretusa, 2021.

Monoson, Sara. *Plato's Democratic Entanglements: Athenian Politics and the Practice of Philosophy*. Princeton: Princeton University Press, 2000.

Montesquieu, Charles de Secondat, baron de. *Persian Letters*. Translated by Stuart D. Warner and Stéphane Douard. South Bend: St. Augustine's Press, 2017.

———. *Pensées*. Edited by Louis Desgraves. Paris: Robert Laffont, 1991.

———. *Œuvres complètes*. Edited by Roger Callois. Paris: Gallimard, 1949.

———. *Oeuvres Completes*. Paris: Gallimard, 1956.

———. *The Spirit of the Laws*. Edited and translated by Anne M. Cohler, Basia Carolyn Miller, and Harold Samuel Stone. Cambridge: Cambridge University Press, 1989.

Nadon, Christopher. *Xenophon's Prince: Republic and Empire in the Cyropaedia*. Berkeley: University of California Press, 2001.

Nehemas, Alexander. *Virtues of Authenticity: Essays on Plato and Socrates*. Princeton: Princeton University Press, 1999.

Nelson, Stephanie. *Aristophanes' Tragic Muse: Tragedy, Comedy, and the Polis in Classical Athens*. Leiden: Brill, 2016.

Neumann, Harry. "Diotima's Concept of Love." *American Journal of Philology* 86 (1965): 33–59.

Nichols, Mary P. *Citizen and Statesman: A Study of Aristotle's Politics*. Lanham, MD: Rowman and Littlefield, 1992.

Nietzsche, Friedrich. *Sämtliche Werke. Kritische Studienausgabe*. 15 Bänden. Edited by Giorgio Colli and Mazzinio Montinari. Munich: Deutscher Taschenbuch Verlag, 1967–1977.

———. *The Gay Science*. Translated by Josephine Nauckhoff and Adrian del Caro. Cambridge: Cambridge University Press, 2001.

———. *The Anti-Christ, Ecce Homo, Twilight of the Idols: And Other Writings*. Cambridge: Cambridge University Press, 2005.
———. *Untimely Meditations*. Translated by R. J. Hollingdale. Cambridge: Cambridge University Press, 1997.
———. *On the Genealogy of Morality*. Translated by Carol Diethe. Cambridge: Cambridge University Press, 1997.
———. *Daybreak: Thoughts on the Prejudices of Morality*. Translated by R. J. Hollingdale. Cambridge: Cambridge University Press, 1997.
———. *Beyond Good and Evil*. Translated by Judith Norman. Cambridge: Cambridge University Press, 2002.
———. *Thus Spoke Zarathustra*. Translated by Adrian Del Caro. Cambridge: Cambridge University Press, 2006.
Nightingale, A. W. *Genres in Dialogue: Plato and the Construct of Philosophy*. Cambridge: Cambridge University Press, 1995.
Nussbaum, Martha. "Compassion: The Most Basic Social Emotion." *Social Psychology and Policy* 13 (1996): 27–58.
———. *The Fragility of Goodness: Luck and Ethics in Greek Tragedy and Philosophy*. Cambridge: Cambridge University Press, 1986.
Orwin, Clifford. "Montesquieu's Humanité and Rousseau's Pitié." In *Montesquieu and His Legacy*, edited by Rebecca Kingston, 139–47. Albany: State University of New York Press, 2009.
Ober, Josiah. *Mass and Elite in Democratic Athens: Rhetoric, Ideology, and the Power of the People*. Princeton: Princeton University Press, 1989.
———. *Political Dissent in Democratic Athens: Intellectual Critics of Popular Rule*. Princeton: Princeton University Press, 2001.
Ober, Josiah, and Charles Hedrick, eds. *Dēmokratia: A Conversation on Democracies, Ancient and Modern*. Princeton: Princeton University Press, 1996.
Ostenfeld, E. N., ed. *Essays on Plato's Republic*. Aarhus: Aarhus University Press, 1998.
Ovid. *Metamorphosis*. Edited by Frank Justus Miller. Cambridge: Harvard University Press, 1971.
Pangle, Thomas L. *Aristotle's Teaching in the Politics*. Chicago: University of Chicago Press, 2013.
———. *Montesquieu's Philosophy of Liberalism: A Commentary on the Spirit of the Laws*. Chicago: University of Chicago Press, 1973.
———. *The Theological Basis of Modern Liberalism*. Chicago: University of Chicago Press, 2010.
Patterson, R. "The Ascent in Plato's *Symposium*." *Proceedings of the Boston Area Colloquium in Ancient Philosophy* 7 (1991): 193–214.
Pelling, Christopher. "Bringing Autochthony Up-to-Date: Herodotus and Thucydides." *Classical World* 102 (2009): 471–83.
Pippin, Robert. *Hegel's Practical Philosophy: Rational Agency as Ethical Life*. Cambridge: Cambridge University Press, 2008.

Plato. *Plato's Philebus: The Tragedy and Comedy of Life*. Translated by Seth Benardete. Chicago: University of Chicago Press, 1993.
———. *The Symposium*. Edited and translated by C. J. Rowe. Oxford: Aris and Phillips, 1998.
———. *The Symposium*, Edited by R. E. Allen. New Haven: Yale University Press, 1991.
———. *The Symposium*. Edited by Kenneth Dover. Cambridge: Cambridge University Press, 1980.
———. *The Republic of Plato*. Translated by Allan Bloom. New York: Basic Books, 1968.
Popper, Karl. *The Open Society and its Enemies*. Princeton: Princeton University Press, 1963.
———. *The Open Society and Its Enemies: New One-Volume Edition*. Princeton: Princeton University Press, 2013.
Radasanu, Andrea. "Montesquieu on Moderation, Monarchy, and Reform." *History of Political Thought* 31, no. 2 (Summer 2010): 283–307.
Radasanu, Andrea, ed. *The Pious Sex*. Lanham, MD: Lexington Books, 2010.
Rahe, Paul A. *Montesquieu and the Logic of Liberty*. New Haven: Yale University Press, 2009.
Rawls, John. *A Theory of Justice*. Cambridge: Harvard University Press, 1971.
———. *Political Liberalism*. New York: Columbia University Press, 1993.
Recco, Gregg. *Athens Victorious: Democracy in Plato's Republic*. Lanham, MD: Lexington Books, 2007.
Reichel, Michael. "Xenophon's Cyropaedia and the Hellenistic Novel." In *Xenophon*, edited by Vivienne J. Gray, 418–38. Oxford: Oxford University Press, 2010.
Reid, Heather, Mark Ralkowski, and Coleen Zoller, eds. *Athletics, Gymnastics, and Agon in Plato*. Sioux City: Parnassos Press—Fonte Aretusa, 2020.
Reid, Heather L., and Davide Tanasi, eds. *Philosopher Kings and Tragic Heroes: Essays on Images and Ideas from Western Greece*. Sioux City: Parnassos Press—Fonte Aretusa, 2016.
Renz, Ursula. "Spinozism as Radical Anti-Nihilism: Spinoza on Being and the Valuableness of Being." *Circolo*, no. 10 (December 2020): 391–406.
Riley, Patrick. "Rousseau, Fénelon, and the Quarrel between the Ancients and the Moderns." In *The Cambridge Companion to Rousseau*, edited by Patrick Riley 78–93. Cambridge: Cambridge University Press, 2001.
Roberts, J. W. *City of Sokrates: An Introduction to Classical Athens*. London: Routledge and Kegan Paul, 1984.
Robinson, Steven. "The Contest of Wisdom between Socrates and Agathon in Plato's *Symposium*." *Ancient Philosophy* 24 (2004): 81–100.
Roochnik, David. *Beautiful City: The Dialectical Character of Plato's Republic*. Ithaca: Cornell University Press, 2008.
Rousseau, Jean-Jacques. *Collected Writings of Rousseau*, 13 Volumes. Edited by Roger D. Masters and Christopher Kelly. Hanover, NH: University Press of New England, 1991–2011.

———. *The First and Second Discourses*. Translated by Roger D. Masters and Judith R. Masters. New York: St. Martin's Press, 1964.
———. *Oeuvres Completes*. Paris: Gallimard, 1964.
———. *Of the Social Contract*. Edited by Christopher Bertram, translated by Quintin Hoare. London: Penguin Books, 2012.
Rosen, Stanley. *Plato's Symposium*. New Haven: Yale University Press, 1968.
Ruprecht, Louis Jr. *Symposia: Plato, The Erotic and Moral Value*. Albany: State University of New York Press, 1999.
Rubin, Leslie G. *America, Aristotle, and the Politics of a Middle Class*. Waco: Baylor University Press, 2018.
Sabine, George. *A History of Political Theory*. New York: Holt Rinehart, and Winston, 1961.
Salkever, Stephen G. *Finding the Mean: Theory and Practice in Aristotelian Political Philosophy*. Princeton: Princeton University Press, 1990.
Saxonhouse, Arlene. *Athenian Democracy: Modern Mythmakers and Ancient Theorists*. Notre Dame: University of Notre Dame Press, 1996.
———. "Democracy, Equality, and Eide: A Radical View from Book 8 of Plato's *Republic*." *American Political Science Review* 92 (1998): 273.
Schaeffer, Denise. *Rousseau on Education, Freedom, and Judgment*. University Park: Pennsylvania State University Press, 2014.
Schaub, Diana J. *Erotic Liberalism: Women and Revolution in Montesquieu's Persian Letters*. Lanham: Rowman and Littlefield, 1995.
Schlacht, Richard, ed. *Nietzsche, Genealogy, Morality: Essays on Nietzsche's "On the Genealogy of Morality."* Berkeley: University of California Press, 1994.
Schuurman, Paul. "Fenelon on Luxury, War and Trade in the Telemachus." *History of European Ideas* 38, no. 2 (2012): 179–99.
Sheffield, F. C. C. *Plato's Symposium: The Ethics of Desire*. Oxford: Oxford University Press, 2006.
Shklar, Judith. *Montesquieu*. Oxford: Oxford University Press, 1987.
Sider, D. "Plato's *Symposium* as Dionysian Festival." *Quaderni Urbinati di Cultura Classica* 33 (1980): 41–56.
Skulsky, Harold. *Staring into the Void: Spinoza, the Master of Nihilism*. Newark, NJ: University of Delaware Press, 2009.
Smith, Steven B. *Hegel's Critique of Liberalism: Rights in Context*. Chicago: University of Chicago Press, 1989.
Solzhenitsyn, Alexander. *One Day in the Life of Ivan Denisovich*. Translated by Ralph Parker. New York: Signet Books, 1963.
Spinoza, Benedict. *Tractatus Theologico-Politicus in Spinoza Opera*. Edited by Carl Gebhardt. Heidelberg: Carl Winters Verlag, 1925.
———. *Theologico-Political Treatise*. Edited by Martin D. Yaffe. Newburyport: Focus, 2004.
———. *Spinoza Reader: The Ethics and Other Works*. Edited by E. Curley. Princeton: Princeton University Press, 1994.

———. *Treatise on Theology and Politics*. Edited by Jonathan Bennett. Early Modern Texts, 2017. https://www.earlymoderntexts.com/assets/pdfs/spinoza1669.pdf.

———. *Political Treatise*. Translated by Samuel Shirley, edited by Douglas Den Uyl, Steven Barbone, and Lee Rice. Indianapolis: Hackett, 2005.

Stadter, Philip. "Fictional Narrative in the *Cyropaideia*." In *Xenophon*, edited by Vivienne J. Gray, 367–400. Oxford: Oxford University Press, 2010.

Stegman, Casey. "Remembering Atlantis: Plato's "Timaeus-Critias," the Ancestral Constitution, and the Democracy of the Gods." *Political Theory* 45 (2017): 240–60.

Strauss, Leo. *Philosophy and Law: Contributions to the Understanding of Maimonides and His Predecessors*. Translated by Eve Adler. Albany: State University of New York Press, 1995.

———. *Persecution and the Art of Writing*. Chicago: University of Chicago Press, 1988.

———. *The Political Philosophy of Spinoza*. Edited by David Wollenberg. Chicago: The University of Chicago, 1959. https://wslamp70.s3.amazonaws.com/leostrauss/s3fs-public/Spinoza%20%281959%29.pdf.

———. *Studies in Platonic Political Philosophy*. Introduction by Thomas Pangle. Chicago: University of Chicago Press, 1983.

———. *Thoughts on Machiavelli*. Chicago: University of Chicago Press, 1958.

Tatum, James. *Xenophon's Imperial Fiction: On the Education of Cyrus*. Princeton: Princeton University Press, 1989.

Taylor, Charles. *Hegel*. Cambridge: Cambridge University Press, 1975.

Tocqueville, Alexis de. *Democracy in America*. Edited and translated by Harvey C. Mansfield and Delba Winthrop. Chicago: University of Chicago Press, 2000.

———. *Democracy in America*. Indianapolis: Liberty Fund, 1990.

Tulpin, Christopher. "Xenophon, Sparta, and the Cyropaedia." In *The Shadow of Sparta*, edited by Anton Powell and Stephen Hodkinson, 127–82. London: Routledge, 1994.

Uyl, Douglas Den. *God, Man, and Well Being: Spinoza's Modern Humanism*. New York: Peter Lang, 2009.

Virgil. *Aeneid*. Cambridge: Loeb Classical Library, Harvard University Press, 1974.

Vlastos, Gregory. *Socrates: Ironist and Moral Philosopher*. Ithaca: Cornell University Press, 1991.

Ward, Lee. *Modern Democracy and the Theological-Political Problem in Spinoza, Rousseau, and Jefferson*. New York: Palgrave Macmillan, 2014.

Weber, Max. *The Protestant Ethic and the Spirit of Capitalism*. Translated by Talcott Parsons. New York: Charles Scribner's Sons, 1958.

White, F. C. "Virtue in Plato's *Symposium*." *Classical Quarterly* 54 (2004): 366–78.

Wood, Allen W. *Hegel's Ethical Thought*. Cambridge: Cambridge University Press, 1990.

Woodruff, Paul. *First Democracy: The Challenge of An Ancient Ideal*. New York: Oxford University Press, 2005.

Xenophon. *Cyropaedia*. Edited by Walter Miller. Cambridge: Harvard University Press, 1914, 1968.

———. *The Education of Cyrus*. Translated by Wayne Ambler. Ithaca: Cornell University Press, 2001.

———. "Regime of the Lacedaemonians." Translated by Catherine S. Kuiper and Susan D. Collins. In *The Shorter Writings,* edited by Gregory A. McBrayer, 107–48. Ithaca: Cornell University Press, 2018.

Youpa, Andrew. *The Ethics of Joy: Spinoza on the Empowered Life*. New York: Oxford University Press, 2020.

Contributors

Ann Charney Colmo is professor emeritus of political philosophy at Dominican University in River Forest, Illinois. She has published "What Sophie Knew: Rousseau's *Émile et Sophie, ou Les Solitaires*," in Pamela Grande Jensen, ed., *Finding a New Feminism*; "Spiritedness and Piety in Aristotle," in Catherine H. Zuckert, ed., *Understanding the Political Spirit: Philosophical Investigations from Socrates to Nietzsche*; and "The Virtues in Aristotle's *Rhetoric*," in the journal *Interpretation*. She regularly presents papers at the conferences of the Association for Core Texts and Courses and the Northeastern Political Science Organization.

Christopher A. Colmo is professor emeritus of political science at Dominican University in River Forest, Illinois. He has published "Theory and Practice: Alfarabi's Plato Revisited" (APSR, 1992) and *Breaking with Athens: Alfarabi as Founder* (Lexington 2005), as well as articles on Plato's Greater Hippias and Shakespeare's *Merchant of Venice*. Other publications include "Reason and Revelation in the Thought of Leo Strauss" (Interpretation, 1990) and "Al-Fârâbî" in *Leo Strauss y Otros Compañeros de Platon* (Ápeiron, 2016) as well as article-length reviews of the work of George Anastaplo and Joseph Cropsey. "Kierkegaard's Disenchanted Christianity" is to appear in *New Approaches to Disenchantment* (Indiana University Press, forthcoming). He reviews regularly for *Choice* and for scholarly journals.

Steven Frankel is the Stephen S. Smith Professor of Political Economy at Xavier University. He currently directs the Smith Scholars Honors Program at Xavier. He received his PhD from the Committee on Social Thought at the University of Chicago in 1997. Upon graduation, Professor Frankel joined the faculty at the American University of Paris, where he received the Board of Trustees Award for Distinguished Teaching in 2001. In 2003, Professor Frankel moved to Xavier where he teaches for the Department of Philosophy and the Honors Programs. Professor Frankel's scholarly work focuses on the relationship between philosophy and religion. In 2014, he published a collection of essays with Prof. John Ray on intellectual and cultural life in France, entitled *French Studies: Literature, Culture, and Politics* (Éditions Honoré Champion, Paris). More recently, he published *Civil Religion and Early Modern Philosophy*, with Martin Yaffe (Pennsylvania State University Press, 2020). He is currently writing a book on the philosophy of Spinoza.

Ryan Patrick Hanley is professor of political science at Boston College. Prior to joining the faculty at Boston College, he was the Mellon Distinguished Professor of Political Science at Marquette University, and held visiting appointments or fellowships at Yale, Harvard, and the University of Chicago. A specialist on the political philosophy of the Enlightenment period, he is the author of *Adam Smith and the Character of Virtue* (Cambridge, 2009), *Love's Enlightenment: Rethinking Charity in Modernity* (Cambridge, 2017), and *Our Great Purpose: Adam Smith on Living a Better Life* (Princeton, 2019). His most recent book is *The Political Philosophy of Fénelon* (Oxford, 2020) and its companion translation volume, *Fénelon: Moral and Political Writings* (Oxford, 2020).

Pamela K. Jensen is professor emerita of political science at Kenyon College, where she taught political philosophy and politics and literature. She has published essays on Rousseau, Shakespeare, and Ralph Ellison. She is contributing editor of *Finding a New Feminism: Rethinking the Woman Question for Liberal Democracy* (Rowman and Littlefield, 1996).

John C. Koritansky is emeritus professor of political science at Hiram College where he has taught since 1970. He is also a founding member and initial chair of Hiram's Garfield Institute for Public Leadership. He has published several articles and book chapters in the areas of American politics, public law, and especially political philosophy, including interpretive comments on Aristotle, Thomas Hobbes, Thomas Paine, and Leo Strauss, in addition to his work on Tocqueville. His book *Alexis de Tocqueville and the New Science of Politics* is in its second edition. He is currently engaged in an attempt to understand how Strauss's reading of Lucretius informs or illuminates his understanding of classical political rationalism.

Stephanie A. Nelson, professor in the Department of Classical Studies at Boston University, teaches widely in Greek and Latin literature and in the classical tradition and has written on subjects ranging from ancient literature and philosophy to narrative time and translation. She is the author of *God and the Land: The Metaphysics of Farming in Hesiod and Vergil* and of *Aristophanes' Tragic Muse: Comedy, Tragedy, and the Polis in Classical Athens* and has written on and given numerous talks on the relation of Joyce's *Ulysses* and the *Odyssey* including a monograph, *Time and Identity in Ulysses and the Odyssey*, from the University Press of Florida.

Mary P. Nichols is professor emerita of political science at Baylor University. She has published numerous articles and books on the history of political philosophy, especially Greek political thought, and on politics, literature, and film. Her books include *Thucydides and the Pursuit of Freedom* (Cornell, 2015), *Socrates on Friendship and Community: Reflections on Plato's Symposium, Phaedrus, and Lysis* (Cambridge, 2009), and *Citizens and Statesmen* (Rowman and Littlefield, 1992). Most recently, she wrote "Plato's Democratic Moment," in *Democracy and the History of Political Thought*, ed. Patrick N. Cain, Stephen P. Sims, and Stephen A. Block (Lexington, 2021).

Timothy Sean Quinn has been a member of the Department of Philosophy at Xavier University, Cincinnati, since 1987. He currently holds the rank of professor of philosophy. Among his recent publications are *Apiqoros: The Last Essays of Salomon Maimon* (Hebrew Union College Press, 2021), *Martin Heidegger and Ernst Jünger: The Correspondence, 1949—1975* (Rowman and Littlefield, 2016) and essays on Machiavelli, Descartes, Jünger, and Maimon.

Andrea E. Ray is a PhD candidate in the Committee on Social Thought at the University of Chicago. Her research focuses on German idealism and its relation to early modern thought. She is currently writing a dissertation on Hegel's critique of Spinoza.

John Ray is associate professor of political science at Xavier University where he teaches political philosophy and constitutional law. He is co-editor with Steven Frankel of *French Studies: Literature, Culture and Politics* (Honoré Champion, 2014). He has published on the question of political leadership in Xenophon's *Education of Cyrus* and George Washington's writings, and on Rousseau's understanding of civil religion.

Frank J. Rohmer is the John D. Moseley Chair of Government and Public Policy at Austin College. He was originally drawn to the college in 1988 by the vision of the formative president after whom the chair he holds is named. As a teacher of political philosophy, American constitutional law, and public administration, Rohmer's professional career has been built around Austin College's commitment to educating students in the liberal arts as a preparation for public service. Consistent with the college's emphasis on the intersection of the theoretical and the practical, Rohmer in addition to his teaching responsibilities serves as prelaw advisor, Truman Scholarship faculty sponsor, and Hatton W. Sumners Scholarship faculty sponsor. He is also the founder of the Dr. Kenneth W. Street Law Symposium, the Austin College Public Administration Symposium, and the Austin College Colloquium on Civil Discourse, three campus events bridging the intellectual and practical.

Nathan Tarcov is Karl J. Weintraub Professor in the Committee on Social Thought, the Department of Political Science, the Committee on International Relations, and the College at the University of Chicago. He has served on the faculty at Harvard, the Policy Planning Staff of the United States Department of State, as Secretary of the Navy Senior Research Fellow at the United States Naval War College, and as Fellow at the Siemens Foundation in Munich. He is author of *Locke's Education for Liberty*, co-translator of *Machiavelli's Discourses on Livy* and of the forthcoming *Complete Tales and Poems of Niccolò Machiavelli*, co-editor of *The Legacy of Rousseau* and Locke's *Some Thoughts Concerning Education and Of the Conduct of the Understanding*, editor-in-chief of the Leo Strauss Transcript Series, and author of articles on Machiavelli, Boccaccio, Locke, the American founders, Strauss, constitutionalism, democracy, and tyranny. He is writing a novel based on Xenophon's *Education of Cyrus*.

Michael Zuckert is the Nancy R. Dreux Professor of Political Science, emeritus, and Thomas Smith Distinguished Visiting Professor, Arizona State University. He works in the two fields of political theory and constitutional studies, in both of which he has published extensively. He has published *Natural Rights and the New Republicanism*, the *Natural Rights Republic*, *Launching Liberalism*, and (with Catherine Zuckert) *The Truth About Leo Strauss* and *Leo Strauss and the Problem of Political Philosophy*, in addition to many articles. He has also edited (with Derek Webb) *The Antifederal Writings of the Melancton Smith Circle*. He is completing *A Nation so Conceived: Abraham Lincoln and the Paradox of Democratic Sovereignty*.

Index

Adams, John, 121
Adeimantus, 24
aesthetic realm of Kierkegaard, 188, 189–91
affectiones, 100n6
Agathon, 11, 15, 17–18, 20, 21
Alcibiades, 2; aristocratic vision of *aretē*, 20–22; idea of *aretē*, 18–20; in *Symposium*, 11, 13, 15
"almost-philosopher," 2, 11, 19, 22
amour-propre, 145–46, 149–50
antiquarian history, 200
Apollodorus, 21
Apology of Socrates (Plato), 15
aristocratic/aristocracy, 81; polity, 83; radicalism, 200
Aristodemus, 20
Aristophanes, 11, 16, 22
Aristotelian principle, 222, 223, 226
Aristotle, 2, 3, 67, 87n8, 217, 219; arguments about virtue, 4; defining lack of excellence, 53; discovery of form or rank in politics, 69; middle-class regime, 88n11; about nature as politicon zōon, 23; nobility concept, 54; about political rule, 67–68; about self-love of munificent, 65n17. See also *Politics* (Aristotle), *Nicomachean Ethics* (Aristotle)
art (*technē*), 54, 60

Attack upon "Christendom" (Kierkegaard), 187–88

bearer of rights. *See* rights-bearers, individuals as
Bennett, Jonathan, 99n1
Berlin, Isaiah, 226
Beyond Good and Evil (Nietzsche), 7, 173, 200, 204–12, 214n24
The Birth of Tragedy (Nietzsche), 213n8
Bloom, Allan, 156n8
Brandes, Georg, 200

caritas (charity), 90, 92, 94–95
Carthaginian polity, 83
Catholic Enlightenment, 106
Charlemagne, 129–31
Charles VII, 128
Christianity, 194; in Carolingian Europe, 129–30; in Fénelon's analysis of ancient and modern virtues, 113–16; "love of neighbor" from, 205; Nietzsche's views about, 203; philosophy in, 90, 190
Chrysantas, 43–44
"City in Words," 12–14, 16, 22, 23, 25n1
"City of Pigs," 13, 16, 23, 25n1, 28n20
commoners (*dēmotoi*), 35

245

"common natures," 202
compassion, 202–3, 205
competition, 21–22
comprehensive doctrines/theory, 216, 217
Condorcet, 121
Considerations on the Causes of the Greatness of the Romans and Their Decline (Montesquieu), 5, 121, 125–27
courage in war, 108–9
Critique of Practical Reason (Kant), 191
Crito (Plato), 15
Cropsey, Joseph, 98, 26n1, 196n2
Cyaxares (king of Medes), 34, 40–42
Cyrus: the Great, 33–34; revolution, 41–45; rule of, 47–48; story of Artabazus's love for, 39–41

D'Alembert, Jean le Rond, 121
Davis, Michael, 87n5
Deleuze, Gilles, 213n12
democracy, 24–25, 78, 81, 82–83, 88n10, 173; Ancient Greek thoughts about, 2–3; freedom, 174–75; honor and, 178–81; manners and, 178; nobility in, 176–77; and public edification, 210; Socrates and, 15–16; in TTP, 89, 97, 100n6; war and, 182–85
Democracy in America (Tocqueville), 6, 174, 186n4; honor and democracy, 178–81; love of equality, 175–77, 181, 182; manners and democracy, 178; self-restraint of democratic majority, 175–76; spiritedness, 182, 184; tyranny of majority, 177, 185n2; war and democracy, 182–85
demos of democracy, 18–25, 56
Den, Douglas, 100n6
Denisovich, Ivan, 193
deontological theory, 217

Descartes, René, 191
desire, 74, 79, 101n16; for immortality, 9; for victory, 43
despair of finite, 191, 192–93, 194
despotism, 72, 181–82, 185n2; democratic, 174; French monarchy, 122–23, 128; Oriental, 132; rule with, 67, 69–71; soft, 1
destiny (*Bestimmung*) of individuals, 167
Diomedes, 79
Diotima, 10, 11, 16; description of ultimate desirability of beautiful itself, 19; "Ladder of Love," 10, 11–12, 15, 18, 21, 25n1; universalizing of eros, 17–18
Discourse on the Origins of Inequality (*Second Discourse*) (Rousseau), 127, 145, 150, 157n13
Discourse on the Sciences and Arts (*First Discourse*) (Rousseau), 143, 154, 155, 158n22
Discourses on Livy (Machiavelli), 34, 50
Divided Line, 10, 11–12, 14
doubt, definition of, 191
Duke of Burgundy, 105, 106

Ecce Homo (Nietzsche), 212n2, 214n20
Eleatic Stranger, 75, 87n7
The Education of Cyrus (Xenophon), 2; autocracy in, 49–50; empire maintenance in, 49–50; equality in, 49–50; excellence in, 49–50; freedom and equality in, 3; purpose and genre of, 33–34; story of Artabazus's love for Cyrus, 39–41. *See also* Xenophon
egalitarian liberalism. *See* Rawls, John
Either/Or (Kierkegaard), 190–91
emancipation of women, 195
Emile, or On Education (Rousseau), 5, 143–44, 158n24; educational

principles in, 144–45; Emile and "the magician-Socrates," 145–49; Emile and Robinson Crusoe novel, 149–54; Rousseau and "the magician-Socrates," 154–56
Enlightenment project, 187–88
epistēmē, 60, 61
equality, 7, 10; admixture of, 3; belief in, 95–96; in *Education of Cyrus*, 49–50; without excellence in Plato's *Symposium*, 16–18; and freedom, 67; indignity of, 212; love of, 175; opposition with, 53; in political life, 81–86; relation with excellence, 2–3; of rights, 164, 167, 170, 190, 193; of rights-bearing, 163–64; role in modern democracies in, 1; tension with excellence, 2; unqualified principle of, 69
Eryximachus, 16, 18, 21, 22
eternal consciousness of finite self, 190, 191–92
Ethical Life. See *Sittlichkeit*
ethical universal approach of Kierkegaard, 188, 189, 191–92
excellence (*aretē*), 1, 6, 7, 9, 10, 12, 53, 54; admixture of, 3; Aristotle's arguments about, 4; awareness of, 126; classical political thought of, 67; courage in war, 108–9; in *The Education of Cyrus*, 49–50; epistēmē, 60; without equality in Plato's *Republic*, 13–15; household management to, 74; of humanity, 111–12, 113, 114; of liberality or generosity (*eleutheria*), 54; munificence, 3; of munificence, 57; opposition between, 53; philanthropic, 104; political, 76, 81–86; priority of right or justice over good, 217–18; Rawls's theory toward, 217; relation between, 2–3; self-command, 107–8; tension between, 2; warrior, 104

"fair equality of opportunity," 217
father–children relationship (*patrikē*), 67, 70, 71–72, 74
Fear and Trembling (Kierkegaard), 188, 194
Fénelon, François de Salignac de la Mothe, 4, 5, 104–17. See also *Telemachus* (Fénelon)
Feuerbach, Ludwig, 190
foolish (*ēlithios*), 59
Forms, 14; pursuit of, 21; theory of, 11–12
Franco, Paul, 168
freedom: to choose, 95; democracy, 174–75; equality of, 170; of free spirits, 212; Hegelian understanding of, 161–62, 168–69; provincial, 175; right to, 164; of speech, 224
free spirits, 206, 207; freedom of, 212
French monarchy, 122–23, 128
friendship, 65n17, 73, 168–69

Galston, William, 226
The Gay Science (Nietzsche), 201–2, 204, 205, 210
Genealogy (Nietzsche), 206
Glaucon, 11, 14
Goethe, Johann Wolfgang von, 189
good: conception of, 217–20, 223–24; duty of mutual respect, 220–23; pluralism of, 226–27
greatness of soul. See magnanimity (*megalopsychia*)
great virtues, 55; greatness of Roman political virtue, 126; magnanimity, 53; munificence, 53–54, 55–63, 63nn2–3, 64n10. See also excellence (*aretē*)

Halper, Edward, 99n2
Hal, Prince, 188
Hegel, Georg Wilhelm Friedrich, 6, 171n11; evaluation of liberalism, 159–60; fundamentality of right to property, 160; about liberalism and its problems, 162–67; about *Sittlichkeit*, 160, 167–70; about slavery and exploitation, 171n10
Heidegger, Martin, 190, 213n7
Helvetius, Claude Adrien, 121
herd morality, 204, 206, 210
hierarchy: defined in Plato's *Republic*, 10, 12; of Socrates's ideal city, 13
Hillenaar, Henk, 117n8
Hobbes, Thomas, 93, 94, 100n10, 104–5, 115, 124, 134, 187
Homer, 5, 19, 21, 72, 77, 106, 107, 111
honor and democracy, 178–81
household management to virtue, 74
human beings, 24, 127, 163, 209; master–slave relationship in, 70; metaphysical longings of mortal, 125; natural condition of, 123–24, 127; physical survival of, 124; political rule, 4, 33, 34, 79, 86; of unequaled intelligence, 131
human dignity, 200, 212; Nietzsche's writings on, 200; of philosophy, 210–11; restoration of, 202
human equality, awareness of, 113
humanity, 207; as equality of rights, 187; virtue of, 111–12, 113, 114
human nature, 5, 17, 126, 187
human self-preservation, 125
human vanity, 124
Hume, David, 34, 112–13, 115
husband–wife relationship (*gamikē*), 67, 68, 71–73, 74

Iliad (Homer), 79, 87–88n9

imagination, 92, 100n6, 101n16
indignity of equality, 212
industrial culture, 202
international law, 134
interpenetration of universality and individuality, 168, 170
inward rebellion, 166

Jefferson, Thomas, 121
justice, 76, 92, 215–16; in *A Theory of Justice*, 215–16; as fairness, 217, 223; principles of, 218–20, 226; theory, 217

Kant, Immanuel, 188, 191
Kaufmann, Walter, 212n4
Keeler, Garrison, 12
Kierkegaard, Søren, 6, 187–88; aesthetic realm, 188, 189–91; dialectical acrobatics, 189; egalitarianism in, 193–94; about emancipation of women, 195; emphasis on indirect communication, 194–95; ethical universal approach, 188, 189, 191–92; religious approach, 188, 189
kingship, 77–78, 80–81
knower (*epistēmoni*), 55, 60

Ladder of Love, 10, 11–12, 15, 18, 21, 25n1
lalein, 51n15
Lampert, Lawrence, 207
Laws (Plato), 88n10
L'Hermite, Tristan, 51n17
liberal democracy, 97, 199, 204
liberalism, 162–67; equality of rights-bearing, 163–64; Hegel vs. Locke's perspectives on, 162–63; and human excellence, 164–65; liberal market-states, 165–67; problems in, 164. See also *Sittlichkeit*

liberal market-states, 6, 159–60, 165–67
Lincoln, Abraham, 225
liturgies (*leitourgiai*), 56
Lives (Plutarch), 185
Locke, John, 89, 104–5, 115, 162–63, 225
logos, 20, 25n1, 35
Louis IX, 131–32
Louis XIV, 105, 106, 122–23
love of equality, 175–77, 181, 182
love of neighbor, 205

Machiavelli, Nicolo, 34, 132, 153
magnanimity (*megalopsychia*), 53
magnificent/magnificence, 63n3
Maimonides (philosopher), 91, 97
Martel, Charles, 129
Marx, Karl, 6, 159–60, 187, 190
master–slave relationship (*despotikē*), 67, 68–70, 71, 72, 74
Media narration in *Education of Cyrus*, 36–39
mediocrity, 6, 193, 201, 202, 206
Metamorphosis (Ovid), 127
metaphysics, 216
middle-class polity, 83–84
middle-class regime, 88n11
Mignini, F., 100n6
Miller, Walter, 51n9, 51n12
Mill, John Stuart, 185n2, 225
moderation (*sophrosunēn*), 35
modern/modernity, 201; enlightenment, 124; liberal state, 164; mature, 6; suppression of human greatness, 200–201, 206–7
monarchy, 88n10
Montesquieu, 4, 5, 103–4, 105, 115, 121; about enlightened science, 122, 124–25, 136; about epistolary style and reversal of perspectives, 122; about European freedom vs. Persian despotism, 122–23, 124–27; about literary novel and philosophic discourse, 127–28; about Ovidian metamorphosis, 128, 131, 135; political science, 121, 131, 135; reflections on complexity of human situation, 121–22; about religious faith and rational knowledge, 129–30, 132; about self-misunderstanding, 122, 123–24; about tragic events and comic wit, 122, 123
morality: concepts of, 217; herd, 204, 206, 210
mores, Tocqueville's discussion on, 176, 177–78, 185
Mozart, Wolfgang Amadeus, 6, 189, 194
multitude (*plēthos*), 44, 89, 90, 91; apt for different regimes, 80; democratic, 82; political, 85; problem of superstition and imagination of, 92
munificent/munificence (*megaloprepeia*), 3, 53–54, 55, 63nn2–3, 64n10; definition of, 55–56; fitting expenditure of, 59–60; great virtue of, 57–59; historical fact about munificent expenditures, 56; magnanimous stands, 60–61; objects of munificent person, 56; and philosophy, 60; and prudence, 60; public scale, 59; in reciprocity, 57; self-love of, 65n17; works of poets, 61–63
mutual esteem, duty of, 225–26

Natur, 214n16
natural law, 94, 101n16
natural rights, 4–5, 89, 91, 93–98, 101n12
naturlich, 214n16

Nicomachean Ethics (Aristotle), 3, 53; magnanimity, 53; munificence, 53–54, 55–63, 63nn2–3, 64n10
Nietzsche, Friedrich, 6–7, 173–74, 177, 187, 199, 212n2, 213n8, 214n20, 219; analysis of modern suppression of human greatness, 200–201, 206–7; association with liberal democracy and socialism, 204; about compassion, 202–3, 205; dignity of philosophy, 210–11; about herd morality, 204, 206, 210; indignity of equality, 212; *Natur* and *naturlich*, 214n16; about nature of nobility and philosophy, 207–10; about noble natures, 205–6; opposition to "the Greeks," 201; and "pathos of distance," 203; psychology of ressentiment, 204; views on human dignity, 200, 202, 212
nobility, 6, 7, 54, 173; in democracy, 176–77; Nietzsche's views about, 173–74; of soul, 173, 185, 199, 203, 207–10
Noble Lie, 23–24, 25–26n1
"nuptial number," 10

oligarchy, 33, 56, 74, 75, 76, 81–84
The Open Society and Its Enemies (Popper), 9
Ovid, 127; Ovidian metamorphosis, 5, 128, 131, 135

Pangle, Thomas, 185n2
"pathos of distance," 203
"pathos of nobility and distance," 203
patriotism, 170, 179
Pausanias, 16–18
Pepin, 129
perfectionism, 219–20
Pericles, 25

Persia in *Education of Cyrus*, 34–36
Persian Letters (Montesquieu), 5, 103, 121, 122–25, 127, 128, 132, 135
Phaedrus, 16, 18, 21, 26n3
Phaedrus (Plato), 26n3, 144
Pheraulas, narration in *Education of Cyrus*, 45–47
Philosopher-Ruler, 11, 12, 14
Philosophical Fragments (Kierkegaard), 190, 196
The Philosophy of Right (Hegel), 6, 26n1, 159, 171n10; individuals as rights-bearers, 160–62; liberalism and its problems, 162–67; liberal market-states as societies, 159–60; *Sittlichkeit*, 160, 167–70
phusis, 212n7, 214n16
physical reality, 14–15
Plato, 2, 9, 24, 84, 144, 189, 217; depiction of democracy, 25; discussion on excellence and universality, 10; physical reality vs. transcendent reality, 14–15. See also *Republic* (Plato); *Symposium* (Plato)
Plutarch, 155, 179, 185
Poetics (Aristotle), 61
political community, 68–69, 84
Political Liberalism (Rawls), 216
political multitude, 85
political rule, 4, 67–74, 79–81, 86, 106, 173
Politics (Aristotle), 2, 3, 57, 58, 67; equality and excellence in political life in, 81–86; equality and freedom in, 4; examining regimes and claims to rule in, 75–81; political rule within family in, 68–74
polity, 4, 15, 68, 75, 80, 82; aristocratic, 83; middleclass, 84
Popper, Karl, 9
Practice in Christianity (Kierkegaard), 188
prejudice, 71, 153

prepeia, 54
primary goods of self-respect, 218, 220–21
The Prince (Machiavelli), 34, 50
"profound levelling" effect, 202
property rights. *See* right to property
prosopopoeia, 155
prudence (*phronēsis*), 4, 45, 60, 79, 85

rationality, 167–68
Rawls, John, 6–7, 215; "basic structure of society," views about, 216–17; comprehensive doctrines/theory, views about, 216, 217; egalitarian liberalism of, 215, 227; endorsement of liberal theory, views about, 225; mutual esteem, duty of, 225–26; mutual respect, duty of, 220–23; pluralism of goods, views about, 226–27; political doctrines/theory, 216; recognition as beings with value, 223–24; theories of justice, views about, 217; treatment of excellence, views about, 224–25
reality: of excellence, 220; physical vs. transcendent, 14
regimes (*politeia*), Aristotle's classification of, 75–81
religious and philosophical doctrines/theory, 216
religious approach of Kierkegaard, 188, 189
"repetition," 192
Republic (Plato), 2, 9, 76, 191; "almost-philosopher," 11, 19, 22; *aretē* (excellence), 13–15, 19–20, 22–23; comparison with Plato's *Symposium*, 10–13; emphasizing hierarchy and Divided Line, 10
ressentiment, psychology of, 204
revelation, 94
revolution (*metabolē*), 74

rich peers (*homotimoi*), 35
rights-bearers, individuals as, 6, 159, 160–62, 188
right to property, 6; fundamentality of, 160; Hegel vs. Locke's perspectives, 162–63
Robinson Crusoe, 5–6, 149–54
Roochnik, David, 11
Rousseau, Jean Jacques, 5–6, 112, 117n11, 124, 143, 156n7, 157n11, 157n17, 158n19, 158n22; *First Discourse*, 143, 154, 155, 158n22; *Second Discourse*, 127, 145, 150, 157n13; *Social Contract*, 127. See also *Emile, or On Education* (Rousseau)

Sakian, 46–47
Scripture, 91–94, 97, 101n12
self-actualization, 6, 165, 168
self-command, 107–8
self-denial, 107, 113, 125
self-esteem, 221–24, 225
self-love, 65n17, 107–8, 145. *See also* amour-propre
self-preservation, 3, 4, 95–96, 125, 134, 154
self-respect, 221; duty of, 220–23; primary good of, 220
self-transcendence, 107
Shakespeare, William, 6, 189
Sickness unto Death (Kierkegaard), 194
Sittlichkeit, 6, 160, 167–70
Smith, Adam, 112–13, 115, 166
Social Contract (Rousseau), 127
socialism, 204, 215
Socrates, 6, 9, 11, 19, 21, 27n4, 189, 191, 194, 195; City in Words, 12–14, 16, 22, 23, 25n1; and democracy, 15–16; about hierarchy of ideal city, 13; Noble Lie of, 23–24; about true excellence, 10

soft despotism, 1
Soleil, Roi, 132
Solzhenitsyn, Alexander, 193
spectacle (*theōrēma, theōria*), 61
spectator (*theōros*), 61
Spinoza, Benedict, 4–5, 89, 104–5, 115; doctrine of natural rights, 94–98; endorsement of democracy, 91; metaphysical and political arguments, 89–90; resolving theological-political problem, 91–93, 98; about theocracy, 101n20
spiritedness, 79, 85, 182, 184
The Spirit of the Laws (Montesquieu), 5, 121, 124–28, 135
Statesman (Plato), 75
statesmen, 97, 98, 206
Strauss, Leo, 94, 196n8, 196n13, 205
summoners, 191
sustenance, 42, 86
sympathy, 111, 114–15, 178
Symposium (Plato), 2, 9; Alcibiades in, 18–25; comparison with Plato's *Republic*, 10–13; Diotima's "Ladder of Love," 10, 11–12, 15, 18, 21, 25n1; equality without excellence in, 16–18

Telemachus (Fénelon), 5, 104, 105, 113–16, 157n17; ancient virtues and modern virtues, 109–13; courage in war, 108–9; disputes over, 105–6; reconciliation of greatness and goodness, 116–17; self-command, 107–8
teleological theories, 217, 219, 220
theocracy, 100–101n11, 101n20
theological-political problem, 91–93
Theological-Political Treatise (Spinoza), 4, 89, 92, 94, 97, 98, 99n1, 11n6. *See also* Spinoza, Benedict

A Theory of Justice (Rawls), 7, 215–16; equality and democracy in, 4–5; equality and excellence in, 217, 220, 222, 224; principles of justice, 218–20, 226; right/justice vs. good, 217–18; self-respect, 220, 221, 223
Thrasymachus, 12, 23
Tocqueville, Alexis de, 6, 7, 25, 174, 213n13, 217; mores, discussion on, 176, 177–78, 185; about nobility in democracy, 176–77; studies on equality and excellence, 1; work on freedom democracy, 174–75. *See also Democracy in America* (Tocqueville)
Tractatus Theologico-Politicus. *See Theological-Political Treatise* (Spinoza)
Tracy, Destutt de, 121
transcendent reality, 14–15
truth, meaning of, 61, 65n23
tyranny, 74; elected, 77; forms of, 81; of majority, 25, 177, 185n2; of timidity, 203

Union, 167
"unnatural cave" concept, 196n8
Untimely Meditation (Nietzsche), 200

Vergil, 106
virtue. *See* excellence (*aretē*)
Voltaire, 121
vornehm, 205–6
vulgar (*banausos*), 59

war and democracy, 182–85
"well-off" (*euporon*), 85
Wilhelm, Judge, 190–92, 194, 195
Wood, Allen, 159, 168
"worthies" (*axiōmati*), 59

Xenophon (Greek philosopher), 2, 3, 33–34, 51n9; Cyrus's revolution, 41–45; Media, narration of, 36–39; Persia, narration of, 34–36; Pheraulas, narration of, 45–47; rule of Cyrus the Great (King of Persia), 47–48. See also *The Education of Cyrus* (Xenophon)

Yaffe, Martin D., 99n1
Youpa, Andrew, 99n2
youths or cadets (*ephēboi*), 35–36

www.ingramcontent.com/pod-product-compliance
Lightning Source LLC
Chambersburg PA
CBHW032031090325
23169CB00011B/51